The Two Wars
of Mrs Duberly

The Two Wars
of Mrs Duberly

An intrepid Victorian lady's experience
of the Crimea and Indian Mutiny

Journal Kept During the
Russian War

Campaigning Experiences in
Rajpootana and
Central India

Frances Isabella Duberly

LEONAUR

The Two Wars of Mrs Duberly: An intrepid
Victorian lady's experience
of the Crimea and Indian Mutiny
Journal Kept During the Russian War and
Campaigning Experiences in Rajpootana
and Central India
by Frances Isabella Duberly

First published under the titles
Journal Kept During the Russian War
and
Campaigning Experiences in Rajpootana
and Central India
During the Peninsula War

Leonaur is an imprint
of Oakpast Ltd

Copyright in this form © 2009 Oakpast Ltd

ISBN: 978-1-84677-698-4 (hardcover)
ISBN: 978-1-84677-697-7 (softcover)

http://www.leonaur.com

Publisher's Notes

In the interests of authenticity, the spellings, grammar and place names
used have been retained from the original editions.

The opinions of the authors represent a view of events in which he
was a participant related from his own perspective,
as such the text is relevant as an historical document.

The views expressed in this book are not necessarily
those of the publisher.

Contents

Journal Kept During
the Russian War

Contents

Now all the youth of England are on fire.
And silken dalliance in the wardrobe lies,
Now thrive the armourers, and honour's thoughts
Reigns solely in the breast of every man.

Je vais où le vent me mène,
Sans me plaindre ou m'effrayer.
Je vais où va toute chose;
Où va la feuille de Rose,
Et la feuille de Laurier.

To the Soldiers and Sailors of
The Crimean Expedition
By an Eye Witness of Their
Chivalrous Valour and
Their Heroic Fortitude,

Frances Isabella Duberly

The writer of this *Diary* accompanied her husband, an officer in the 8th Hussars, who left England, with his regiment, on the breaking out of the war, and she is now with him in the Crimea.

The Editor.

FRANCES ISABELLA DUBERLY AND "BOB"

Preface

I am aware of many deficiencies in this *Journal*. It was kept under circumstances of great difficulty. I have always put down information as I received it, as nearly as possible in the words of my informant, in letters which I did not myself witness. I have endeavoured to keep free from comment or remark, thinking it best to allow the facts to speak for themselves. When this *Journal* was first commenced I had no intention whatever of publishing it; nor should I have done so now, had it not been for the kind interest manifested in it by many of my friends.

CHAPTER 1

The Voyage

The sails were fill'd and light the fair winds blew,
As glad to waft us from our native home,
And fasr the white rocks faded from our view,
And soon were lost in circumambient foam.
Byron.

Monday, April 24th, 1854.—Left the New London Inn at Exeter at ten o'clock in the evening, with sad heart and eyes full of tears. The near approach of this long voyage, and the prospect of unknown trials and hardships to be endured for I know not how long, overwhelmed me at the last moment; and the remembrance of dear friends left behind, whom I never more might return to see, made me shrink most nervously from the new life on which I was to embark. We reached the Royal Hotel at Plymouth at midnight, after a bitterly cold journey.

Tuesday, 25th.—After making a few purchases necessary for our comfort during the voyage, we embarked about three o'clock on board the *Shooting Star*, lying in the Plymouth dockyard; and towards evening, amid indescribable hurry, confusion, and noise, we weighed our anchor, and dropped down the river, where we lay till three o'clock on Wednesday morning; and then, with a fair and gentle breeze, and every prospect of a prosperous voyage, we stood out to sea.

Friday, 28th.—The breeze, which had been gradually freshening during yesterday, increased last night. I, sick and almost helpless in my cabin, was told the disastrous news that both the mizzen-top and main-top gallant-masts were carried away; that fragments of the wreck—masts, ropes, and spars—strewed the deck: one poor fellow was lying seriously injured, having broken his leg, and crushed the bone.

Saturday, 29th.—Weak and nervous, I staggered up on deck, to see it strewn with spars, ropes, and blocks. During the night the gale had fearfully increased, and the morning sun found two of our poor horses dead. The groans of the boy, who was lying in one of the cabins, and the gloom caused by the death of our horses, threw us all into depressed spirits, which were not cheered by looking at the ugly, broken mast aloft. I heartily thank God, who brought us safely through last night's gale.

Although weakened almost to delirium by seasickness and awed by the tremendous force of wind and sea, I could not but exult in the magnificent sailing of our noble ship, which bounded over the huge waves like a wild hunter springing at his fences, and breasted her gallant way at the rate of sixteen knots an hour.

Sunday, 30th.—How unlike the quiet Sundays at home! How sadly we thought of them—of pleasant walks to church, through sunny fields and shady lanes! After we had read the service, Henry and I went on deck, and sat there quietly. The wind had dropped to a dead calm; and our good ship, as though resting after her late effort, dozed lazily along at barely two knots an hour. Towards evening, we saw several whales and porpoises, and phosphorescent lights gleamed like stars on the calm, dark sea.

Monday, May 1st.—The wind still very quiet, and our ship hardly making any way.

Tuesday, 2nd.—We signalled a vessel which, after much delay, replied that she was the *Blundel*, from Portsmouth, bound to Gallipoli. At ten o'clock tonight we arrived off Gibraltar. For some hours previously we were in sight of the Spanish coast; and, notwithstanding the lateness of the hour, the clear atmosphere and brilliant moon enabled us to discern the town of Gibraltar and the Rock rising behind it. It was a cause of much disappointment to us that we had not passed it earlier, as we hoped to have conveyed to our friends at home the news of our safe arrival thus far. Another horse died from inanition, having eaten nothing since he came on board.

Wednesday, 3rd.—An almost entire calm. Our lazy ship scarcely vouchsafed to move at all. Such a glorious day, succeeded by a night which realised all one's dreams of the sweet south!—the Spanish and African coasts still visible, and on the former, mountains capped with snow. We put up an awning on the deck, as the heat was very great. During the night, however, a fresh breeze sprung up, filling our flapping sails, and bearing us on at the rate of fifteen knots an hour.

Thursday, 4th.—The breeze continued, and our good ship went cheerily on her course. A fourth horse died last night. They tell me he went absolutely mad, and raved himself to death. The hold where our horses are stowed, although considered large and airy, appears to me horrible beyond words. The slings begin to gall the horses under the shoulder and breastbone; and the heat and bad atmosphere must be felt to be understood. Every effort to alleviate their sufferings is made; their nostrils are spunged with vinegar, which is also scattered in the hold. Our three horses bear it bravely, but they are immediately under a hatchway where they get air.

Friday, 5th.—A day of much sorrow and suffering to me, as I was awoke by our servant (Connell) coming to our door at seven o'clock, and saying that the "Grey Horse"—"Missus's Horse"—my own dear horse, was very ill. Henry ran to him directly, and after examining him, fancied his attack was different from that of the others, and that he might live.

How deeply one becomes attached to a favourite horse! Never was a more perfect creature, with faultless action, faultless mouth, and faultless temper.

Saturday, 6th.—My horse still lives, and they tell me he is a thought easier; but last night was most unfavourable to him, there being a fresh wind and rolling sea. During the forenoon I came on deck, heavy at heart. We passed the island of Galita, of volcanic formation and rocky appearance: it appears to be covered with a rusty brown moss.

During the afternoon we exchanged signals with vessels which had been respectively twenty-eight, seventeen, and fourteen days at sea. We have been ten.

Sunday, 7th.—A lovely morning, and a quiet sea. Although the *Shooting Star* makes but seven knots an hour, we hope to arrive at Malta by dark. Had the wind held, we should have been off the town in time for afternoon service. My letters are ready for S., W., and Mrs. F. Would that we could receive news from home! I hear we passed the Island of Pantelaria this morning, but was not on deck in time to see it; indeed, I had no heart for the distractions of outward objects, for my horse, though he still lives, is at the point of death.

Monday, 8th.—We were awoke at four o'clock by the sound of a matin bell, and knew by it that we were off Malta. Looking through the stern windows, we found ourselves at anchor in the harbour; the massive fortifications bristling with guns were close on either side of us, as we lay quiet and motionless on the waveless sea. At eight o'clock Henry went on deck, and soon after returning, put his arms round me, and I knew that my darling horse was out of pain!

Henry went ashore with Captain Fraser, and, amid the sultry heat, sweltered up the "*Nix mangiare*" stairs, and through the blinding streets of the town. At ten we received orders to put to sea forthwith; but the wind lay ahead of us, and at five we were barely moving out of port. Shortly after, when the calm evening was dressed in all the gorgeous colours of a southern sunset, and whilst the military calls were sounding those stirring notes he loved to hear, my good horse was lowered to his rest among the nautili and wondrous sea flowers which floated round the ship.

A small French brig, containing a detachment of the Chasseurs d'Afrique, lay becalmed close to us. They told us that their vessel was one of 150 tons; that they had twenty-eight horses on board, and had lost none, although they provided no stalls for them, but huddled them into the hold as closely as they could stow them away.

Tuesday, 9th.—Our orders are to proceed to Cape Matapan, where, if the wind should be against us, a steamer will tow us to Scutari. Some of our crew, having bought spirits from the bumboats off Malta, became mutinous, and several passed the night in irons.

Friday, 12th.—Last night ominous banks of clouds loaded the horizon, and soon proved the truth of my quotation—

> *There's tempest in yon horned moon,*
> *And lightning in yon cloud.*

A hurricane of wind thundered in our rigging, and a deluge of rain came down. Endeavouring to make head against the gale, Captain Fraser tried our good ship to the utmost, but was at last obliged to let her drive before the storm

It was a fearful night to us who are unaccustomed to the sea; the rolling was very heavy and wearisome. Neither Henry nor I undressed all night. Today has been a day of as much suffering as I ever wish to experience. Sick incessantly, too weak to turn, I was lying towards night almost unconscious, when I was roused by a most tremendous roll. The ship had heeled over till her deck was under water. Candlesticks, falling from the table, rolled at their leisure into the corners. Captain Fraser rushed on deck, Captain Tomkinson into the hold, where every horse was down, one being pitched half over the manger. I was shot from the stern locker, on which I was lying, to the far corner of my cabin, and every box and portmanteau came crushing over me.

Saturday, 13th.—Happily, the violent motion abated during the night, though the thunder and lightning were terrific. And this is the "Sweet South! whose sky rains roses and violets, and whose weary, fragrant heat, combined with gorgeous colours, dazzles the senses so that one feels like a phœnix burning on spice wood." This is all very fine, but Singleton Fontenoy must have been more fortunate in his time of year. To me, for the last three days, the Mediterranean has been arid and sickly as the first approach of fever—heaving, nauseating, as the deadly approach of plague. Those who are good sailors may linger over it if they will. Give me the smallest house in England, with a greenhouse and a stable, and I will sigh no more for the violet waves of a Mediterranean sea, nor the brilliant stars of a sometimes golden heaven.

Sunday, 14th.—Ran on deck to take my first longing look at Greece. We were close under the Arcadian shore, about four miles from the Island of Stamphane. The high, bold coast lay hazy and crowned with misty clouds in the early sunlight. I watched for an hour, my mind dreaming poetic fancies: "I, too, have been in Arcadia." A brilliant day coloured the blue waves once more. We had service for all hands on deck. Mr. Coull, the Admiralty agent, officiated; and being somewhat unaccustomed to acting chaplain, he read the prayer for Queen Adelaide straight through.

Monday, 15th.—Almost a calm. We sighted the *Maryanne*, with Major De Salis and a detachment of 8th Hussars on board. She sailed a week before us, and our having overtaken her is a great triumph to our ship. The Messenian coast lay close to us all day—snow-capped and cloud-wreathed mountains lying in a half indistinct and dreamy haze, a very Eleusinian mystery in themselves.

Tuesday, 16th.—After dark we passed the Straits of Cerigo; and all this morning have been gliding amongst the islands of the Archipelago, leaving Rock St. George upon our left, and the fertile and beautifully cultivated Zea on our right. They lay in beauteous sleep upon the bosom of the ocean, in colouring half intense, half languid, like the tints of the dog-rose and wild violet. Silently and swiftly our good ship held her way. We sighted the *Echinga*, which had sailed ten days before us, but we did not overtake her before nightfall (star-rise would be a better word); but we followed on her track as surely as evil destiny follows a foredoomed soul.

Wednesday, 17th.—As I write we are off Mitylene, an apparently uncultivated island, but full of beauty of outline and colour nevertheless; and after coasting for two hours the fertile and well-wooded shores of Asia, we came to the narrow passage between Tenedos and the mainland. This passage is dangerous, from a reef of rocks; but we spanked through it at eleven knots, closely followed by the *Echinga*, while they saluted us from the batteries. Three hours later, our favouring breeze had whispered its own lullaby, and we were lying helpless and becalmed at the mouth of the Dardanelles. A strong current, acting on the ship, swung her round broadside to the forts. The glory of the sunset, the gaily painted little Turkish vessels, with the brilliant fez and long pipes of the sailors, the still water, reflecting every beautiful colour like a lake of mother-of-pearl, made a landscape such as I had never hoped to see save in a picture. The current in the night drifted us twelve miles back, and towards morning we "let go our anchor, and prayed for" a steamer.

Thursday, 18th.—Made up our lost way with infinite difficulty, going at the rate of eight knots for five minutes, and then drifting back for ten with the current. We made a triumphant entry into the Dardanelles, in company with the *Maryanne*, *Echinga*, a man-of-war the name of which we did not know, a French transport, and a steamer. The coast is well wooded and fertile. We saw many Turks assembled on the fort on the left-hand side, and several women, all attracted by the novel sight of so many fine English vessels inside their unknown sea.

The current here is so strong that at eight o'clock we cast anchor; and though every eye was strained towards Gallipoli, looking for the steamers, none appeared; and during the night the ship drifted from her moorings, and we were obliged to lower the bower anchor in forty fathoms.

Saturday, 20th.—Yesterday we opened the sealed book of the Dardanelles, and what beauties did it not disclose!—a hilly, rocky coast, with interstices of lovely and fertile valleys clothed in rich green, and shaded with luxuriant trees; forts at every point; some of considerable strength, others more picturesque. Numbers of cattle and mules were grazing on the shore; and a string of camels, led by a mule with a bell, reminded one more forcibly than anything else, that we were really in the East. Gallipoli, which was visible from a long distance, is a large and apparently a good Turkish town, which means an execrable English one, and is finely situated on a high cliff. It is surrounded by a large English and French encampment. Gallipoli has now many French and four English regiments stationed there.

We hove to for orders, and were immediately despatched to Scutari, for which place we started with the evening breeze, and by eight-o clock we were well into the Sea of Marmora. At three o'clock today we caught our first sight of Constantinople, and by nine at night were anchored in the harbour. A Maltese pilot, who came on board at five o'clock, told us that the *Echinga*, *Pride of the Ocean*, and *Ganges*, had arrived a few hours before.

We hear that there are barracks at Scutari capable of holding 6000 men, and that 16,000 can be quartered there by being encamped in the enclosure. Towards sunset we watched the *Imaum* ascend the minaret close to us, and presently the town echoed with the call to prayer. Coming to us across the water, the effect was very musical, and somehow it touched me.

Sunday, 21st.—A cold, wet, miserable day, during which we remained at our anchorage. Everyone except myself went on shore: Henry tells me that the filth, stenches, and dogs on shore are indescribable. The prospect from the deck is not tempting certainly. The captain returned with news of a steamboat tomorrow to disembark the horses, and also a quay for them to land on. I never was more completely *désillusionée* in my life than with my first day in Constantinople.

Tuesday, 22nd.—Disembarked at last! The tug came alongside very early, and towed us to the quay near Kulali. Such a quay, after our dockyard at Plymouth!—a few old rotten planks, supported on some equally rotten-looking timbers, about three feet above the water's edge. However, they must have been stronger than they looked, for they resisted the plunges and kicks of our horses, as they were tumbled out of the ship, without giving way. No accident befell the disembarkation.

Our horses were in wonderfully good condition, and appeared fresh and in good heart. I went ashore, and went up to "Bob;" but the sight of him, and the memory of his lost companion, completely upset me, and I could only lay my head on his neck and cry. A good Greek, who, I suppose, fancied the tears and the horse were someway connected, came and stroked the charger's neck, and said, "*Povero Bobo!*"

After dinner, Mr. Philips, Henry, and I rowed up to the barracks in Mr. Coull's gig. They appear from the outside to be a very fine building, close to the sea, and with a very handsome façade; but the inside—the dilapidation! the dirt! the rats! the fleas!! These last are really so terrible that several officers have been fairly routed by them, and obliged either to pitch their tents on the common, or to sleep on board the ships.

No provision whatever has been made for the soldiers; and if Captain Fraser had not put a basket of provisions in the *caïque* that took the baggage, neither officers nor men would have broken their fast tonight. The stables into which I went first, of course, are more like the crypt of a church than anything else— dark, unpaved, unstalled, of enormous size, and cool: no straw and no mangers!

Wednesday, 24th.—Our orders are to have the ship ready for sea tomorrow, and to re-embark the horses on Friday, to proceed to Varna. We hear that an English frigate has been run on shore by a Greek pilot, and blown up by Russians or Austrians, no one is very clear which. Today, for the first time since I left England, I induced Mrs. Williams, the sergeant-major's wife, who came out as my maid, to wash a few of the clothes which had accumulated during our voyage. I mention this, as being the first assistance she has ever thought fit to render me since I left England.

Thursday, 25th.—At five this morning a tug came alongside, and took us to the quay at Kulali barracks. Steamers which arrived yesterday evening, confirmed the intelligence respect—the *Tiger.* We are under orders to proceed to Varna without delay. A more brilliant morning never smiled upon the earth; and I think I never can forget the *coup d'œil* that presented itself as I ran up on deck. Behind us on either side lay the beautiful city of Constantinople, embowered in trees, and surmounted by its tall and slender minarets.

The gay-coloured houses, painted in every imaginable colour, lit up the already brilliant scene; while the picturesque costumes of the Turkish and Greek boatmen, rowing down the current in their gaudy and well-poised *caïques*, with the long line of Kulali barracks, with its avenue of shady trees, formed a picture of light and shadow truly fascinating. The horse artillery were ranged on the quay, in marching order, with guns mounted, and several pack horses loaded, waiting the signal to embark on their transport, which was moored alongside. Our horses were being exercised beneath the spreading trees.

Turkish dogs, lazy and dirty, were lying about in all directions; while horribly filthy beggars were hovering everywhere, interspersed with Turkish soldiers and Greeks. The little harbour is filled with cabbages, and refuse of every description,—a dead dog floating out, and a dead horse drifting close to the shore, on whose swollen and corrupted flanks three dogs were alternately fighting and tearing off the horrible flesh.

Beyond this lay the sea,—quiet, blue, serene, and beautiful beyond all words!

We hear that our troopers are to return to their stalls in the hold, and that we are to take government horses on our decks. We expected to have to convey an infantry regiment, so we are let off cheaply.

Friday, 26th.—Lord Lucan, who commands the cavalry, sent an order to Major De Salis, yesterday, to the effect that, "unless

Mrs. Duberly had an order sanctioning her doing so, she was not to re-embark on board the *Shooting Star*, about to proceed to Varna."

Major De Salis returned for answer, that "Mrs. Duberly had not disembarked from the *Shooting Star*, and he had not sufficient authority to order her to do so."

Up to this time (ten o'clock) I have heard nothing further about it. My dear husband has worried himself into a state of the greatest uneasiness. He looks upon the order as a soldier: I look upon it as a woman, and laugh at it. Uneasy, of course, I am; as, should the crew refuse to assist me, I must purchase a pony, and ride 130 miles (up to Varna) through a strange and barbarous country, and over the Balkan.

Should I find that Lord Lucan has taken other steps to annoy me, I have settled with two of the ship's company, who have agreed to put me on shore and bring me off again after dark, and allow me to remain either on the main-deck or in the hold until we reach Varna; and once landed, and once on horseback, I shall be able to smile at this interference; which is in every way unwarrantable, as I left England by permission of the Horse Guards, and with accommodation provided by the Admiralty.

Our horses re-embarked today from a temporary quay made of boats and planking. I spent this lovely day imprisoned in my cabin,—thinking it wisest not to appear on deck.

Saturday, 27th.—Major De Salis let me out of durance by telling me that Lord Raglan had been applied to by Lord Lucan, and had stated that he had no intention of interfering with me; so, after luncheon, Henry, Mr. Coull, and I started in Mr. Coull's gig for Pera, and went to Mr. Seager's store, where we met Captain Tomkinson and Dr. Mackay, and all went together to the Stamboul bazaar. What a walk we had! Alas that the beautiful illusion of this fairy city, as seen from the harbour, should vanish the moment one sets foot in the streets,—paved with small rocks, against which you cut your feet while stumbling over every imaginable abomination!

Ownerless dogs lying and prowling about in all directions,-

horses and men heavily laden with enormous weights push through the streets, regardless of your shoulders or your toes.

The bazaar is certainly worth seeing, but will be too often and too well described to make it necessary for me to enlarge upon it here. It is amusing, if only to listen to the enormous prices asked, and the very small ones taken. I bought some crimson slippers embroidered in gold, and Henry bought a *chibouque*, and then we all started to walk up to the Hotel de Bellevue for our dinner. The dinner was a failure, though the walk was not; for it was a scramble up a perpendicular hill, repaid with an exquisite view from a graveyard at the top. The row home at night refreshed me both in body and mind.

Sunday, 28th.—Our orders are to be ready tomorrow to sail for Varna. Someone brought a report that, immediately on landing, we were to go three days' march up the country. Nothing is arranged until the last moment;—the authorities do not appear to know their own minds. The subject was discussed at grog-time, and the clamour of opinions and tongues,—some witty, some discontented, some facetious, and some fuddled,—was the most amusing thing possible.

Monday, 29th.—King Charles's day! And never had King Charles more vexations to encounter on that day than we! At half-past seven came the major, with an order that all extra tents, picket poles, &c., should be landed without delay (they having all been embarked the day before). I, not feeling well, remained in bed until ten o'clock. Although the *Megæra* steamship was ordered to be alongside to tow us at nine this morning, she has not made her appearance, and it is now four. Neither the commanding officers afloat or ashore appear to have the least idea of what they are about.

The 17th Lancers have had no order to re-embark; while we, who are only part of a regiment, and without our head-quarters are sent up to encamp at Varna, within sixty miles of the Russian force. Fifteen ponies are purchased to carry the baggage of the regiment; and the allowance for officers is only sufficient to allow Henry and me a bullock-trunk apiece,—rather different to our notions of the *impedimenta* of a regiment! They report the commissariat at Varna as being so ill-arranged that we must not expect to get anything but salt meat for some weeks after our arrival. The *Megæra* has just passed us with the 7th Fusiliers on board. I waved my hand to Colonel Yea as they passed, the decks crammed with soldiers. I find, by the shaking of the ship that we are weighing anchor, and that the *Megæra* is going to take us in tow.

The *Maryanne* and *Echinga* have both passed us on their way up the Bosphorus;—transports are coming up fast alongside Kulali barracks; and, in about an hour, we too shall have looked our last upon the (outwardly) fair city of Stamboul

Wednesday, 31st.—"In about an hour!" Why, we began to weigh anchor at four o'clock on Monday, and at one o'clock today it is only just out of the water. Our ship, fitted up in such unseemly haste, has not a rope or a cable on board worth sixpence. The anchor, when half out of the water yesterday, slipped, and the cable breaking disabled two of our best men. Our captain, after running through various courses of rage—swearing and cursing—has become philosophical and smilingly indifferent. Captain Johnson, of the *Megæra*, who began at the other end is going rapidly mad.

We, the *Clipper*, the finest ship afloat, who were the first to receive orders to get under weigh, are the last to leave the harbour. Let me shut up my journal, the subject is too disastrous. Oh, the creaking of that windlass! the convulsive shivering of the ship! the grinding of the hawsers! However, at four o'clock we are off at last; and I think there is not one who does not regret leaving the gay and lovely Bosphorus, and Pera, near which we have been anchored so long, refreshing ourselves with strawberries, oranges, and sherbet, lying lazily on the burning deck, and feeling as though excess of beauty overcame our languid pulses.

Eight o'clock.—We have all been on deck, watching the beauties of the coast as they disappeared behind us: Therapia—where

is the Hotel D'Angleterre, the resort of the wives of English naval and military officers, who have "accompanied their husbands
to the seat of war;" the stone bridge and plane trees of seven
stems; the noble viaduct overlooking Beikos Bay, and, finally,
the broad surface of the Black Sea. The huge engines and filthy
smoke of the *Megæra* made our vessel heave and filled us with
nausea.

CHAPTER 2

Disembarkation and Encampment at Varna

Quanti valorosi uomini li quali non che altri ma Galieno, Ippocrate o Esculapio avrieno giudicati sanissimi, la mattina desinarono co' loro compagni et amici, che poi la sera vegnente appresso nell' altro mondo cenarono colli loro passati!—Boccaccio.

On Thursday, June 1st, our disembarkation commenced. We came in sight of Varna about nine o'clock. It is a small but clean-looking town, and certainly, from the harbour, gives one no idea of the impregnable fortress which resisted the Russians in 1828-29. Here the disembarkation of horses was dangerous and awkward, for they were obliged to lower them into boats, and row them ashore.

All were frightened—some very restive. One trooper kicked two men, bit a third, and sent a fourth flying overboard. At half past four Henry and I came ashore in Mr. Coull's gig. We took leave of Captain Fraser and the officers of the *Shooting Star* with great regret, and, as we rowed off, all hands came aft and cheered. It was kindly and heartily done, and I did not expect it; it overcame me, and filled my eyes with tears. The landing-place gave me a greater realisation of the idea of "war time" than any description could do.

It was shadowing to twilight. The quay was crowded with Turks, Greeks, infantry, artillery, and hussars; piles of cannon balls and shells all around us; rattle of arms everywhere; horses kicking, screaming, plunging; and "Bob," whom I was to ride, was almost unmanageable from excitement and flies. At length, horses were accoutred, and men mounted, and, nearly in the dark, we commenced our march, Henry and I riding first. Luckily, our camp was merely about a mile off. I looked at the streets, vilely paved, full of holes, and as slippery as glass; but feeling how useless was any nervousness, now that the die was cast, I gave the dear old horse his head, and he carried me without a trip to the camp. Our tent had to be brought up with the *impedimenta*.

It was pitch dark, and the dew fell like rain. Major De Salis most kindly came to meet me, and, taking me to his tent, gave me some ham, biscuit, and brandy and water, and allowed me to lie down until my own tent was erected.

Friday, 2nd.—A broiling day. There is no tree or shelter of any sort near our encampment, which is finely situated on a large plain fronting the lake. Artillery, Turkish cavalry, and eight regiments of infantry compose our camp at present, though, through the dust on my right hand, I can discern French troops marching in fast. Some of our infantry tents are pitched on mounds, which mounds are the graves of those Russians who fell in the campaign of 1828-29.

Saturday, 3rd.—About ten o'clock Major De Salis brought us some milk in a bottle, and we broiled a slice of the ham kindly given us by Captain Fraser, of the *Shooting Star*, and so, over the camp fire, we made our breakfast. Our dinner at night consisted of the same, as no other rations than bread have been served out; and but for our ham we should have had no meat at all. Later, a welcome sight presented itself in the shape of Captain Fraser and some bottles of beer, one of which I drank like a thirsty horse. The horses are wild with heat and flies, and they scream and kick all day and night.

Lord Cardigan and staff rode into our lines. Henry went into Varna, and bought a very fine grey cob pony, of the British consul, for twenty guineas. Captain Eden, of the *London*, called on me and invited me to church and luncheon tomorrow. Captain

Tomkinson, Mr. Philips, Dr. Mackay, Henry, and I dine on board the *Shooting Star.* Am I not hungry?

Sunday, 4th.—We started on horseback at half-past nine to meet the "gig," which was waiting for us in the harbour. Lady Erroll, whom I am curious to see, was also asked, but as Lord Erroll was detained in camp she could not leave. After service we inspected the ship, a magnificent two-decker of ninety guns, and partook of a most refreshing luncheon. Lord George Paulet, who had written to me in the morning, came and carried us off to the *Bellerophon,* and entertained us most hospitably. When we rode home at night, we found the 17th Lancers disembarking.

Captain Wallace, 7th Fusiliers, who was killed yesterday by a fall from his pony, was buried today—the first-fruits of the sacrifice! We march tomorrow morning at five to Devna, a village about nineteen miles up the country. After I had packed, I sat down outside the tent, and wrapped myself in the novel beauties of the scene—the great plain bordered by the vast lake; the glorious colours of sunset; the warlike confusion of foreground; hussar and artillery horses picketed; infantry encamped; Turkish soldiers galloping here and there on their active little horses; *Bashi-Basouks* all round us, and the smoke of the campfires throwing a blue haze over the whole.

Monday, 5th.—Was awoke by the *reveille* at half-past two; rose, packed our bedding and tent, got a stale egg and a mouthful of brandy, and was in my saddle by half-past five.

I never shall forget that march! It occupied nearly eight hours. The heat intense, the fatigue overwhelming; but the country-anything more beautiful I never saw!—vast plains; verdant hills, covered with shrubs and flowers; a noble lake; and a road, which was merely a cart track, winding through a luxuriant woodland country, across plains and through deep *bosquets* of brushwood.

A most refreshing river runs near our camp, but we have no trees, no shelter. Captain Tomkinson made me a bed of his cloak and sheepskin; and drawing my hat over my eyes, I lay down under a bush, close to "Bob," and slept till far towards evening.

Tuesday, 6th.—The major was busy in arranging and settling the men; but towards the afternoon, Captain Tomkinson, Henry, and I rode into the village, to try to procure some *vin du pays* for our dinner (wherein we failed); and to the hills, to try for some green forage for our horses, as the straw brought us by the natives is little else than old bed stuffing, and full of fleas. We met one of the commanders of the Turkish army going with an escort to Schumla. His belt and holsters were most magnificently chased. He was on the small horse of the country, and had just mounted a fresh relay.

His escort looked like a collection of beggars on horseback; but the little active horses sprang into a gallop at once, and kept it up over tracks that would puzzle many a clever English hunter. After our horses had fed on long grass and flowers, we came home to our dinner. A French colonel in the Turkish service, Colonel Du Puy, called on us in the evening, and interested us much by his account of his last winter's campaigning in this comfortless country.

Wednesday, 7th.—Captain Tomkinson and Mr. Clutterbuck, each with eight men, went out to patrol: they went about ten miles, in different directions, but saw no Cossacks.

Lord Cardigan joined this detachment of the brigade today.

Part of the 17th Lancers also marched in.

Saturday, 10th.—The head quarters and Captain Lockwood's troop have arrived at Varna, and were expected up today; but as they had no baggage ponies, nor any means of conveyance for the baggage, they were detained until we could send down our ponies to bring them up. This does not strike me as being well arranged. Whose fault is it? The infantry of the Light Division were also ordered up to Devna today, to form a large camp in conjunction with us; but as it poured with rain they could not march. Captain Tomkinson, with a sergeant and nine men, has been away on patrol these three days, but is expected back tonight. Lord Cardigan forbids them to take their cloaks to wrap round them at night, as he considers it "effeminate."

Luckily it is summer, though the dews fall like rain. Our camp is most picturesque, in the midst of a large and fertile plain, near a sparkling river, and carpeted with brilliant flowers—burrage, roses, larkspurs, heather, and a lovely flower the name of which I do not know. Henry and I wandered among the hills this afternoon; and "Bob" sped over the long grass and delicate convolvuli, neighing with delight at being loosed from his picket rope, where he has been rained and blown upon incessantly for two days and nights.

Monday, 12th.—Captain Tomkinson returned today from Basardchick, bringing me a handful of roses from the ruined village, observing, as he gave them to me, that I now possessed roses from nearer the enemy than anyone else.

Thursday, 15th.—A mail came up today, brought up by an orderly from Varna. I received letters from S., F., and E. I also got a *Devizes'* paper, which pleased me much. The morning wet and chilly; the noon hot and sultry.

Friday, 16th.—A report was rife in camp that 57,000 Austrians were marching to our assistance against the Russians; also that the whole force, English and French, will be under immediate marching orders for Silistria, as 90,000 Russians are investing the town.

Saturday, 17th.—Weather intensely hot—no shade, no breeze. Head-quarters marched up today from Varna. Mr. Philips left today for Tirnova, where he was sent to purchase 500 horses. They inform us today that the Austrian force is 300,000, and it is uncertain upon which side they will fight. What a comfort we find in our double marquee tent! The lining excludes the heat more effectually than anything else, and it is so much more easy of ventilation than a bell tent.

The Bulgarian pony "Whisker," proving too active with his heels, was obliged to be picketed by himself, and not liking it, amused himself, and bothered us, by untying the knot with his teeth, and scampering all over the country.

The Light Division are really expected up on Monday, when it is supposed we shall begin our march in earnest. Such an expectation fills all minds with excitement and hope: I pity the Russian army which encounters our men as they are now. We hear wonders of the valour of the Turks. Every day the Russians make breaches in the walls, and rushing on to the attack, are beaten off every day by these dauntless men at the point of the bayonet. The Russians, a few days since, sent in a flag of truce to bury their dead: the Turks not only agreed, but sent a party to assist.

Wednesday, 21st.—The 5th Dragoon Guards and two troops of the 13th Light Dragoons marched to join our encampment today. The former took up a position nearer the river, but the 13th came up on our right, between the 17th Lancers and ourselves. Yesterday we performed a "grand march:" we shifted our ground, and went about 200 yards further up the valley. This movement occupied us from six, a.m., to three, p.m. The ground, which had not been previously marked out, took some time to choose, and Lord Cardigan and *aides-de-camp* were a wearisome time in arranging it; and when it was arranged, we were put more than a mile from the water; whereas, by a different disposition of the troops, all might have been equally near to the river bank.

Thursday, 22nd.—Henry and I started at half-past twelve to ride over to the infantry camp; Captain Lockwood mounted me on his roan horse, and Henry rode the grey. We missed our track, and made thirteen miles out of seven. We wandered through most exquisite woodlands, through sunny glades and banks of sweet spring flowers, passed trees through whose green leaves the golden sunlight fell dropping in a shower, and through deep shadows and thickets, beneath which our horses could hardly force their way.

Arrived at the camp, we inquired for about a dozen of our friends, and found they had every one, without a single exception, "gone into Varna;" so there was nothing for it but to turn our horses' heads homewards through the weary heat. Hurrying home to be in time for dinner (we had had nothing but a piece of bread and a glass of water, kindly given me by a good commissary), we found only disappointment for the bottom of the pot had come out, and all the stew was in the fire.

Friday, 23rd.—The 17th Lancers got up some pony races to-day, over a tolerable course of a mile. Captain Morgan won gallantly, on a pony for which he had paid 50s.

Sunday, 25th.—Was awoke at four o'clock from a profound sleep, by the words, "A general order for the regiment to be prepared as soon as possible to march thirty miles." All the camp was alive No tents were to be struck, but everyone was to move. We could make nothing of the order, until we heard that a courier had arrived to say that the Russians had abandoned the siege of Silistria, and had crossed the Danube. We still dressed in hot haste, wondering at the order, when an *aide-de-camp* came up to say that only a squadron of the 8th and a squadron of the 13th were to go; and that they were to march towards Silistria to make a reconnaissance of the Russian army.

The order to "bridle and saddle" was given, and all was ready for a start, when a counter-order arrived—"The squadrons are to wait until three days' provisions are cooked;" so that of the whole regiment roused at four, two troops went away at half-past ten. If it takes six hours and a half to get two squadrons under weigh, how long will it take to move the whole British force? At six o'clock Henry, Major de Salis, and I rode over to the Turkish camp to dine with Colonel Du Puy. We met Mr. G——, the correspondent of the *Daily News*, also M. Henri, and another officer, *aides-de-camp* to Maréchal St. Arnaud. These two last were returning from Schumla, whither they had conveyed a fine Turkish horse, as a gift from the *maréchal* to Omar Pasha. I saw the little horse.

He was about fourteen hands, black, with the exception of two white marks and a white foot. Omar Pasha returned him, as a Turkish superstition prevents the soldiers from riding horses not entirely of a colour. He who rides a black, bay, or chestnut horse with white marks, or a white foot behind, will assuredly be slain in battle. A Turkish officer joined our party during the evening; and after sitting for some time in silence, smoking his *chibouque*, he informed me, through his interpreter (he had been staring at me for half an hour previously) that it was only permitted him to sit in my presence during war-time; under any other circumstances he could not sit down with a woman who was unveiled.

Monday, 26th.—Henry rode into Varna to procure money from the commissariat chest. I went out to meet him in the afternoon, and Captain Chetwode rode with me. We went as far as the infantry camp at Aladyn, and on our way passed the head-quarters of the 13th, marching up to join our camp. The lovely evening and clear sky induced us to prolong our ride so far, and we found Henry among the officers of the 23rd Welsh Fusiliers, who most hospitably pressed us to stay and partake of their excellent dinner, which we did.

On our way home, in the almost impenetrable twilight, we passed close by Captain Tomkinson's poor horse, which fell under him last night as he was returning from Varna. There he lay stark and stiff, a white mass amid the dark shadows—as fine a fencer as ever strained upon the bit on a hunting morning; and, hark! the gallop and baying of the wild dogs, even now trooping over the hills to feed upon his almost palpitating heart! Ah! mournful sight, that he should lie there, so ghastly and so still!

Thursday, 29th.—Two troops of the 11th Hussars joined us today. We had no news of Lord Cardigan's patrol until after dinner, when Bowen rode into the lines on Captain Lockwood's roan horse, who bore him feebly to the picket ropes, and then fell down. For many minutes he appeared dying of exhaustion, but eventually we revived him with brandy and water. Bowen tells us that the squadrons will not return for some days; that their fatigue has been excessive, and their hardships very great. They appear to have been marching incessantly, for which hard work neither men nor horses are fit.

A French colonel on his way to Silistria dined with us this afternoon, and interested us much by his accounts of the Turkish army. He told us no army cost so much to maintain, with such infamous results. The soldiers are neither fed nor clothed. All the money which passes through the hands of the pashas sticks to their fingers. Often, when halting after a long march, they inquire whether any meat is to be served out to them.

"No!"

"Any bread?"

"No!"

They shrug their shoulders and betake themselves to cold water and a pipe. A more wretched appearance than that which they present cannot be imagined; but at Silistria they have proved their courage.

Friday, 30th.—Part of the Light Division marched up this morning, and encamped on the opposite side of the valley. The Rifles marched in first; next followed the 33rd, playing "Cheer, boys, cheer;" and cheerily enough the music sounded across our silent valley, helping many a "willing, strong right hand," ready to faint with heat and fatigue. The 88th Connaught Rangers gave a wild Irish screech (I know no better word) as they saw their fellow countrymen, the 8th Royal Irish Hussars, and they played "Garry Owen" with all their might; while the 77th followed with "The British Grenadier." A troop of R. H. A. also came up to Devna. The accession of 7,000 men will be like a plague of locusts: they will eat up our substance. We can get little else but stale eggs, tough chickens, and sour milk, and now we shall not get even that; and the cries of "Yak-mak Johnny!"

"Sud Johnny!"

"Eur mooytath Johnny!" will be transferred from the cavalry to the "opposition lines."

Sunday, July 2nd.—Captain Tomkinson returned today from Silistria, whither he had been sent to ascertain the best road for marching troops. He described the whole Russian force, although they have lately raised the siege of Silistria, as being still in sight of the town, and speaks much of their numerous field pieces. He brought back a Russian round shot, and told me he had seen two of the enemy, but lying cold and still. I hear the Turks are hardly to be restrained from mutilating their dead foes. If they can do so unseen, they will cut off three or four heads, and, stringing them together through the lips and cheeks, carry them over their shoulders, like a rope of onions. [1]

The Turks inform us that the Russians say they will treat the Turks whom they make prisoners, as prisoners of war, but the French and English will be treated as felons, and sent to Siberia; and really, if the Russians are as uncleanly, smell as strong, and eat as much garlic as the Turks, it will be the best thing that can happen to us under the circumstances. We have had a hurricane all day, filling our tents, eyes, dinners, hair, beds, and boxes with intolerable dust. Our chicken for dinner was so tough that not even our daily onions could get it down. We were forced to shake our heads at our plates, and relinquish the dinner. The black bread, which is kneaded on the ground, is a happy mixture of sand, ants, and barley—and it is besides so sour that it makes my eyes water.

Monday, 3rd.—At three o'clock we were ordered to turn out as quickly as possible in light marching order, to receive Omar Pasha, who wished to inspect the troops, and was on his road from Schumla to Varna, where he was to hold a council of war. In ten minutes the cavalry were mounted, and Henry and I started upon "Bob" and the great grey, to see the man whom war had made so famous. His appearance struck me as military and dignified. He complimented all our troops, and insisted on heading the Light Cavalry charge, which made me laugh, for he was on a small Turkish horse, and had to scramble, with the spurs well in, to get out of the way of our long striding English horses. He was loudly cheered; appeared highly gratified; made me a

---

1. Although this may have been true of some of the irregular troops in the Turkish army, such a practice is utterly abhorrent to the Turks themselves, who know how to command the highest degree of bravery with the most chivalrous humanity.—Ed.

bow and paid me a compliment, and proceeded to his carriage to continue his journey.

Thursday, 6th.—Reports of a more peaceful nature reach us. We hear that Omar Pasha is the only counsellor for war. The Russian force is retreating daily. Now the "shave" is, that Austria is beginning to be afraid lest the English and French armies should decline to leave this fertile land, and all the powers, inimical or neutral, appear desirous to hush the matter up. The party which returned today from Silistria inform us of the good feeling shown by the Turks to their Russian prisoners. They feed them with their meat and rice, and treat them with every mark of kindness and consideration.

The peaceful reports which reach us give dissatisfaction. We are all for one good fight, to see which is the better man; all for one blow, struck so effectually as to crush all warlike propensities against us forever. We hear today of the terrible fate of the *Europa*. Report at present speaks so vaguely that we know not what to believe. At first we were told that every soul had perished, and afterwards that only Colonel Willoughby Moore and the veterinary surgeon fell victims to this terrible catastrophe.

A more frightful tragedy could scarcely occur than the burning of a transport ship—soldiers ignorant of seafaring, and horses crammed in the hold! Omar Pasha returned again today, and on his way inspected the Heavy Cavalry and Artillery. Lord Raglan also came up, and the staff made a brilliant-display. Omar Pasha again expressed himself in the most complimentary manner; and after it was all over, Henry and I turned our horses' heads and went for a ride.

Tuesday, 11th.—The reconnaissance, under Lord Cardigan, came in this morning at eight, having marched all night. They have been to Rassova, seen the Russian force, lived for five days on water and salt pork; have shot five horses, which dropped from exhaustion on the road, brought back an *araba* full of disabled men, and seventy-five horses, which will be, as Mr. Grey says, unfit for work for many months, and some of them will never work again.

I was out riding in the evening when the stragglers came in; and a piteous sight it was—men on foot, driving and goading on their wretched, wretched horses, three or four of which could hardly stir. There seems to have been much unnecessary suffering, a cruel parade of death, more pain inflicted than good derived; but I suppose these sad sights are merely the casualties of war, and we must bear them with what courage and fortitude we may. One of these unfortunate horses was lucky enough to have his leg broken by a kick, as soon as he came in, and was shot. There is an order that no horse is to be destroyed unless for glanders or a broken leg.

Thursday, 13th.—A long morning was spent in investigating the state of the horses by Colonel Shewell, Lord Cardigan, and Mr. Grey. I despatched letters to Captain Fraser, of the *Shooting Star*, and Lady Duberly.

A sad event closed this day. One of our sergeants, who had been ill for some days previously, left the hospital tent about three o'clock, a.m., and when our watering parade went down to the river, they found his body in the stream: he was quite dead. He was a steady and most respectable man: could he have had a foreboding of the lingering deaths of so many of his comrades, and so rashly have chosen his own time to appear before God? The band of the Connaught Rangers came at seven o'clock to play him to a quieter resting-place than the bed of the sparkling, babbling stream—a solitary grave dug just in front of our lines, and near enough for us, during our stay, to protect him from the dogs.

Three more of the reconnoitring party's horses are lying in the shadow of death. I had been pained by all this, and Henry and I, ordering our horses, rode out, in the cloudless summer evening, to a quiet little village nestled among the hills, where the storks build their nests on the old treetops that shade the trickling fountain where the cattle drink. Colonel Shewell met us as we rode into camp with a radiant face, telling us that all the transports are ordered up from Varna, and that we are to embark immediately for Vienna, as the Russians are so enraged with Austria for taking part against us that they have determined on besieging that place.

Saturday, 15th.—The Vienna "shave" turned out false; instead, came an order desiring that all our heavy baggage should be sent to Varna, to be forwarded to Scutari. Heavy baggage! when we are already stript of everything but absolute necessaries, and are allowed barely sufficient ponies to transport what we have!

Letters arrived last night, but were not delivered till today. Yesterday evening Henry and I took a lovely ride to Koslud-sche, a small town about eight miles from the camp. The pastoral scenes, in this land of herds and flocks, speak in flute-like tones of serenity and repose—the calm, unruffled lives of the simple people, the absence of all excitement, emulation, traffic, or noise; valley and hillside sending home each night its lowing herds, and strings of horses, flocks of sheep and goats.

The lives of the inhabitants are little removed above the cattle which they tend; but to one who "has forgotten more life than most people ever knew," the absence of turmoil and all the "stale and unprofitable uses of the world," the calm aspect of the steadfast hills, the quietude of the plains, and the still small voices of the flowers, all tell me, that however worn the mind may be, however bruised the heart, nature is a consoler still; and we who have fretted away our lives in vain effort and vainer show, find her large heart still open to us, and in the shadow of the eternal hills a repose for which earth has no name.

Sunday, 16th.—Henry and I took a new ride this evening. We turned into the gorge to the left of our camp; but leaving the *araba* track, we struck into a narrow footpath, embowered with trees, and frowned over by stern and perpendicular rocks, at whose foot ran the narrow fissure along which we rode slowly. Emerging at last, we came on an open plain covered with heavy crops of barley; crossing this for a short distance, we came presently into another thick copse of underwood, down which we had to ride, over precipitous and rocky ground, where the horses could barely keep their footing, and where a false step must have been fatal. The stars lighted our track, and we descended safely. We found ourselves on the road to Devna, and, waking up our horses, we cantered over the plain to our camp.

Wednesday, 19th.—I have mentioned nothing that has happened since Sunday; as, except the usual routine of parades and camp-life, and perpetual fresh reports as to our eventual destination, nothing has occurred. But today we lost one of the poor fellows who had returned ill from the reconnoitring expedition. He came back with low fever, and, after being two days insensible, expired this afternoon. Henry and I, accompanied by Captains Hall Dare and Evans of the 23rd, rode today to Pravadi. We started at one o'clock, and returned soon after eight.

Next to Silistria, Pravadi is the strongest fortified town in Bulgaria. The town lies in what (approaching from the Devna side) appears to be an abyss. High, perpendicular rocks, like the boundaries of a stern sea-coast, enclose it, east and west. Fortifications protect it on the south, and a fortification and broad lake on the north. We rode to it through lovely home scenery, softened by the blue range of the Balkan in the distance. We saw almost to Varna. In the town we found shops, and purchased damson-cheese and some Turkish scarfs.

My pony, "Whisker," cast a shoe in going, and Captain Hall Dare started without one; so we stopped at a farrier's and had them shod. My saddle excited immense curiosity. They touched and examined it all over; and several men tried to sit in it, but Henry prevented them. We went to a café, where we got a cup of first-rate coffee; and at about half-past four, we started to ride home. Oh, the heat! We made a ride of about twenty-two miles, but its beauty well repaid us for our trouble.

The Turks have a unique way of shoeing horses. One man fastens a cord round the horse's fetlock, and so holds up his leg; a second man holds aside the animal's tail, and with a horse-hair flapper keeps away the flies; a third man holds his head and talks to him; while the fourth, squatting on the ground, with his head on a level with the horse's foot, hammers away with all his might at eight nails, four on each side.

Friday, 21st.—News came that Sir G. Brown had gone to the Crimea, to discover the best place for landing troops, and that we should follow him before long—at which we were glad.

Sunday, 23rd.—The cholera is come amongst us! It is not in *our* camp, but is in that of the Light Division, and sixteen men have died of it this day in the Rifles.

We hear the whole camp is to be broken up; the Light Division are to march to Monastir, and *we* are under orders to march to Issyteppe tomorrow. I regret this move very much, as it will separate me from Lady Erroll, whose acquaintance has been the greatest comfort and pleasure to me; but I trust we shall soon be quartered together again, as no one but myself can tell the advantage I have derived from the friendship of such a woman.

Monday, 24th.—The march is postponed, owing to the difficulty of finding sufficient water at Jeni-bazaar, which is to be our destination. Captain Lockwood volunteered to ascertain for Lord Cardigan what were the supplies of water, and started for that purpose this afternoon. I, acting on Lady Erroll's suggestion, rode down to the 11th lines this evening to call on Mrs. Cresswell, who has arrived with her husband, Captain Cresswell, of the 11th Hussars. I could not but pity the unnecessary discomforts in which the poor lady was living, and congratulated myself and Henry, as we rode away, on our pretty marquee and green bower.

Present orders say we do not march till Wednesday. Lord Cardigan has been searching unsuccessfully for another camping-ground. Mr. Macnaghten, who rode into Varna, tells me that the transports are all being ordered up, but that the *Shooting Star* had been cast on account of defective rigging. Henry rode into Varna. Towards evening I started on horseback with Captain Chetwode to meet him, and we rode to Aladyn. The infantry of our division moved today eight miles over the hills. They move, in the hope of averting that fearful malady which has crept among them. We hear it is raging at Varna, and that a quarantine is established between that place and Constantinople. For ourselves, we have had a solitary case of smallpox; but the poor fellow has been taken to the hospital at Varna today.

Tuesday, 25th.—Orders to march tomorrow morning to Issyteppe.

Two o'clock, p.m.—Captain Lockwood having returned, and reported an insufficiency of water, he was ordered to repair again to the place to endeavour to discover water in the neighbourhood.

Three o'clock.—March postponed till tomorrow night at soonest, Lord Cardigan having taken a fancy to a night march. There is no moon just now.

Five o'clock.—March definitely settled for tomorrow morning at six.

Thursday, 27th.—The cavalry of the Light Division, with Captain Maude's troop of Horse Artillery, marched this morning to Issyteppe,—a wretched village, situated in a large plain about twelve miles from Devna.

A most uninteresting country led to it,—flat and bare, destitute of trees or water, except one half-dried fountain, with a rotting carcass lying beside it. When we attempted to water our thirsty horses, only few could drink; the rest had to hold on, as best they could, till they reached their journey's end.

A now dry, boggy ditch, which runs through the village, brought a plague of frogs to our camp; and a heavy thunderstorm, rattling on our heads as we sat on the sward at dinner, drove us, drenched and uncomfortable, to our tents, and wetted our boxes. Captain Lockwood and I walked down to the village before sunset, to endeavour to procure an araba wheel (ours had come off), also a chicken for tomorrow's breakfast; but we failed in both: there was nothing but old women, cats, and onions in the place.

Friday, 28th.—My husband's birthday! and he is likely to be, for today at least, miserable enough. We were roused, wet and dreary, at three o'clock. At six we were in our saddles; and a very distressing march I found it, though it did not exceed fourteen miles. The heat was intolerable, the sun blinding. The horses again started without water, nor was there any between Issyteppe and Jeni-bazaar. We reached the latter place about half-past eleven; and immediately after the piquet poles were put down, there was a simultaneous rush to the fountains of the town to water the horses. Poor wretches, how they rushed to the water!

Poor old Hatchet (Captain Lockwood's horse) nearly went head foremost down the well, while others upset bucket after bucket, by thrusting their heads into them before they reached the ground. There was a fine group of trees near a fountain opposite our lines, and under their refreshing shade the brigadier pitched his tent. A feeling of great dissatisfaction was caused by the troops being forbidden either to water their horses, or to obtain water for the use of the officers, from the fountain in question, although the other fountains are so far off. The fountain, being so little drained, overflowed in the night, and a fatigue party were put in requisition to make a drain. If Æsop were alive, I wonder if this would inspire him with another fable? Tonight I am thoroughly exhausted with fatigue.

Sunday, 30th.—Lord Cardigan tells us today that we shall remain here until we go into winter quarters at Adrianople.

Tuesday, August 1st.—Our tents not being pitched on the right (our place as senior regiment out), Lord Cardigan changed us today, causing us to change places with the 13th Light Dragoons. Our tents when changed were not quite in a line, though I confess it was barely perceptible; but at evening we had to strike and move all our tents about a foot and a half further back. We hear today that the Light Division have lost 100 men and four officers.

Friday, 4th.—I regret to say that poor Captain Levinge, of the R. H. A., is dead. The report is, that having been suffering from

45

incipient cholera, he took an overdose of laudanum. He is much regretted. An artilleryman of Captain Maude's troop died of cholera, and was buried yesterday. This is our first case of cholera. Captain Stevenson, 17th Lancers, took me for a ride this evening to a wondrous gorge, about three miles from our camp.

We passed suddenly from a sunny landscape, laden with grain, into Arabia Petræa. It was as though the hills had been rifted asunder, so high, narrow, sombre, and stern were the gloomy walls that almost threatened to close over our heads. A small torrent ran at the foot, tumbling over huge masses of rock, which had fallen from the grim heights above. I felt oppressed; and reaching the open fields once more, put "Bob" into a canter, which he seemed as willing to enjoy as myself.

Saturday, 5th.—"I never watched upon a wilder night." At evening-tide it was hot and sultry, but at midnight up came the wind, sweeping broadly and grandly over the plain. We feared for our tent, although well secured; and presently across the hurricane came booming the great guns of the thunder. The lightning seemed to pierce our eyelids. By morning every trace of storm had vanished, and day looked out smiling as before, though her lashes were gemmed with heavy tear-drops, and the deep trees near us at intervals shivered out a sigh.

The adjutant-general came to camp today. He says the infantry are under orders to embark on the 16th for the Crimea. Are we to go too? or are we to be left out here, to constitute a travelling Phœnix Park for Lord ——?

Thursday, 10th.—Rose at half-past three, and by five, Henry, Captain Tomkinson, Captain Chetwode, Mr. Mussenden, and I were starting for Schumla. We broke into a canter after leaving the village of Jeni-bazaar, and in two hours and five minutes reached Schumla, a distance of fifteen miles. Here we met Captain Saltmarshe, Mr. Trevelyan, and Mr. Palmer, of the 11th, and Mr. Learmouth of the 17th, and had a joint breakfast, and a very nasty one, at the Locanda, kept by Hungarians. That over, we walked about the town. It is very picturesque; the houses are nestled in trees, but are irregular, dirty, and mean.

In the Greek shops we succeeded in making a few purchases, such as a glass tumbler, five china plates, a soup ladle (tin), and some Turkish towels. I tried hard to procure some tea, lemons, or arrowroot for our sick in hospital, but I might as well have asked for a new-fashioned French bonnet. They did not know what I wanted. I bought a fine Turkish bridle, and we returned to the Locanda, where I lay down on the boards (Oh, how hard they were!) to try to sleep for an hour. It was impossible.

The bugs took a lease of me, and the fleas, in innumerable hosts, disputed possession. A bright-eyed little mouse sat demurely in the corner watching me, and twinkling his little black eyes as I stormed at my foes. Our dinner was tough meat and excellent champagne, which we did not spare; and after admiring the sunset tints on the fine forts of the town, we again got into our saddles; and a great moon, with a face as broad, red, round, and honest as a milkmaid's, shed her hearty beams over us and lighted us home, and afterwards to bed.

Poor Major Willett lies sick in the village of Jeni-bazaar, where he has been moved for the sake of quiet.

Friday, 11th.—Ilinsky (or some such name), the Hungarian commandant, came over and dined with us. Two or three funerals today. The 5th Dragoon Guards are suffering terribly from cholera. Two days ago eleven men died. The report of the great fire in Varna, which reached us two days since, proves to be quite correct. It seems to have ravaged the town. Various rumours are afloat concerning its origin; some suppose it was set on fire by the Greeks, at Russian instigation. Many shops, and much of the commissariat stores, are burnt; and the plunder during the fire was said to be enormous. Our supplies must in future be drawn from Schumla.

Why has there been no branch commissariat at Schumla? Varna is a two-days' march from us. It is also a fact, that the commissariat chest in Varna was guarded by one slovenly Turkish sentry. Our sad sickness increases. Our hospital tents are full. Poor Mr. Philips is now attacked with fever; and the sun sets daily on many new-made graves. A second hospital marquee arrived for our regiment today.

Wednesday, 16th.—Today's mail brought us the sad news of the death of Miss D., Henry's step-sister,—loved and regretted by us all. This took away the pleasure we felt in the arrival of our letters.

Thursday, 17th.—Henry and I took a long ride, to endeavour to shake off the depression which this perpetual sickness forces upon one. We had never before seen suffering that we could not alleviate; but here there are no comforts but scanty medical stores, and the burning, blistering sun glares upon heads already delirious with fever. I am sure that nervous apprehension has much to do with illness; and, indeed, if the mind abandons itself to the actual contemplation of our position, it is enough to make it quail.

Friday, 18th.—Poor Mrs. Blaydes (my servant), after recovering from an attack of fever, brought on a relapse today from over-anxiety to attend to my comforts. She endeavoured to work till her health absolutely forbad it; and a great assistance she was to me. Poor woman! she has been insensible since morning.

A woman of the 13th died today. Hospital marquees were shifted to fresh ground, as it was observed that men put into them almost invariably died. Henry and I rode to where Captain Chetwode and Mr. Clutterbuck were shooting; and on our return we met Lord Cardigan, who tells me all the talk is of Sebastopol; and he thinks the Light Cavalry will be under orders before long. Another mail, laden with heavy news. Poor little W.! F.'s only son! I have so many feelings in my heart; and yet they must all be absorbed in sympathy for the sorrowing father and mourning mother!

Saturday, 10th.—Rode with Henry to a village on the left of our camp, about six miles off, the name of which I do not know. What a ride that was!

What a day it was that day,

Hills and vales did openly
Seem to heave and throb away
At the sight of the great sky,
And the silence as it stood
In the glory's golden flood,
Audibly did bud and bud.

After climbing up the sides of an interminable hill, we reached the table land—oaks, walnuts, filberts, a very wilderness of trees! We plunged down into a deep and leafy gorge, stopped at the wayside fountain, and finally emerged into the broad plain of the camp.

Sunday, 20th.—Poor Mrs. Blaydes expired this morning! Truly, we are in God's hands, and far enough from the help of man! Insufficient medical attendance (many of the doctors are ill), scanty stores, and no sick diet—we must feed our dying on rations and rum! As far as I am concerned, I feel calm, and filled with a tranquil faith: I have the strongest trust in the wise providence of God.

Monday, 21st—Went out with Henry over the stubble to shoot quail; Captain Chetwode had the gun, and killed several brace.

Tuesday, 22nd.—Henry made a salami of the quail for breakfast that was truly delicious: I could be a gourmet, if I could always feed on such salamis. Mr. Clowes, Henry, and I went out today; Henry shooting, Mr. Clowes and I beating from our ponies with long whips.

Wednesday, 23rd.—Mr. Maxse, *aide-de-camp* to Lord Cardigan, who has returned today from Varna (sick-leave), says the troops are embarking fast; that the harbour is filled with transports; that siege guns are being put on board, and every preparation making for an expedition to the Crimea. We are reanimated! The sickness decreases; cooler weather is coming on; things look more cheerily now.

We rode today with Captain Tomkinson—such a pretty ride!

Going south for five miles, we turned to our right on smooth, long turf, by a little stream whose course was only marked by the flowers along its banks. Then came large trees bowed down with foliage, and hill sides matted with creeping plants, clematis and vine. Turning homeward, we saw fields of tobacco and Indian corn. We were a long way from home; so waking up our ponies, we left the Turkish camp and conical hill on our left, and galloped over the turf to Jeni-bazaar, and then uphill to our lines.

Thursday, 24th.—Returning from a ride among the filbert trees—how the nuts fell into our hands and laps!—we met Mr. Maxse riding at a gallop. He bore orders for our immediate embarkation at Varna for Sebastopol. The artillery and 11th Hussars are to march tomorrow; we, and the 13th and 17th, follow on Saturday. The order was heard silently; not a single cheer: we have waited in inaction too long. Sickness and death are uppermost in our thoughts just now. I also am not well—the hard food tells on me; and to become well, rest and change of diet are necessary: but I don't see much chance of getting either.

Saturday, 26th.—We started at ten o'clock on our first day's march. We left our poor colonel on the ground, too ill to be moved. Mr. Philips and Mr. Somers were also left behind in the village, to follow as they best could. We halted at Issyteppe, where we had also stopped on our way up. Here the 13th and 17th remained until Monday; and we fondly hoped to do the same, but are ordered to march on tomorrow to Gottuby. Both our servants, Connell and Hopkins, are ill; and I am very suffering, so much so as to doubt my ability to march tomorrow.

Sunday, 27th.—Marched to Gottuby, and encamped on the cholera-stricken ground just vacated by the Heavies. We had appalling evidence of their deaths! Here and there a heap of loose earth, with a protruding hand or foot, showed where the inhabitants had desecrated the dead, and dug them up to possess themselves of the blankets in which they were buried.

Nevertheless, we gladly halted, for the heat was very distressing; though it would have been better if the sick had gone on to Devna, as they will now have no halt in their march tomorrow. The 13th who remained at Issyteppe, lost a man of cholera. He was taken ill at four, and buried at six o'clock. We do not start before nine o'clock tomorrow. I hope to be able to ride.

Monday, 28th.—A cold, showery morning refreshed us all, and made the horses' coats stare. Oh, how much have I, though only slightly ill, felt the miseries attendant on sickness out here! It depresses one to know that every remedy is out of one's power. Come rain, come heat, on you must go: were it not for my trust in the Great Strength my heart would fail. We reached Devna about eleven, glad to see the old place again. And the river! how we walked the horses up and down in it, and how they thrust their parched heads into the stream, than which no stream ever seemed so limpid or so sweet!

Tuesday, 29th.—"March at half-past six to Varna." March delayed till half-past seven, at which time we started (I with an ether bottle) over the hills to Aladyn, and so to Varna by the upper road. The colonel was unable to leave his bed, and followed in an *araba*. The ride was beautiful. We passed a singular geological formation of large rocks, resembling the ruins of a huge temple with many towers. We reached our camping ground (the middle of a stubble field) at twelve o'clock.

We passed two camps on the road—one Sir De L. Evans's; the other a part of the Light Division, consisting of the 19th, 77th, and 88th. The 88th seemed in sad spirits: they lost their surgeon yesterday of cholera, and the major was then supposed to be dying. All round us are camped the various regiments—French and English cavalry, infantry, and artillery, and Turkish infantry and cavalry. The Rifles embarked today.

I heard that Lady Erroll was seen riding into Varna, to embark with them. Colonel Yea (7th Fusiliers) called on me, and told me that his regiment was to embark tomorrow in the *Emperor*; he also said his regiment was to be the first to land. At five o'clock we saw no chance of getting anything to eat (we had had nothing since six in the morning), and I could not bear it any longer; so we saddled the ponies, and cantered into Varna.

Here of course we found all the shops closed, but at length discovered a small restaurateur in a back street, who gave us some excellent soup, vile cutlets, and good macaroni. In the almost pitchy darkness, we felt for our ponies, and were groping our way home, when we passed the hospital in which Dr. Mackay, who came out with us in the *Shooting Star*, and who was appointed to the staff from the 12th regiment, resides. We ran upstairs, and found him, with one or two brother medicos, drinking rum-and-water, and "smoking a weed."

He made us most welcome; and, from his account of his patients, appears to be working hard and most self-sacrificingly in the good work of trying to alleviate pain. We soon left him to continue our way home. Lord Cardigan, immediately on my arriving at Varna, went to head-quarters to ask Lord Raglan's permission for me to accompany the troops to the Crimea. Lord Cardigan was at the trouble of bringing me Lord Raglan's answer himself.

It was a decided negative. "But," added Lord Cardigan (touched perhaps by my sudden burst of tears, for I was so worn and weak!), "should you think proper to disregard the prohibition, I will not offer any opposition to your doing so."

Wednesday, 30th.—Too weak to rise. I thank God we remain here today, and perhaps tomorrow, as the *Himalaya* has not yet come in. Captain George and Major Eman called on me, but I was not able to see them. Two men who marched in with us yesterday are dead of cholera today. "Oh God, in whose hands are the issues of life and death!"

Thursday, 31st.—I was congratulating myself on the chance of another quiet day, when an *aide-de-camp* galloped up to say that the *Himalaya* had arrived in harbour, and we were to turn out immediately to embark. It was then one o'clock. I tried to rise, but at first could hardly stand, and gave up all hope of packing. As soon as they could be got under weight, the bullock wagons started for the quay. Wrapped in an old hat and shawl, Henry lifted me on my dear, gentle pony's back, and we crept down to Varna. But no embarkation for us that night. Till ten o'clock I waited before our *arabas* arrived, and our tent was pitched; a kind-hearted woman of the regiment gave me a boa, and at half-past ten we got a little dinner, and turned into bed.

CHAPTER 3

The Expedition to the Crimea

He that has sail'd upon the dark blue sea
Has view'd at times, I ween, a full fair sight,
When the fresh breeze is fair as breeze may be,—
The white sails set the gallant frigate tight—
Masts, spires, and strand retiring to the right;—
The glorious main expanding o'er the bow,—
The convoy spread, like wild swans in their flight—
The dullest sailor wearing bravely now,—
So gaily curl the waves above each dashing prow!

Byron.

Ἔπειτα δὲ Κιμμερίοισιν
Νῆα θοὴν ἐπάγοντες ἱκάνομεν.

The Argonauts.

September 1st.—The embarkation began at six o'clock. Whilst the troops were filing down, Captain Lockwood, one of Lord Cardigan's *aides-de-camp*, rode up with an order from Lord Lucan that no officer was to embark more than one horse; those who had embarked more were to send them ashore again. Pleasant news this for me! However, I had no time to grumble, but hoisting myself into an *araba* full of baggage, and disguised as much as possible, I went down to the shore. Lord Lucan, who was there, scanned every woman, to find traces of a lady; but he searched in vain, and I, choking with laughter hurried past his horse into the boat.

Here the crew received me very hospitably, gave me some water, and a compliment on the clearness of my cheeks, which "did not look as though I had done much hard work in the sun," and finally put me safely on board the *Himalaya*, where I was immediately handed down to my cabin.

Monday, 4th.—We hoped to sail today.

Tuesday, 5th.—I have remained in my cabin ever since I came on board. Well may we pray for "all prisoners and captives." After my free life under the "sweet heavens," to be hermetically sealed up in the narrow cabin of a ship—I cannot breathe, even though head and shoulders are thrust out of window.

Since I have been here death has been amongst us. Poor Captain Longmore, who on Friday helped me up the ship's side, was dead on Sunday morning—

Stretch'd no longer on the rack of this rough world.

Death with such inexorable gripe appears in his most appalling shape. He was seized but on Friday with diarrhœa, which turned to cholera on Saturday, and on Sunday the body was left in its silent and solemn desolation. During his death struggle the party dined in the saloon, separated from the ghastly wrangle only by a screen. With few exceptions, the dinner was a silent one; but presently the champagne corks flew, and—but I grow sick, I cannot draw so vivid a picture of life and death. God save my dear husband and me from dying in the midst of the din of life! The very angels must stand aloof. God is our hope and strength, and without Him we should utterly fail.

Today the signal came to proceed to Balchick Bay; and having hooked ourselves on to No. 78., with the Connaught Rangers on board, we steamed to join the flight of ships sailing from Varna. About two hours brought us to Balchick; and the appearance of the bay, crowded with every species of ship, from the three-decker man-of-war down to the smallest river steam-tug, filled the mind with admiration at the magnificent naval resources of England.

Delay prevails here as everywhere. The fleet are all collected and awaiting the order to proceed. Sebastopol is within thirty-six hours' sail, and apparently there is no impediment: but not a vessel has weighed anchor.

Wednesday, 6th.—Some say we are waiting for the wind to change, or lull; others that we are to wait until the *Banshee* arrives with despatches from England. Many more are betting that peace is proclaimed, and that we shall be met at Sebastopol by a flag of truce. I incline to the opinion that we are waiting for the *Banshee*." The weather continues lovely. The master of the *Echinga* came on board tonight, and tells me that Lady Erroll is in his ship, and that she intends remaining on board during the siege. I had fully made up my mind to, and until this unhappy order of "only one horse" threw over all my plans. My husband, too, seems to think that I could not encounter the fatigue on foot, so I fear I must (most reluctantly) consent to follow him by sea to Sebastopol. Our sick list increases frightfully.

Thursday, 7th.—We sailed in company of the fleet, a truly wonderful sight! News arrived last night of the taking of Bomarsund, which put us all in spirits; and as no accident occurred beyond the snapping of a hawser, we made a successful start.

Friday, 8th.—No motion is perceptible in this magnificent ship, though her mighty heart throbs night and day, and there is sufficient sea to make the transport behind us pitch disagreeably. Were it not for the rush of water beneath the saloon windows, I should fancy myself on land. Walking on the deck, between the lines of horses, I cannot fail to have made friends with two or three—one in particular, a fine large Norman-headed chestnut, with a long flowing mane, and such kindly eyes.

Saturday, 9th.—At a signal from the flag-ship, we pulled up to anchor, in order to concentrate the fleet and allow the laggards to come up. Ignorance concerning our movements prevails everywhere, and conjectures are rife. Many absolutely doubt whether Sebastopol is to be our destination or not. Henry has been very far from well these last few days, and is laid up with an attack of lumbago, particularly unwelcome just now. Dr. Evans, who has been appointed to the regiment, shows very humane feeling; and I trust, under his kind care, my dear husband will soon recover. Poor Connell, our soldier-servant, still lies sick and suffering; but I hear from Sergeant Lynch that he is, if anything, better.

Sunday, 10th.—Still at anchor, 160 miles from Sebastopol. Yesterday, when we stopped our engines, we were nearly meeting with a serious accident. The transport ship behind us, having too short a hawser, and too much way on her, ran into us, smashing our jolly boat, and crashing through our bulwarks and taffrail like so much brown paper.

Monday, 11th.—The *Caradoc* and *Agamemnon* have returned. Signals fly from the mast-head of the flag-ship: "Prepare to get under weigh." Discussion of our unknown destination; some say Odessa—some Sebastopol.

Sunshine above, and smooth water below. On board not half-a-dozen men feel "as if they were on the eve of fighting."

Tuesday, 12th.—At 9, a.m., we came in sight of the Crimea. We have been on board twelve days today. Twelve days accomplishing 300 miles! The delay puzzles as much as it grieves and disgusts. Lord Cardigan, too, is growing very impatient of it. Towards evening the ships drew up closer together. Magnificent two- and three-deckers sailed on each side of the transport fleet. A forest of masts thrust their spear-like heads into the sunset clouds. Birnam Wood is come to Dunsinane! At even-fall, the *Brenda*, a little *Danube* boat, drawing four feet of water, was ordered off to Sebastopol to reconnoitre. An answering pendant was run up to her peak: a puff of smoke, a turn of her paddle-wheels, and away flew the little craft, shaking out her white wings like a bird.

Wednesday, 13th.—The entrance to the harbour of Sebastopol is distinctly visible. Everyone is roused up and full of energy, except my dear husband, who lies sick and full of pain in his cabin. I much fear he will not be able to land. A signal at twelve o'clock to "Keep in your station." We are near enough to the shore to see houses, corn, cattle, and a horse and covered cart.

Not a shot has been fired; all is tranquillity in the serene sky above, and the unrippled waters beneath. All are quiet except Lord Cardigan, who is still full of eagerness. Poor Connell is not nearly so well. There is a soldier's wife on board, too, suffering severely from fever. What will become of her when the troops disembark!

Thursday, 14th.—Leaving Eupatoria behind us, we hauled close in shore, about nine o'clock, about thirty miles from Sebastopol. The French began to disembark forthwith, and by ten o'clock the tricolour was planted on the beach. I have a painful record to make. During last night our poor servant Connell, after struggling long with fever, succumbed to it, and closed his eyes, I trust, in peace. I did not know of his danger till I heard of his death. Today he was committed to the keeping of the restless sea, until the day when it shall give up its dead.

Friday, 15th.—English troops disembarking in a heavy surf. The landing of the horses is difficult and dangerous. Such men as were disembarked yesterday were lying all exposed to the torrents of rain which fell during the night. How it did rain! In consequence an order has been issued to disembark the tents. The beach is a vast and crowded camp, covered with men, horses, fires, tents, general officers, staff officers, boats landing men and horses, which latter are flung overboard, and swum ashore. Eleven were drowned today. I am glad to say we lost none. Lord Cardigan begins to be eager for the fray, and will be doing something or other directly he has landed, I fancy. He landed today at five.

Saturday, 16th.—All our horses were ashore by half-past ten, and started immediately on outpost-duty, for which they tell me Lord Cardigan has taken a force of rifles and artillery as well. At ten o'clock today, with failing heart, I parted from my dear husband, and watched him go ashore; whilst I, alas! having no horse, cannot follow him, but must go on board the *Shooting Star*, and get round by sea. How I hate it! How much rather I would endure any hardship than be separated from him at this time! But my reason and strength both tell me it is impracticable, and so I must make up my mind to it. Captain Fraser received me with his usual most considerate kindness, and tried by every means to make me forget my wretched position.

Sunday, 17th.—Artillery disembarking all day from the *Shooting Star*. One poor fellow caught his hand in a block, and tore it terribly.

Monday, 18th.—Today I set my foot in the Crimea.

A lovely day tempted me to disembark and try to see my dear husband on shore. Captain Fraser and I started at twelve o'clock. On landing amongst the artillery, we first inquired for the poor fellow who was hurt yesterday, and then for the Light Cavalry. "They are seven miles inland!!" I never can forget, or be sufficiently grateful to the officers of artillery for, the kindness they showed me this day. After looking about for a quiet horse to carry me, they decided on stopping a party of horse artillery, and getting them to give us seats on the gun-carriage.

Mr. Grylls, who had charge of the party, most courteously assented, and by his kindness I was able to reach the outposts. Here I surprised my husband, who shares a tent with five officers, and who was delighted to see me. Whilst I remained there, a patrol of the 13th Light Dragoons came in, commanded by Colonel Doherty. They had seen a body of about six hundred Cossacks, who had fired at them, but without effect. These same Cossacks, a few minutes later, had set two of the neighbouring villages, and all the corn, on fire.

After about an hour spent in camp, Henry put his regimental saddle on his horse, and I mounted him, Henry and Captain Fraser walking by my side, and we returned to the shore. Our road was lurid with the red glare of the vast fires. This country is as fertile as Bulgaria, and has all the advantages of cultivation.

In the village close to the outposts, of which the Rifles had possession, were found comfortable and well-furnished houses, with grand pianofortes, pictures, books, and everything evincing comfort and civilisation. Several of our Riflemen have been killed by the Cossacks, who hover round the army like a flying cloud. We reached the beach at dusk; and again taking leave of my husband, with a heavy heart I stepped into the boat and was rowed on board.

Tuesday, 19th.—The troops have all advanced today; and about half-past three we heard the heavy sound of the guns booming across the water, as we lay quietly at anchor. What can those guns mean? I wonder if, among the annals of a war, the sickening anxieties of mother, wife, and sister ever find a place. Let us hope the angel of compassion makes record of their tears.

Wednesday, 20th.—Left Kalamita Bay, and, with several other ships, joined the rest of the fleet off Eupatoria.

Thursday, 21st.—Captain Tatham, of the *Simoom*, took me ashore in his boat. It was a lovely day. We walked about Eupatoria; and Captain Tatham introduced me to the governor, Captain Brock, who showed me great kindness and attention. In his house (a very comfortable one, with polished oak floors and large windows) he had safely secured in "durance vile" two prisoners, the land steward and shepherd of Prince Woronzow. After leaving Captain Brock, we met a Russian *propriétaire*—one of the very few who remained in the town.

He conversed with us in French for some time, and showed us over the Greek church. Nearly all the inhabitants, terrified at the apparition of an enemy's fleet, had fled. Captain Brock, in the hope of procuring prompt supplies, has fixed a tariff regulating the price of all kinds of stock; and the Tartar population, delighted at the ready and large circulation of money, bring in provisions freely and willingly. Eupatoria is rather a pretty town, interspersed with trees, with large, low, comfortable-looking, detached houses.

Friday, 22nd.—Was awoke from a restless sleep by the entrance of my maid—a soldier's wife—with her apron over her eyes. I naturally asked what was the matter. "Oh, ma'am! Captain Tatham has sent to say he has received despatches, which will oblige him to leave Eupatoria today. And there has been a dreadful battle—500 English killed, and 5000 Russians; and all our poor cavalry fellows are all killed; and, the Lord be good to us, we're all widows."

God, and he only, knows how the next hour was passed—until the blessed words, "O thou of little faith," rang in my heart.

At breakfast I asked Captain Fraser for the particulars of the message; but he, from a feeling of kindly wishing to save me anxiety, assured me he had heard nothing about the battle, and did not believe a word of it. However, at two o'clock, I went ashore to see the Governor, and ascertain the words of the despatch. He told me that there had been a severe battle at the river Alma, but no official particulars had yet reached him.

Saturday, 23rd.—I heard more particulars of this great fight, though very few: 2090 English killed and wounded; the 7th and 23rd Fusiliers almost destroyed, and, thank God! the cavalry not engaged. How can timorous, nervous women live through a time like this!

The guns which we heard as we were breasting our swift way from Kalamita to Eupatoria, were merely messengers to us of the heavy firing inland, causing wounds, blood, and sudden death—lives, for which we would gladly give our own, extinguished in a moment; hands flung out in agony, faces calm and still in death; all our prayers unavailing now: no more speech, no more life, no more love.

Sunday, 24th.—Again awoke by the guns. Captain Fraser assured me they were the guns of the fleet. The Cossacks, last night, made a descent upon Eupatoria, and having secured some plunder, fired on our soldiers. Their fire was returned with such interest that they were soon glad to retire.

The *Danube* steamboat went this afternoon to Katcha, laden

with sheep, and taking with her a Russian prisoner—a gentleman—and supposed to be a spy. I met him directly after he was taken, as he was walking from the guard to the shore.

Monday, 25th.—A steamboat came in this morning, and Captain Fraser immediately sent off a boat to the *Simoom* (which had not left, as she threatened, on Friday) to ascertain the news.

Until as late as six o'clock we had been listening to the guns, but were little prepared for such news as Captain Tatham sent back to us.

The fleet are at the Katcha, and the army also. The fleet stood in yesterday, and fired about twenty shots. The Russians sunk five line-of-battle ships and two frigates across the harbour. Three remain, which cannot get out, nor can we get in. A prisoner reports that all is consternation—Menschikoff in tears. At Eupatoria news flies from mouth to mouth. They say that, at Alma, the charge of Highlanders was most magnificent; that they swept over the Russian entrenchments like a sea. Our Cavalry being so weak we were unable to follow up our advantage, or we might have cut off the enemy in their retreat. It is said that the whole garrison of Sebastopol was engaged at Alma—50,000 Russians to about 45,000 English and French. I hear the English bore the brunt of the fight.

Went ashore this afternoon, and rode with Captain Brock, who most kindly provides me with both horse and saddle. After we had finished our ride, we went to one of the deserted houses, where we found a grand pianoforte—the first I had played on for so long! It was like meeting a dear and long absent friend.

The house and garden were soon filled, and echoing to the magnificent chords of "Rule Britannia;" whilst Tennyson's sweet words, "Break, Break, Break," and the "Northern Star," fitted both the occasion and the place.

One more song and I must hasten back, to be on board my ship by twilight. Heavy guns are pouring their dull broadsides on our straining ears. What shall the song be, sad and low, or a wild outburst of desperate courage? I have it:—

Non curiamo l'incerto domani:

Se quest' oggi n' è dato goder.

Tuesday, nine o'clock.—The day rose foggy and gloomy, and my heart, notwithstanding its elation yesterday at the brilliant conduct of our troops, was dull, anxious, and sad. I am engaged to ride with Captain Brock, and am restless to go ashore, in the hope of hearing news. Oh this suspense! How could I be so weak as to allow myself to be separated from my husband? A life-time of anxiety has been crowded into these ten days.

Eight o'clock found me on board the *Danube*, steaming, trembling, rushing through the water towards the fleet at Katcha. A note from Captain Tatham, brought up by the *Danube*, at three o'clock, induced me to go and see whether I could not get on board the *Star of the South*, and so go down to Balaklava with the siege train. I had one hour to decide; and, packing up a few things in a carpet bag, and taking my saddle, I went on board at four o'clock.

September 27th.—Mr. Cator having duly reported my arrival to Admiral Dundas, the admiral did two things: first, he sent on board some excellent white bread, milk, eggs, &c. &c., for breakfast; and, secondly, he proposed either that I should go down to Balaklava in the *Simoom*, and so be passed to the *Star of the South*; or else, if, as was most probable, this latter ship had been sent to Scutari with wounded, that I should return to Eupatoria, and be sent down by the earliest opportunity. I decided, therefore, on availing myself of Mr. Cator's kind offer to take me back to Eupatoria, and we started at eleven o'clock. Today we stood close in shore, on the coast of Alma. On our right stood heights occupied by the Russian army; on our left the place where our army bivouacked. Huge volumes of thick, smouldering smoke still rolled heavily over the plain. The *Albion*, close in shore, was occupied in removing wounded. Here and there dark masses lay about, war's silent evidence; and overall was the serene heaven, smiling on a lovely landscape, sunny and bright. And I, too:

Smil'd to think God's greatness shone around our incompleteness,

And round our restlessness—His rest.

The cabin of the *Danube* was full of trophies of the fight-helmets pierced with shot and dabbled in blood, little amulets of brass, all blood-stained and soiled, muskets, bayonets, and swords stained with the red rust of blood. We hear that our army have taken Balaklava, after a slight resistance. Balaklava is a small harbour to the southward of Sebastopol, affording, from its depth and shelter, a wonderful anchorage for ships. This we suppose will be the base of operations; here all our ammunition stores, troops, &c., will be disembarked.

They compute the number of men inside Sebastopol at about 16,000. On arriving at Eupatoria I heard, with feelings of great sorrow, that Colonel Chester and Captain Evans, of the 23rd, are both killed; that Lord Erroll is wounded; and that poor Mrs. Cresswell is a widow. God help and support her under a blow that would crush me to my grave! The last tidings heard of Mrs. Cresswell were, that she had gone down to Varna in the *War Cloud*. I conclude by this time she has gone home, as Captain Cresswell died of cholera on the Monday of the march. Major Wellesley also died about that time, on board the *Danube*; and his boxes, sword, hat, &c., were lying in the cabin—a melancholy sight! How full of anxiety I am!

About two o'clock we were safely at anchor off Eupatoria. We went ashore. Captain Brock very kindly mounted Mr. Cator and me, and we three rode round the fortifications. Captain Brock received information, last evening, of 1800 Cossacks within a few miles of the town. We, too, shall have to record the Battle of Eupatoria. The ride over, I adjourned to the *Shooting Star*, but during the afternoon I met, and was introduced to, Captain King, of the *Leander*, who very kindly asked me to dine tomorrow. Thus ends my birthday!—day ever to be remembered, as on it I saw my first battlefield. How many more shall I see ere I am a year older? Shall I ever live to see another year? Look on into the winter, with its foreboding of suffering, cold, privation, and gloom!

What wilt thou become through yon drear stretch of dismal wandering?

September 28th.—The *Leander's* boat came for me at two o'clock, and I had a very rough and wet passage on board. I met the captain of the *Jena*, a French man-of-war, Colonel D'Osman, in command of the French troops, Captain Brock, &c.; a very agreeable party, at which we were most hospitably entertained.

Friday, 29th.—I take a letter to Henry ashore with me today, as I trust to find some means of forwarding it, and I cannot bear the suspense any longer.

Today I am all unnerved; an indefinable dread is on me.

Captain Fraser caught a magnificent Death's-head moth, and gave it to me. I shivered as I accepted it. This life of absence and suspense becomes at times intolerable. Oh, when shall I rejoin the army, from which I never ought to have been separated! Any hardship, any action, is better than passive anxiety.

A friend of Captain Fraser's, who came on board, tells me that none have had the courage to acquaint Mrs. Cresswell with her loss; and she is actually coming up to Balaklava with troops. Cruel kindness!

Saturday, 30th.—*Oh that my grief were thoroughly weighed, and my heaviness laid in the balances together, for the sorrows of the Almighty are within me, and terror sets itself in array before me.*

Sunday, 1st October.—The *Shooting Star* is under orders for Katcha; and I am engaged to ride with Captain Brock ashore. Not a ripple stirred the water; so, trusting to Captain Fraser's assurance that the ship would not move today, I went ashore after breakfast. It was indeed a heavenly day! Our horses sauntered along, and my heart involuntarily looked up, through the radiant sky, to the universal God of peace and war, sunshine and storm!

We saw an immense cloud of locusts making for the sea. The air was quite obscured by them. Returning about one o'clock, what was my dismay to see the *Shooting Star* spreading her white wings, and dropping quietly out to sea! Fortunately, the *Danube* was going down at two o'clock. I did not lose a moment, but after taking a most regretful leave of pleasant, cordial Eupatoria, I went once more on board the *Danube*, and started in pursuit of the *Star*. The breeze had got up considerably, and favouring her, we found her at anchor at Katcha when we arrived.

Monday, 2nd October.—Today my adventures have been more amusing still. Not liking a dull day alone on board, I wrote a note to Lord George Paulet, who called on me immediately after breakfast, and took me away to the *Bellerophon*. Here I was in the middle of a most agreeable, lazy morning, looking out on the sparkling sea, and listening to the wondrous harmonies of a most perfect band, when Admiral Dundas sent on board to say, that if I wished to go down to Balaklava, the *Pride of the Ocean* was then passing with troops, and he would order her to be hove to; but Mrs. Duberly must not keep her waiting a moment longer than necessary."

My transit from the *Bellerophon* (through one of the lower ports), laden with a ham, some miraculous port wine, and all sorts of good things provided by Lord George's kind hospitality, was accomplished in a very short space. The admiral, however, was impatient, and Captain Christie more so. Mr. Cator was sent in the *Britannia's* galley to take me on board; and after accomplishing my packing in ten minutes, and taking my desk and carpet bag, I started in the galley and had some difficulty in overtaking the *Pride of the Ocean*.

Tuesday, 3rd.—We expected a three hours' sail; but the wind dropped, and we were becalmed for four-and-twenty. By three o'clock we were lying almost stationary before the forts of Sebastopol, and within range of the guns. It was a moment not altogether free from nervousness; but no guns molested us, and we passed unharmed. Presently we passed the light off Chersonese. We lay off the point beyond the Monastery of St. George all night; and at morning, the *Simla* came to tow us to our anchorage just outside Balaklava harbour.

This anchorage is a wonderful place; the water is extremely

deep, and the rocks which bound the coast exceed in ruggedness and boldness of outline any that I ever saw before. The harbour appears completely land-locked. Through a fissure in the cliffs you can just see a number of masts; but how they got in, or will get out, appears a mystery; they have the appearance of having been hoisted over the cliffs, and dropped into a lake on the other side.

At three o'clock, tugs came alongside the *Pride of the Ocean*, to disembark her troops, the 1st Royals, who, horses and all, were landed before dark.

At dinner, whilst I was quietly eating my soup, I heard some-one enter the cabin, and looking up saw Henry, who had heard of my arrival, and had come on board. I need not say that the evening passed happily enough! He brought me a handful of letters, which occupied me till late at night.

CHAPTER 4

Balaklava

Frigida me cohibent Euxini littora ponti;
Dictus ab antiquâ Axenus ille fuit.
Nam neque jactantur moderatis æquora ventis;
Nec placidos portus hospita navis adit.
Sunt circa gentes, quæ prædam sanguine quærunt:
Non minus infidâ terra timetur aquâ.
Nec procul a nobis locus est ubi Taurica dirâ
Cæde pharetratæ pascitur ara Deæ.

Ovid

Opfer fallen hier, Weder Lamm
noch Stier, Aber Menschen-Opfer
unerhört.

Gœthe.

Wednesday, October 4th.—This morning I landed at Balaklava, having left the *Pride of the Ocean* with regret, after endeavouring to express to Captain Kyle my deep sense of the great consideration and kindness he showed me whilst on board his ship.

Mr. Cunningham, the admiralty agent, was going on shore, and I availed myself of a seat in his boat, notwithstanding the day was a rough one; and then I learned the entrance to this wonderful harbour, where the ships lay side by side, moored to the shore as thickly as they could be packed.

In the afternoon, Henry came down to see me; and scrambling into his regimental saddle—for I had left my own on board the *Shooting Star*—we rode up to see the cavalry camp. Here I was obliged to confess, though sorely against my will, that it was impossible I could live in the camp. Henry shares his tent with three men. The cold—the impossibility of getting a separate tent, has made me resolve to remain on board ship, and go daily to the camp.

Thursday, 5th.—I rode all over the camp; went on to the Light Division, to the 63rd and 68th; took my first look at Sebastopol from the land as it lay in a hollow about two miles from us. It is a much finer town as seen from the land. The fortifications appear of great strength and number, and the buildings struck me as being large and handsome. They were busy throwing shell into our lines, but the range was too long to do us any harm.

The shells fell into a hollow at our feet; and all that I saw exploded harmlessly; though two days before one had burst in a tent of the 68th, killing one man, and wounding two. We returned through the French lines. The French soldiers seemed astonished at the apparition of a lady in their lines, and made various but very flattering remarks thereon. Late at night Mr. Cator arrived in Balaklava, and came on board the *Star of the South* to see me.

Friday, 6th.—The *Shooting Star* arrived outside Balaklava last evening. Mr. Cator sent off a gig to her for my saddle, which came ashore about twelve, and will save me much fatigue, as I find the big grey and the regimental saddle very tiring, especially in trotting.

I hear today of poor Dr. Mackay's death with great regret. He died from the effects of over-exertion in the zealous discharge of his arduous duties amongst the sick.

Sunday, 8th.—Lord Cardigan very kindly lent me a horse, and Mr. Cator and I rode up to the front. Here we saw Captain Hillyar, of the Naval Brigade, who is working hard to get his guns into position.

These seamen appear to work with the greatest energy and goodwill. One meets a gang of them harnessed to a gun, and drawing with all their might and main; or digging at entrenchments, singing, laughing, and working heartily and cheerily. But their experience of camp-life is short indeed in comparison with that of our poor soldiers, with whom they contrast so gaily.

Returning home, we met Sir Edmund Lyons, to whom I was introduced, and who asked me to dine with him tonight on board the *Agamemnon*, where I met a very old and valued friend, Captain Drummond, of the *Retribution*.

Today an affair took place which was severely canvassed at dinner. Some Russian cavalry drove in our outlying piquet in the morning, and in consequence all the cavalry, and Captain Maude's troop of H. A., turned out under Lord Lucan. By judicious generalship, they say, the whole force might have been taken, or severely punished; but a hesitation at the wrong moment allowed them all to retire out of range, after having killed two or three of our men, while they escaped unhurt.

Monday, 9th.—Walked up to camp with Mr. Bosanquet. Found Henry, who accompanied us part of the way back, and then went on board the *Danube* to luncheon. Henry and I dined there at six o'clock. In the afternoon I walked along the ridge of the stupendous rocks overlooking the sea. The spray dashed into my face—the sea foamed far beneath my feet. There was something in the strong wind, the beetling cliffs, the churning sea, and boundless view that filled me with glorious admiration and delight. Last night our dear horses "Bob" and "Whisker" arrived from Varna, and were taken to the camp this afternoon. I look forward to tomorrow, when I shall see them again.

Tuesday, 10th.—Henry brought down the grey horse, and "Whisker." The day was intensely cold, a bitter wind swept through us, chilling every pulse. When we reached the camp, we found poor "Bob" half dead with cold; so, shifting the saddles, Henry got on his back, and we stretched away at a rapid canter for the front.

Here we met Major Lowe, of the 4th Light Dragoons, and Captain Portal, who asked us to dine. We gladly accepted; and while dinner was preparing, he rode with us to the extreme right, to show us Sebastopol from a fresh point of view.

Close to us, hid in brushwood, was our own piquet; about 1000 yards from us was the Russian piquet. From the forts of Sebastopol the shot and shell came hissing every two minutes.

I could not but feel a high degree of excitement, and I think it was not unnatural. We were standing on the brow of a hill, backed by our magnificent troops, and fronting the enemy; the doomed city beneath our feet, and the pale moon above: it was indeed a moment worth a hundred years of everyday existence. I have often prayed that I might "wear out my life, and not rust it out," and it may be that my dreams and aspirations will be realised.

Wednesday, 11th.—A French transport got aground yesterday before Sebastopol. The Russians fired at her, and carried away her bowsprit. The crew deserted her, but endeavoured to get her off during the night. The garrison made a sortie this morning with the bayonet, but retreated as soon as our men turned out.

Friday, 13th.—A report was current that the fire of the siege was to open today, but hardly a shot disturbed the warm serenity of the air. What a variable climate! Three days ago the cold was intense, today the sun is oppressive. Captain Lockwood rode down to call on me. He told me with a melancholy face, that the Russians had made a successful descent on Eupatoria, and had wrested the place from us; but a lieutenant in the navy who came in shortly after, declared this information was false, as, although driven back, the force had returned, and effectually driven out the enemy.

The arrival of ships from Eupatoria laden with supplies, would seem to say that at any rate the Russians had not possession of it. The *Cambria* and *Medway* arrived today, each with a regiment of 1300 Turks.

Saturday, 14th.—Since last night two yachts have come into harbour, the *Dryad* (Lord Cardigan's) and the *Maraquita* (Mr. Carew's). What a satire is the appearance of these fairy ships amidst all the rough work of war! They seem as out of place as a London belle would be; and yet there is something very touching in their pretty gracefulness.

Henry, Captain Fane, Mr. Goss, R.N., and I started on horseback for the camp. We lunched at our own tent. Our ride took in nearly the whole front line of the camp, commencing on the right, at the ground lately occupied by the 4th Light Dragoons, passing the Rifles and the 23rd, and then returning by the French.

The entrenching work progresses rapidly, under a heavy and continuous fire. I hear that Lord Raglan was in the foremost trench last night till one o'clock. A rifleman standing near him had his head taken off by a round shot.

Either today, or yesterday, a rifleman, seeing a shell light in the entrenchment, knocked out the fuse with his rifle. He was mentioned in general orders. I cannot but think it a pity that our service provides no decoration, no distinctive reward of bravery, for such acts as this. If it were only a bit of red rag, the man should have it, and wear it immediately, as an honourable distinction, instead of waiting for a medal he may never live to obtain, or may only obtain years hence, when it shall have lost half its value.

Guns are run into position tonight; the wheels were being muffled in sheepskin when I was in camp. I heard of a sortie on the French this morning, but no particulars.

Sunday, 15th.—Awoke exhausted.

What an exhaustion! It seemed to me as though my life was ebbing away, my sands running quietly down; so I lay for a long time, becalmed in soul and body. I cannot account for this at all. I remained in this state all the morning, and did not get up till twelve o'clock; at which time Captain Nolan came in, and we had a long and interesting conversation. After discussing my afternoon's amusement, I determined on accepting his horse and saddle, with a tigerskin over the holsters; while he borrowed a pony, and we rode together to see Henry at the camp. After spending an hour in his tent, Henry and I walked down to the

Star of the South to dinner, Henry returning on foot at night.

Monday, 16th.—For three days the firing has been continuous. Captain Nolan told me yesterday that the siege would open in earnest on Tuesday. A party of us sat till late on deck, watching the flashes of the guns.

All night they kept it up, but now, 11 a.m., are quiet. The *Agamemnon* steamed out yesterday from Balaklava to join the fleet. The French are at this moment landing a fresh regiment of cavalry, and the *Medway* is being cleared of her cargo of Turks. We wait, with some little excitement, for tomorrow. I have ordered my horse at eight o'clock in the morning.

Tuesday, October 17th, 10 p.m.—At half past six o'clock began that fearful rain of shot and shell, which poured incessantly on the forts and batteries of Sebastopol, until night befriended the city, and threw her shade over it. At a quarter past seven the Round Tower was silenced, though the battery at its foot still kept up a fire from two guns, which we could not enfilade. Soon after ten Henry and I had arrived, and took our place opposite the Fourth Division.

At ten o'clock a French powder magazine exploded, which dismounted fifteen guns, and killed about forty of their men.

At half-past one, the French and English fleets, with the *Mahmoudie*, brought in their fire. The *Agamemnon*, with Sir E. Lyons on board, went close in, followed by the *Sanspareil*. The *London, Albion, Bellerophon, Retribution*, were all more or less severely mauled, as they poured in broadside after broadside, with incredible and incessant noise. I merely mention the names of such ships as I know something of. There were many others, amongst them the *Rodney, Arethusa, Trafalgar*, and the *Tribune*. The *London* was twice on fire. The *Albion* had a shell which, by unlucky chance, pitched into Captain Lushington's stores, destroying his cellar and his clothes. The *Bellerophon* had a shell through Lord George's cabin; the *Retribution* lost her mainmast.

At ten minutes past three a magnificent sight presented itself—a huge explosion in the Mud Fort (Redan), the smoke of which ascended to the eye of heaven, and then gathering, fell slowly and mournfully down to earth. I thought of torture and sudden death, and was softened to tears, while round me cheers burst from every throat—

All down the line one deafening shout.

Officers and men were carried away with enthusiasm, and I felt myself half cheering too. Three quarters of an hour after a smaller explosion caught our eye. Again the cheer rang out. "Men! Men, for God's sake! It is ours!" and an ammunition-wagon sent up its contents to form a fierce cloud in the serene sky.

We left at dusk, and rode slowly down to Balaklava, our hearts and ears filled with the magnificent din of war. Our casualties have been very few. Poor Captain Rowley and the assistant-surgeon of the 68th are dead. The gathering twilight prevented our seeing much of the damage done to the town. We fancied it greater than it proved. One of our Lancaster guns burst today; the other is doing good work. The shot rushes with such vehement noise through the air that it has been surnamed the "Express Train." We fired 170 rounds a gun yesterday (so they say). I was not sorry to find rest on board ship, being tired out with the excitement and exertion of the day.

Wednesday, 18th.—Did not intend going out early, but at nine o'clock I saw my horse saddled on the beach. A large Russian force is collected on the plains, at whom, as is evident, we are firing hard. I dressed in all haste, and started to the front. Here I found cavalry, artillery, and Turks drawn up beyond our camp, and a Russian force in the valley, at some 1,800 yards distance, standing gazing at them. The firing had all ceased, and the greater part of the Russians had retired under shelter of a hill. As soon as we were tired of looking at them, and tired of waiting for them to advance, we left the field battery, behind which we had taken our places, and went slowly on to the front.

The French batteries were unable to reopen fire. The ships were a great deal too much mauled yesterday to be able to go in again for some time. The English guns were firing, and we had some red-hot shot, in the hopes of setting fire to the town; but the town appears built of incombustible materials, although it was twice slightly on fire yesterday, the flames were almost immediately extinguished I am told that the men of Captain Lushington's battery last night refused to be relieved, though they had been at work all day. They said they had "got their range, and were doing good work, and would not go away,—all they wanted was something to eat, and some grog."

Sir George Cathcart sent them down immediately all the food and grog he could muster.

"Ah!" exclaimed one of the riflemen who had been firing at the gunners in the Mud Fort before the explosion took place, "When it blew up, in the confusion, there was beautiful shooting!"

We had luncheon in Major Wynne's tent, of the 68th, and left again about three o'clock to ride back to Balaklava. Passing the fortifications between the front and rear, we found the French mustered in rather a strong force in the battery overlooking the Russian army. No movement had been made by the Russians. They will probably remain in the shelter of the hill until they are drawn. Artillery and cavalry were coming slowly home as we approached our lines. The heavy guns of the siege still follow us with their ceaseless sound.

Colonel Hood, of the Guards, was killed today, and the ambulance corps brought down forty sick, to be embarked on board ship at Balaklava. I saw, with the aid of glasses, today a loose horse going with a strange halting gait before the batteries of the Russian forts. He was thought to be an English artillery horse wounded yesterday; strange that, among all that thunder of shot and shell, not one bullet could be spared for him.

Thursday, 19th.—We thought Sebastopol to stand, perhaps, a three days' siege—more likely a single day's; while some, more arrogant still, allowed it eight hours to resist the fury of the allies!

Now there are orders that no shot is to be fired into the town for fear of destroying the houses. Is this because Lord Raglan is confident of the speedy possession of the town, or from the estimable amiability of his private character, which makes him shrink from inflicting wanton damage or death? This order to spare the town is much commented on. However commendable the greatest humanity may be, we cannot but remember that the blood of 2090 men, lying on the field of Alma, calls to us from the ground. Were we besieged, the Russians would not show the like consideration to us.

Today we moved our camp, so as to be out of the way of the batteries we have erected on the heights round Balaklava.

I did not go to the front today. I got sick with anxiety, and deaf with the guns.

Friday, 20th.—Today the French siege-guns are in good play, and firing with good aim. They commenced their rocket-practice about two o'clock, and created a fire in the direction of the harbour. The battery at the foot of the Round Tower is still working away, though the Round Tower itself has been silenced since seven o'clock in the morning of the siege.

The French silenced a square fort on the left early today. As we rode home, we found the Russian army had moved out again, and all our forces were outposted in the batteries and at the top of the hills. However, I was too hungry to stay and watch them, and left them to look at each other at their leisure.

There is a talk of storming the town tomorrow. I fancy, if it was intended, it would not be talked about beforehand. A deserter reports that the troops inside are in fear and disheartened; if so, an assault may not be necessary.

Major Norcott, of the Rifles, to whom I was talking today, gave me a most affecting account of the death of his favourite horse at Alma. He spoke with his eyes filled with tears; and, indeed, he could hardly have found a more sympathising auditor, for I never think of my own dear grey without a sharp and cruel pain. A sailor in one of the naval batteries was wounded yesterday. But "he wasn't going to be carried about as long as he could walk;" and he actually crawled to the 68th camp, and asked for a "drink of water." Individual instances of courage are too many for me to record separately.

Saturday, 21st.—Hearing that nothing more than the usual fire was going on at the front, I did not hurry forward today, but reached my usual ground of observation in time to see an explosion behind the Round Tower, followed by a heavy fire from the two unsilenceable guns, which they kept up viciously for some time. The Russian fire was slack, and principally directed on the French lines. The French batteries are firing well. Sir George Cathcart, with whom I was in conversation for some time, tells me that no attempt must be made to storm the town *now*, until the French are ready to act in concert with us. All appear to concur in thinking that the Crimea will be our winter quarters. A very promising officer, Mr. Greathed, was killed in the naval battery today.

Sunday, 22nd.—Guns as usual.

Monday, 23rd.—Rode up to the battery on the left; I do not know which it was. Last night the men were making a new parallel, 500 yards in advance of the present ones. At what an enormous range (it appears to me) we have placed our guns! Will this long range answer? I think the siege progresses very slowly. They ran the Lancaster in and pointed it on the dockyards.

A sortie was made this morning on the French. Their first intimation of it was from a party of soldiers appearing on the embrasures, crying out, "*Ne tirez pas! nous sommes Anglais!*" Before the French discovered their mistake they had spiked three guns. A sortie was also made on our piquets, led on most gallantly by a Russian officer. He was shot in the mouth, and taken prisoner. Captain Brown, of the 44th, lost his right arm and two fingers of his left hand.

Tuesday, 24th.—Awful confusion, hurry, and noise in the harbour of Balaklava, facilitating (?) the disembarkation of twenty-four pound shot and powder.

Some artillery officers, who lunched on board the *Star of the*

South, speak much of the fatigue consequent on the work in the trenches. Our batteries succeeded in setting fire to a part of the town at half-past three, p.m., which burnt fiercely for a short time, but was eventually extinguished. A flag of truce was sent to our head-quarters today, to say that the sick and wounded were distributed in various houses in Sebastopol, which should be distinguished by a yellow flag, and to request that they might be exempt from fire; but Lord Raglan, fancying this merely a scheme to make magazines of such houses, refused to comply with the proposal.

Wednesday, 25th.—Feeling very far from well, I decided on remaining quietly on board ship today; but on looking through my stern cabin windows, at eight o'clock, I saw my horse saddled and waiting on the beach, in charge of our soldier-servant on the pony. A note was put into my hands from Henry, a moment after. It ran thus:

"The Battle of Balaklava has begun, and promises to be a hot one. I send you the horse. Lose no time, but come up as quickly as you can: do not wait for breakfast."

Words full of meaning! I dressed in all haste, went ashore without delay, and, mounting my horse "Bob," started as fast as the narrow and crowded streets would permit. I was hardly clear of the town, before I met a commissariat officer, who told me that the Turks had abandoned all their batteries, and were running towards the town. He begged me to keep as much to the left as possible, and, of all things, to lose no time in getting amongst our own men, as the Russian force was pouring on us; adding, "For God's sake, ride fast, or you may not reach the camp alive."

Captain Howard, whom I met a moment after, assured me that I might proceed; but added, "Lose no time."

Turning off into a short cut of grass, and stretching into his stride, the old horse laid himself out to his work, and soon reaching the main road, we clattered on towards the camp. The road was almost blocked up with flying Turks, some running hard, vociferating, "Ship Johnny! Ship Johnny!" while others came along laden with pots, kettles, arms, and plunder of every description, chiefly old bottles, for which the Turks appear to have a great appreciation. The Russians were by this time in possession of three batteries, from which the Turks had fled.

The 93rd and 42nd were drawn up on an eminence before the village of Balaklava. Our cavalry were all retiring when I arrived, to take up a position in rear of their own lines.

Looking on the crest of the nearest hill, I saw it covered with running Turks, pursued by mounted Cossacks, who were all making straight for where I stood, superintending the striking of our tent and the packing of our valuables. Henry flung me on the old horse; and seizing a pair of laden saddle-bags, a great coat, and a few other loose packages, I made the best of my way over a ditch into a vineyard, and awaited the event. For a moment I lost sight of our pony, "Whisker," who was being loaded; but Henry joined me just in time to ride a little to the left, to get clear of the shots, which now began to fly towards us.

Presently came the Russian cavalry charging, over the hillside and across the valley, right against the little line of Highlanders. Ah, what a moment! Charging and surging onward, what could that little wall of men do against such numbers and such speed? There they stood. Sir Colin did not even form them into square. They waited until the horsemen were within range, and then poured a volley which for a moment hid everything in smoke. The Scots Greys and Inniskillens then left the ranks of our cavalry, and charged with all their weight and force upon them, cutting and hewing right and left.

A few minutes—moments as it seemed to me—and all that occupied that lately crowded spot were men and horses, lying strewn upon the ground. One poor horse galloped up to where we stood; a round shot had taken him in the haunch, and a gaping wound it made. Another, struck by a shell in the nostrils, staggered feebly up to "Bob," suffocating from inability to breathe. He soon fell down. About this time reinforcements of infantry, French cavalry, and infantry and artillery, came down from the front, and proceeded to form in the valley on the other side of the hill over which the Russian cavalry had come.

Now came the disaster of the day—our glorious and fatal charge. But so sick at heart am I that I can barely write of it even now. It has become a matter of world history, deeply as at the time it was involved in mystery. I only know that I saw Captain Nolan galloping; that presently the Light Brigade, leaving their position, advanced by themselves, although in the face of the whole Russian force, and under a fire that seemed pouring from all sides, as though every bush was a musket, every stone in the hill side a gun. Faster and faster they rode. How we watched them! They are out of sight; but presently come a few horsemen, straggling, galloping back. "What can those skirmishers be doing? See, they form up together again. Good God! it is the Light Brigade!"

At five o'clock that evening Henry and I turned, and rode up to where these men had formed up in the rear.

I rode up trembling, for now the excitement was over. My nerves began to shake, and I had been, although almost unconsciously, very ill myself all day. Past the scene of the morning we rode slowly; round us were dead and dying horses, numberless; and near me lay a Russian soldier, very still, upon his face. In a vineyard a little to my right a Turkish soldier was also stretched out dead. The horses, mostly dead, were all unsaddled, and the attitudes of some betokened extreme pain. One poor creamcolour, with a bullet through his flank, lay dying, so patiently!

Colonel Shewell came up to me, looking flushed, and conscious of having fought like a brave and gallant soldier, and of having earned his laurels well. Many had a sad tale to tell. All had been struck with the exception of Colonel Shewell, either themselves or their horses. Poor Lord Fitzgibbon was dead. Of Captain Lockwood no tidings had been heard; none had seen him fall, and none had seen him since the action. Mr. Clutterbuck was wounded in the foot; Mr. Seager in the hand. Captain Tomkinson's horse had been shot under him; Major De Salis's horse wounded. Mr. Mussenden showed me a grape-shot which had "killed my poor mare." Mr. Clowes was a prisoner. Poor

Captain Goad, of the 13th, is dead. Ah, what a catalogue!

And then the wounded soldiers crawling to the hills! One French soldier, of the Chasseurs d'Afrique, wounded slightly in the temple, but whose face was crimson with blood, which had dripped from his head to his shoulder, and splashed over his white horse's quarters, was regardless of the pain, but rode to find a medical officer for two of his *camarades*, one shot through the arm, the other through the thigh.

Evening was closing in. I was faint and weary, so we turned our horses, and rode slowly to Balaklava. We passed Mr. Prendergast, of the Scots' Greys, riding down to the harbour, wounded in the foot; the pluck with which an Englishman puts pain out of the question is as wonderful as it is admirable. Time would fail me to enumerate even the names of those whose gallantry reached my ears. Captain Morris, Captain Maude, both cut and shot to pieces, and who have earned for themselves an imperishable name!

What a lurid night I passed. Overcome with bodily pain and fatigue, I slept, but even my closed eyelids were filled with the ruddy glare of blood.

Thursday, 26th.—They are sending as many ships as possible out of harbour. On board the ship in which I live are 400 tons of gunpowder, and she is to be gradually filled up.

The Russians, to the number of 5000, made a sortie on the French lines this morning, but were repulsed with loss.

Two Russian officers, wounded yesterday, were brought down and embarked today from Balaklava. No tidings of Captain Lockwood. They tell me that there is a chance that Captain Morris may survive, and that poor Maude, though seriously, is not mortally wounded. I wrote to his wife today, to endeavour to break to her, as best I could, the fact that he was only wounded!

My poor servant, whose husband was in the 8th, has been in deep anxiety and distress, as, when I left last night, her husband had not been seen. One man told me he thought he saw him fall; but, of course, I would give her no information but facts. Today, hearing that he had returned wounded, and was in hospital, she started to see if it was true. Alas, poor woman! all she heard was tidings of his death.

Mr. Cator walked over from Khersonnese tonight, and arrived about nine o'clock.

Saturday, 28th.—What an anxious night. Guns firing incessantly from the batteries round Balaklava! and occasional volleys of musketry seemed to say that the enemy were having another try for it. I lay awake, a little anxious and doubtful. The harbour was astir—steamers getting up their steam, anchors being weighed, and all made ready for departure. If they should be able to shell the harbour!

The *Star of the South* is full of powder, and every ship has more or less on board.

Daylight brought news that upwards of 200 horses had escaped from the Russian lines, and galloped towards our entrenchments and those of the French. The marines, thinking, in the dark, that it was a charge of cavalry, fired right and left; the affrighted horses, turning off, dashed over the plain towards the French, who opened on them immediately. Many were killed, but many more, rushing over everything, were caught in the camp, and distributed—a welcome windfall after the 25th.

A flag of truce went into Sebastopol today, to enquire the number of officers taken, and their fate and names. The answer was, that eleven officers were captured, of whom only two survive. Who may those two be? We are to send again tomorrow to learn their names. Lord Cardigan tells me, that the loss of the Light Brigade in the charge was 300 men, 24 officers, and 354 horses. Twenty-seven wounded horses have since been shot. Lord Cardigan received a slight lance wound in the side; he distinguished himself by the rapidity with which he rode.

Shifted camp today to be out of the way of the French guns.

Sunday, 29th.—Tremendous gale of wind all last night. Fortunately it blew off shore, or it might have caused serious damage among the ships lying outside.

Why are the ships allowed to lie outside? All the transport masters object to the anchorage. Why are they kept there against their judgments and their will?

Saw Colonel Lake and Mr. Grylls yesterday, for the first time since they so kindly assisted me in my search for Henry, at Kalamita.

The flag of truce went in again today, and returned answer that Mr. Clowes, 8th Hussars, and Mr. Chadwick, 17th Lancers, were the only survivors. Poor Lockwood!

Wednesday, November 1st.—A bright, cheery day in harbour tempted me to ride to the camp. Oh, false valley of Balaklava, to conceal amongst thy many surrounding hills the bitter cold of the higher lands! Auctions of deceased officers' effects occupied almost every one today. The prices were fabulous. An old forage cap fetched 5*l*. 5s. 0d.; an old pair of warm gloves, 1*l*. 7s. 0d.; a couple of cotton nightcaps, 1*l*. 1s. 0d.: whilst horses sold as absurdly cheap—one fetched 12*l*. 0s. 0d. and another, 9*l*. A common clasp knife fetched 1*l*. 10s. 0d.

Reinforcements of French troops, Guards, and Highlanders, to the amount of 2000, arrived today. Osten Sacken, with a force of 20,000 men, has come to the relief of the besieged city. We are doing nothing particular today beyond firing red-hot shot. All are in expectation of the storming, and all, meanwhile, shivering with cold. Henry succeeded in purchasing a very large waterproof wrapper for "Bob," which makes me much easier on his account; but, Oh! how anxious do I feel as often as I look at that dear old friend, and think of the hardships he has to undergo.

Sunday, 5th.—I heard very heavy and continuous firing, which lasted all the morning; but as I saw no one from the front, and Henry was there with his regiment, I could learn nothing about it before twelve o'clock. Then, indeed, news came in fast. At five o'clock this morning, in the middle of a dense fog, our outlying piquets suddenly found themselves surrounded and fired at from all sides—heavy guns, of large calibre, with shell and musketry, ploughing in every direction.

How can I describe the horrors and glories of that day? It was a hand-to-hand battle, wherein every man fought for his life. Stunned, and confused for a moment, our troops rallied with inconceivable energy and courage. From five, a.m., till three in the afternoon they fought with all the acharnement of wild beasts—

> Groom fought like noble, squire like knight,
> As dauntlessly and well.

But I!—I only knew that Henry was there; and begging Captain Buckley, of the Fusilier Guards, who was recovering from his wound at Alma, and on board the *Star of the South*, to accompany me, we started on foot for the front.

With such work going on, reports were not likely to be slack.

I had barely left the town before I was told of the utter destruction of the cavalry, which had "remained the whole day passive under a galling fire." But I had learnt experience, and this did not trouble me much. We pushed on, and met a cart coming down slowly: in it was Sir George Brown, wounded in the arm. A melancholy train of ambulance was winding slowly down to Balaklava. Alas! I well knew its ghastly freight. An hour later, and Henry was giving me himself an account of the terrible casualties of the day. He spoke with grief of Sir George Cathcart, who bravely met with a soldier's highest honour—a death won with such impetuous courage that the memory of it must last throughout all time. The brigade of Guards has suffered cruelly. General Strangways is dead; poor Major Wynne, of the 68th; Major Dalton, of the 49th, who leaves a young widow and children alone at Constantinople.

But who is not among the list of dead? Poor young Cleveland, with his fair, boyish face! Ah me! how ruthless is the sword!

I cannot hope to glean full and correct particulars of this day, wondrous in the world's history, until time has allowed the feeling of excitement a little to subside.

Monday, 6th.—Henry and I rode up to our camp, which is

situated near the windmill at the front. Here we met le Baron de Noe, who, with Henry, rode on to inspect the battle-field.

I could not go. The thought of it made me shudder and turn sick. On his return, Henry told me that the field of Alma was child's play to this! Compressed into a space not much exceeding a square half-mile, lay about 5000 Russians, some say 6000; above 2000 of our own men, exclusive of French, of whom, I believe, there were near 3000; lines upon lines of artillery horses, heaps upon heaps of slain, lying in every attitude, and congregated in masses—some on their sides, others with hands stiffening on the triggers of their muskets; some rolled up as if they died in mortal pain, others smiling placidly, as though still dreaming of home: while round the batteries, man and horse piled in heaps, wounds and blood—a ghastly and horrible sight!

We were taken by surprise, attacked where we had no intrenchment or fortification of any kind. We fought as all know Englishmen will fight; and our loss was in proportion to the carelessness that permitted the attack, rather than to the magnificent courage that repelled it.

Wednesday, November 8th.—The 46th, under Colonel Garrett, arrived in Balaklava today, and disembarked this afternoon. They are a particularly fine looking regiment; two companies are already here. They landed 750 strong.

Thursday, 9th.—Rode up to the front today with Captain Sayer and Mr. Rochfort, who took up their quarters yesterday on board the *Star of the South*; the former having come out to see his brother, who was wounded at Alma, and the latter as an amateur. They went to inspect the horrors of the battlefield; Henry and I went to Sir George Cathcart's grave—fit resting-place for the heart of such a soldier. In the centre of what has been a ruined fortification, in front of the division he led so gallantly, almost within range of the guns of Sebastopol, surrounded by those officers of his division who fell by his side, he sleeps until the *reveille* of the Great Day. A cross, rudely built of rough stones, stands at the head of his grave.

Friday, 10th.—A heavy gale of wind made terrible distur-bance among the shipping, both inside and outside the harbour, so much so that several ships' masters outside protested at not being admitted to the shelter of the harbour. [2] Owing to the heavy rain, the roads were nearly impassable on Wednesday and today. I hear that several of the poor, starved, worn-out artillery horses died on the road, vainly endeavouring to drag up guns to the front.

Saturday, 11th. The 62nd regiment landed today at Kamiesh Bay.

The severe weather affects both men and horses terribly; of the latter, I fear, few will survive to feel the warm breath of spring.

These horses have no clothing, and very insufficient food; and the men live in a state that few of our paupers in England would endure.

Monday, 13th.—The *Jura* arrived today. It is still blowing as if it never blew before, and raining in torrents. The Russians made a sortie last night on the French, and were repulsed—with what loss, on either side, I am unable to learn.

Tuesday, 14th.—The most terrific gale commenced blow-ing at about five o'clock this morning. At seven o'clock, when I looked through the stern-cabin windows, the harbour was seething and covered with foam, and the ships swinging terribly. By nine it had increased to a frightful extent, and I could hardly, even when clinging to the ship, keep my footing on deck. The spray, dashing over the cliffs many hundred feet, fell like heavy rain into the harbour. Ships were crushing and crowding to-gether, all adrift, all breaking and grinding each other to pieces. The stern-work of the *Star of the South* was being ground away

---

2. It would have been well indeed had this warning and remonstrance been attend-ed to. Not only the crews who perished on the 14th, but many brave soldiers, who afterwards died of cold and hunger, might still have survived, had the stores in the *Prince* and other vessels been saved. No inquiry has been made public, but the officer who appears to have been responsible for this catastrophe has been rewarded.—Ed.

by the huge sides of the *Medway*, which was perpetually heaving against her.

By ten o'clock we heard that the most fearful wrack was going on outside amongst the ships at anchor, and some of the party—Captain Sayer, Mr. Rochfort, and Captain Frain—started for the rocks to try if by any means they could save life. The next tidings were, that the *Prince* and the *Resolute*, the *Rip van Winkle*, the *Wanderer*, the *Progress*, and a foreign barque, had all gone down, and, out of the whole, not a dozen people saved. At two o'clock, in spite of wind and weather, I managed to scramble from ship to ship, and went ashore to see this most disastrous sight. Ah me! such a sight, once seen, who can forget!

At the moment after my arrival, the devoted and beautiful little clipper ship *Wild Wave* was riding to her death. Her captain and crew—all but three small boys—had deserted her at nine o'clock; and she was now, with all her masts standing, and her helpless freight on board, drifting with her graceful outlines and her heart of oak, straightway to her doom. She is under our feet. God have mercy on those children now!

Captain Frain, Captain Liddell, and some seamen heave a rope downwards, at which one boy springs, but the huge wave is rolling backwards, and he is never seen again.

A second time they hurl it down to the boy standing on the stern frame, but the ship surging down upon the ruthless rocks, the deck parts beneath his feet, and he is torn, mangled, and helpless; but clinging still, until a wave springs towards him eagerly, and claims him for the sea.

The third and last survivor catches at the friendly rope, and swooning with exhaustion and fear, he is laid upon the rock; while in a moment, with one single bound, the little ship springs upwards, as though she, too, was imploring aid, and falls back a scattered mass, covering the sea with splinters, masts, cargo, hay, bread, and ropes.

Meantime the *Retribution*, the *Lady Valiant*, the *Melbourne*, the *Pride of the Ocean*, the *Medora*, the *Mercia*, and several more, are all more or less damaged, and most of them entirely dismasted, riding it out as best they may. The greatest praise is due to the crew of the *Avon's* lifeboat, who went out fearlessly to endeavour to render aid; but were unable, owing to the heavy sea, to get near the ships. Let me shut up my book; for the more I contemplate it, the more terrible the disaster appears.

Captain Jennings, who came on board ill today, talks of beds and clothing carried bodily into the air, and of tents being split to ribbons, or torn from the ground, and hurled away.

This is nine o'clock, p.m. The *Medway, Marmion, Brenda*, and *Harbinger* are still hard at work on the sides of our unlucky ship; and I much fear the figure-head of the *Medway* will be into my cabin to-night.

Wednesday, 15th.—The sky is serene and blue, and nature, weary of her hurricane of tears, has sobbed herself into quietness. Captain Kyle, of the *Pride of the Ocean*, came into harbour this morning, having, together with his crew, abandoned his ship. How beautifully she rode through yesterday's gale! all her masts cut away, and her long black hull, with its graceful lines, sitting on the troubled water like a bird. The *Retribution* rode out the gale safely, though holding by only one cable.

Thursday, November 16th.—Report mentions twelve ships lost at Katcha, and thirteen at Eupatoria, but as yet this wants confirmation.

Today one of the crew of the *Star of the South*, Welsh by name, has been indefatigable in endeavouring to save the lives of some poor fellows who had been cast on the lower rocks, where they were scarcely to be got at from the heights above. About twelve o'clock, we heard that this fine fellow, in endeavouring to reach a sailor below him, lost his balance, and was lying with a broken leg close to the man he had risked his life to save. A party went to fetch him in, and found him suffering only from contusion, and not from a broken limb. The man appears to have behaved with wonderful courage and good feeling, and is deserving of unqualified praise.

Saturday, November 18th.—A day like the renewal of youth!-

cloudless, warm, and so bright! Captain Howard, of the 44th, took pity on me, a prisoner on board ship, and sent down a white Spanish horse for me to ride. I went to the camp, and found them all spreading themselves out to dry in the sunshine, like so many torpid flies. Henry applied to be allowed an office in Balaklava, so as to secure a stable for "Bob," who is half starved and as rough as a terrier. The grey horse was stolen two days ago, and is not yet recovered.

Sunday, 19th.—A mail has arrived. I thirst for letters from England, as a feverish man thirsts for a draught of water. On Friday the cavalry horses had one handful of barley as their day's food.

Yesterday they had the same.

Monday, 20th.—Heavy rain. The 97th landed today. They look fresh and well; but I should fancy few will be so tomorrow morning, if this is to be their inauguration day in camp.

Wednesday, 22nd.—Yesterday the *Queen of the South* disembarked draughts of Guards, &c., to the amount of 800 men. They were hardly disembarked before nightfall, and as we were returning at dusk from a ride to the camp, we met them marching up.

Henry and I had an adventure today, exciting though harmless. We were riding slowly across the plain, under the French batteries, but in full view of the Russian force, when I saw a fragment of shell lying on the ground, and forgetting all about the Russian artillery, requested Henry to pick it up; he dismounted for the purpose, when luckily I turned round in time to see the smoke of a piece of field artillery. I need hardly say we lost no time in taking ourselves out of range! We were both on white horses, and afforded a conspicuous mark. Lord George Paget is gone home. Thirty-eight other officers, profiting by his example, have sent in their papers.

Thursday, 23rd.—Perpetual sounds of heavy firing during the night told us that something was on hand; and next morning we heard that the Rifles had attacked a battery of twenty guns, but owing to insufficient numbers, they were three times driven back, until a French reinforcement enabled them to hold it. A very intelligent French soldier of the 20*ième de la Ligne* came into our tent today, when we were up in camp. He had read part of *Byron*, and the *Vicar of Wakefield!*

He told us that on the 5th several of our men, in the confusion, lost their regiments, and placing themselves in the French ranks, fought side by side with their neighbours and allies. Poor Colonel Shewell, overcome at last by the rough life, has been obliged to make up his mind to remain for some days on board ship. The appearance of the officers very much resembles that of the horses; they all look equally thin, worn, ragged, and out of condition in every way.

Sunday, 26th.—A brilliant morning induced us to try and attend church on board the *Sanspareil*. Arrived there, we were told there was no service, all the men being employed ashore. We stayed for some time in the ward room, looking at the many scars left in the good ship's timbers by the shells on the 17th of October, when she followed the Agamemnon so closely into action.

In the afternoon Captain Anderson, Mr. Goss, and I went to service in the chaplain's room in Balaklava,—an interesting congregation enough, composed entirely of soldiers who had come fresh from the noise of war. The quiet voice of the chaplain was inexpressibly soothing, and the words he chose peculiarly applicable to the excited and half-tired state of my mind—"There remaineth therefore a rest." He spoke for ten minutes, though at times his voice was barely audible amidst all the din and noise on the quay, the flogging of jaded and dying horses, and the voices of the soldiers, cursing with every imaginable oath their exhausted cattle.

The grey horse, "Job," died this evening of sheer starvation: his tail had been gnawed to a stump by his hungry neighbours at piquet. Misfortune appears to haunt us, as this is the third horse we have lost since leaving England: but we will "live misfortune down," with that dreary and desperate courage that the terrible scenes of this terrible life impart. Poor "Job!" he earned his name from his exhaustless patience under innumerable afflictions: he was an enormous, powerful, and hungry horse, and he sold his life by inches. There was no help for it: had it been myself instead of him, I must have died.

Tuesday, 28th.—Captain Dawson Damer came down this afternoon; and I rode back with him to Kadekoi, where the officers of the Guards have a house, and dined there, Henry joining us from the camp. The excellent dinner and kindly hospitality put us quite in spirits, after the ship food and our long fit of depression. Major Hamilton lent me his white pony. Oh, dainty pony! with black lustrous eyes, and little prancing feet, and long white tail dyed red with henna, like the finger tips of the most delicate lady in Stamboul!

We rode home at dark, along the rotten, deep, almost impracticable track. The dead horses lying right across the road, as they fell, and the dead and dying bullocks, filled me with horror, and the white pony with spasms of fear. Now we trod upon the muddy carcass of a horse; now we passed a fallen mule, and a huge bullock, sitting up, with long ghastly horns pointing upwards in the moonlight, awaiting his death.

No horse is permitted to be destroyed without a special order from Lord Lucan, except in case of glanders, and, I believe, a broken leg. Some horses in our lines have been lying steeped in mud, and in their death-agony, for three days!

Thursday, November 30th.—Tempted by the sunshine, I left my work, and walked over the cliffs with Captain Damer. My work (what will the young ladies at home say to my fingers?) is an enormous canvass sheet and breastplate, which I have made to cover up "Bob," and which I must take tomorrow to the *Sanspareil* to have waterproofed. I was scarcely over the ship's side, when the boat drifted—oh, horror!—against a dead body, one of the many that were floating in from the wrecks outside. It was the first I had happened to see.

The *Times* of the 13th is in harbour, and somebody, I forget who, tells me that my name appears in it. I wish they could put in that I had left the ship, and was established on shore, if only in a single room. Of this, however, I fear there is but little chance, as I hear Balaklava is to be given up to the sick. The place stinks already with the number of sick Turks, who have turned it into a half-putrid hospital. I never saw people die with such a dreary perseverance as these Turks. Two hundred of them were buried in one day a short time since.

I am happy to hear that it is at last arranged to bring the Light Cavalry down from the front, and quarter them near Balaklava, it being found impossible to convey forage up to them at the front.[3] Fifteen of our horses died last night.

Sunday, December 3rd.—It rained viciously all day. Captain Buckley came down to see me in the afternoon. I hear the sick are dying at an average of eighty *per diem*. I know that the mortality amongst the newly-arrived regiments is very great; nor can any one wonder at it! We, who are acclimatised, can hardly make head against the hardships of the life, what, then, must those feel who have just left an English barrack, or even the crowded discomforts of a transport! With some little horror (not much), and a great deal of curiosity, I watched from over the taffrail of the *Star of the South*, the embarkation of some Russian prisoners and English soldiers (all wounded) for Scutari.

The dignified indifference of the medical officer, who stood with his hands in his pockets, gossiping in the hospital doorway,— the rough and indecent way in which the poor howling wretches were hauled along the quay, and bundled, some with one, and others with both legs amputated, into the bottom of a boat, without a symptom of a stretcher or a bed, was truly an edifying exemplification of the golden rule, *Do to others as you would be done by.*

On board the steam-ship *Avon*, I hear the sights and sounds are too dreadful to imagine. An officer, who was sick on board, tells me the wounded men were laid on the deck with noth-

3. How inconceivable it seems to us at home that our commanders should have suffered the surviving horses of our Light Cavalry Brigade to die of starvation and cold on the heights, when they could have moved them to Balaklava, where they would have found both forage and shelter.—Ed.

ing but a blanket between them and the boards. Oh, how their wounded limbs must have ached! He said the groans and moans of these poor creatures, on the first night he spent on board, were heart-rending; but by the next night the noise had considerably decreased—death had been more merciful to their pain than man. Independently of the wounded soldiers, with whom our hospitals are full—the dreary, weary Turks have got a kind of plague amongst them, which infects the air.

If anybody should ever wish to erect a "Model Balaklava" in England, I will tell him the ingredients necessary. Take a village of ruined houses and hovels in the extremest state of all imaginable dirt; allow the rain to pour into and outside them, until the whole place is a swamp of filth ankle-deep; catch about, on an average, 1000 sick Turks with the plague, and cram them into the houses indiscriminately; kill about 100 a-day, and bury them so as to be scarcely covered with earth, leaving them to rot at leisure—taking care to keep up the supply.

On to one part of the beach drive all the exhausted *bât* ponies, dying bullocks, and worn-out camels, and leave them to die of starvation. They will generally do so in about three days, when they will soon begin to rot, and smell accordingly. Collect together from the water of the harbour all the offal of the animals slaughtered for the use of the occupants of above 100 ships, to say nothing of the inhabitants of the town,—which, together with an occasional floating human body, whole or in parts, and the driftwood of the wrecks, pretty well covers the water—and stew them all up together in a narrow harbour, and you will have a tolerable imitation of the real essence of Balaklava. If this is not *piquante* enough, let some men be instructed to sit and smoke on the powder-barrels landing on the quay; which I myself saw two men doing today, on the Ordnance Wharf.

Monday, December 4th.—The *Europa*, steam-ship, came in this afternoon with draughts, and the 97th regiment—1100 men in all. Last night the Russians from Kamara made an attempt to get into the town and fire the shipping. They were intercepted,-some shot, and some taken prisoners. It was well they were; for had they not been, Balaklava by this time would have existed only in the past tense, as I should also have done most probably myself—an event on which I do not wish to calculate just yet.

There are Russian residents permitted in Balaklava; amongst them a Mr. Upton, son of the engineer who constructed the forts of Sebastopol, and who was taken prisoner when we first marched down upon that place.

Thursday, December 7th.—The *Queen of the South* came in today with Turks on board, but was sent on to Eupatoria to disembark them. The *Sydney* also arrived with part of the 34th on board, and Mr. Chenery, the *Times* correspondent at Constantinople.

Several men dined on board, and we had no lack of intelligent conversation for that evening at least, whatever the case may usually be. Captain Hillyar, of the *Agamemnon*, came down from the trenches today and called on me. He tells me the French were repulsed last night in attacking a Russian battery; and also that the Russians made a sortie on our trenches, from which we drove them back.

It appears that the Russians are every day improving their position, as far as new batteries, new trenches, and fresh guns go. A story is current in Balaklava (but people in Balaklava are apt to be scandalous) that one of the Engineers, whose business it indubitably is to watch the various points of attack, being in a battery this morning (whose battery I will not mention), a new mud fort, with sixteen guns mounted and in position, was pointed out to him. "God bless my soul; so there is! I never knew anything about that!" was his exclamation.

A Maltese man and a woman were found murdered on the rocks just outside Balaklava yesterday. I have not heard that anything has been done towards tracing the crime; indeed, such a process would be impossible in such a crowd and confusion of all nations, languages, and peoples.

Sunday, December 10th.—A mild, warm, damp day. I write so seldom in my journal now, because I have nothing to say, except to grieve over the cruel detention of the mail, now four days overdue.

Tuesday, 12th.—Heavy firing last night from nine o'clock till twelve—followed this morning by an exquisite specimen of Balaklava reports. They said, "The Russians had come down last night in force, and had established themselves (or endeavoured to do so, I forget which) between the army in front and the army in the rear; that the Rifles had fired away all their ammunition; and that the Russian loss was (as usual) tremendous!" An artillery officer, who came down this evening from the trenches, in which he had passed all the previous night, was considerably astonished to hear of this wondrous battle; but said that the Rifles certainly fancied they heard the sound of approaching troops, and blazed away as hard as they could—firing all their ammunition;—the result being, I believe, one dead Russian!

Saturday, December 16th.—Torrents of rain have fallen. The country is more swampy than any words of mine can convey an idea of. Fresh Russian reinforcements have arrived, both to the army in Sebastopol and the army in the field. Today two steamers arrived; one full of artillery, and the other with the 89th regiment on board. The French have been landing troops very fast, the last few days, at Kherson; and there is a sort of vague idea floating about in the minds of men that a battle is in meditation on the 19th.

The French, who the other day put their admirable walking ambulance at our disposal to bring down our 1300 sick, have today lent us sixty horses to assist to drag up the *munitions de guerre*. Finding it impossible, by any amount of curses and blows, to get as much strength out of a dying horse as out of one in full vigour, they have at last agreed to give up the attempt; and 400 Turks are to be stationed on the hills to unload the carts at the bottom, and load them again at the top, passing their shot and shell up from hand to hand.

A few Russian prisoners are also employed in assisting the French to mend our roads. Their countenances are wonderfully alike, all with flat noses and short chins; but they seem cheerful and wondrously willing to work. I hear they receive one shilling a-day, and a ration of rum.

Sunday, 17th.—Went to morning church; afterwards walked with Mr. Anderson, and, returning through a deluge of mud, met the 89th and 17th regiments, which had disembarked at an hour's notice, as an attack is expected tomorrow, it being St. Nicholas's day, when the Russian soldiers are supposed to have an extra ration of *rakee*; and as they never fight unless half drunk, the argument is not so bad after all.

Monday, 18th.—A brilliant, warm day tempted us out; and, at eleven o'clock, Henry, Mr. Rochfort, Mr. Aspinall, and I, found ourselves on horseback starting for the Monastery of St. George. After about three miles of extremely heavy riding, we got upon the downs, and broke our wearisome walking-pace. The monastery soon came in sight. Built on the edge of a rock, with a precipitous and wooded descent to the sea, it stands quite alone, a solid and rather fine building, surrounded by massive rocks and high cliffs. We tied our horses to the railings of a church outside the precincts, and, guided by a Zouave, penetrated to the gardens within.

A few monks were amusing themselves on the terraces, and against the rails, over which we leaned to take in the beauty of the abrupt cliffs, which sloped, laden with trees and foliage even at this time of year, down to the water's edge. Mr. Rochfort left us, and presently returned with a handful of Russian stocks in bloom, which he gave to me. Several Russian families have taken refuge here from the lines of the English and French armies. One Englishman interested us all; a Mr. Willis, who had been for five-and-thirty years head caulker in the harbour of Sebastopol. He grumbled sorely at the advent of his countrymen, who, as he said, had pulled down his house, and loop-holed it, and had destroyed his vineyard—his 999 trees!

General Bosquet and staff rode up as we left, and several English officers were leaving at the same time as ourselves. We had a cheery canter home, during which one of us put up a hare, which, although we had a very speedy greyhound with us, we could not catch. I rode the white Spanish horse.

Tuesday, 19th.—Rode my dear old horse today, for the first time since his starvation, and nearly cried with joy as I felt him straining on the bit. A few days ago, when he came down from the front, a mere skinful of bones, and with an expression of human woe and suffering in his large sad eyes, he haunted me night and day; but, remembering my former loss, I would neither mention him in this book, nor would I inquire whether he was dead or alive, as each morning came, and today he was able to canter for a couple of dozen yards.

Wednesday, 20th.—Rode the white Spanish horse, and hearing that the French were intending to make a reconnaissance, we cantered into the plain and joined them. The Chasseurs d'Afrique, the 6ième Dragons, and another regiment (which, I do not know) were riding towards Kamara and Canrobert's Hill. As they approached the latter, the enemy showed themselves on the top; mutual skirmishers were sent out; several shots were fired. One *dragon* was killed, a *chasseur* wounded, and a *chasseur* horse destroyed; and then, after sitting and looking at each other for some little time, we turned and rode slowly back.

The object of this reconnaissance was to endeavour to ascertain the number of the enemy, and also to try to recover the batteries abandoned by the Turks on the 25th of October. Whether either of these objects was accomplished, I cannot tell, but I think not. It seemed to me cruel enough to leave the one poor fellow in the middle of the great plain, lying on his face, in his gay-coloured uniform, to be either prodded to death with the Cossack lances, or eaten by the eagles and the wild dogs. The scene haunted me for days—aye, even in my dreams.

Friday, 22nd.—Incessant rain.

Saturday, 23rd.—*Ditto*, only twice as hard.

Sunday, 24th.—The two previous days condensed in one; and

this is Christmas eve. How many hearts in our sodden camp must feel sad and lonely today! How many pictures of home, and how many faces (how much loved we never knew till now) rise before our hearts, all beaming with a happiness probably unpossessed by them, but in which our imagination loves to clothe them!

Alas! how many assembled round the blazing fires at home drink no healths, but meet in sorrow to pour out the wassail as a libation to the many honoured dead!

Heavy firing today from the ships. Sir Edmund Lyons has been but three days in command. He is popular, and much is expected of him.

Christmas Day.—A brilliant frosty morning. After church Henry and I walked up to the cavalry camp, and invited Lord Killeen and Colonel De Salis to join our dinner party on board the *Star of the South*, which somehow was prolonged far into the night.

Wednesday, 27th.—We started intending to ride up to head quarters, but the roads were so deep and rotten, so full of holes that seemed to have no bottom, the day was so raw, and our progress so slow, that, notwithstanding my endeavours to keep my habit short and temper long, I was too much disgusted and wearied to struggle further than our cavalry camp.

The cold tonight is intense, and as we have no fire on board this ship our sufferings are very great. But "there is in every depth a lower still," and we should be worse off in the trenches. It is when suffering from these minor evils of cold and hunger (for our table is very much neglected), that I feel most how much my patience, endurance, and fortitude are tried. The want of fire, of a carpet, of even a chair, makes itself terribly felt just now.

Friday, 29th.—Lieutenant Ross, of the *Stromboli*, called on me this afternoon, and joined us in a charming walk to the ruins of the Genoese Fort, whence we watched the sparkling sunlight on the sea; and then turning to our left, we stretched across the hills to the Marine and Rifle camp, and returned by descending the precipitous cliff into Balaklava.

Saturday, 30th.—The French cavalry, a regiment of Zouaves, and some of the Highlanders of Sir Colin Campbell's division, made a reconnaissance today over the ground supposed to have been occupied by the Russian army under Liprandi. This force they found had almost entirely vacated the plain, owing, as we suppose, to the severe weather cutting off their supplies of provisions. The French set fire to all the huts they found, and the party returned about dusk, having met with very few casualties.

I did not go out with the reconnaissance, as our horses require rest rather than work, and would never have carried us through the deep mud for so many hours. Instead, we walked up to the camp, where the sale of the late Major Oldham's kit was in progress. We were fortunate enough to find some excellent soup, manufactured by Captain Jennings, of the 13th Light Dragoons, of which I am afraid we left him very little.

We hear that Lord George Paget has started on his return to the Crimea.

Monday, January 1st, 1855.—Day cruelly cold, but very bright. Henry and I walked to the Genoese Fort, and watched the ships sailing harbourwards on the calm and shining sea.

The 39th regiment arrived in the *Golden Fleece,* and Mr. Foster shortly after came on board the *Star of the South;* and we discussed the merry old days spent together at Weymouth, until the sound of the old waltzes rang in my ears, and the horn of Mr. Farquharson's huntsman came up echoing from far over the sea.

Wednesday, January 3rd.—The quay covered with French soldiers, whom I watched with the greatest amusement, as they absolutely plundered our shot and shell, so rapidly did it disappear under their hands for conveyance to the front. Before our men can collect their wits for the work, 100, 200, 250 shell are passing from hand to hand into the wagons waiting to receive them.

But, as their officer remarked to me, "*Les Anglais sont de très bons soldats, mais ils ne savent pas faire la guerre. Ils se battent très bien (Allons, mes enfans, vite! vite!), mais ils n'aiment pas travailler. Ils ont peur de se souiller les mains. (Nous voilà prêts pour le départ.) Nous sommes aussi prêts pour aller à Sevastopol; mais les Anglais— c'est eux qui nous font toujours—attendre—attendre. Madame, j'ai l'honneur de vous saluer;*" and away went the whole corps, every two men carrying a 10-inch shell. Ah, how have our resources been wasted!—our horses killed!—our men invalided; while over it all broods the most culpable indifference!

Tuesday, January 9th.—A day of miraculous escape. Henry and I were writing in the cabin, and I was just finishing a note which a sergeant of the 62nd was waiting to take up to the front—our ship had been engaged for some days previous in taking in powder and ammunition, and she had on board nearly 1000 tons—when suddenly the sergeant put his head in at the door, and asked if the note were ready. I said, "Not yet; you must wait a moment."

The reply was, "I cannot wait—for—the ship's on fire!"

A moment after, and the noise and hurry showed us it was too true. The fire was in the lower hold, and burning within six feet of the magazine!

At such a time there was no thought of fear. It had been raining; and Henry and I, unwilling to add to the crowd forward, after getting some galoshes, went on deck. We were then advised to go and stand on shore, and to take my poor maid, who was screaming, and praying to every saint in the calendar, by turns. We were soon overboard, and watching the exertions of the men at the pumps. The hose of the steam-ship *Niagara* was in a few moments at work, as well as our own, and in a short time the alarm was over, and the fire extinguished.

Moored next us was the *Earl of Shaftesbury*, also a powder ship; and a little ahead of us lay the *Medora*, likewise with powder on board. All felt that their last moment was come; and yet, a strange exultation possessed my heart in contemplating so magnificent a death—to die with hundreds in so stupendous an explosion, which would not only have destroyed every vessel in harbour, and the very town itself, but would have altered the whole shape of the bay, and the echoes of which would have rung through the world!

Wednesday, January 10th.—Not liking the anchorage, after yesterday's experience, I endeavoured to ride up to head quarters, to petition for rooms on shore, but the heavy rain stopped all that.

Saturday, 13th.—Frost, snow, and bitter cold. This morning I ran up on deck, for the day was bright and sunny, in spite of the cold, keen air. It was a wondrous sight!—everything buried in a foot of snow; rocks, houses, gun-limbers, plants, and tents, all covered. The ships in harbour were the prettiest: they were all dressed in purest white; the capstan tops looking like huge twelfth cakes; the yards and spars glittering like rods of ice bound together by fairy ropes of snow; the whole glistening in the sunlight like an illumination.

I thank God heartily that I can see and appreciate beauty of every kind. How many have eyes which see not; ears which ear not; hearts which cannot understand!—men who perpetually remind one of the character described by Wordsworth, of whom he says—

> *The primrose by the river's brim*
> *A yellow primrose was to him,*
> *And it was nothing more.*

Monday, 15th.—Took the dear old horse's bridle over my arm, and walked him up to camp, as he has not been out for some days, and it is too slippery to ride.

Appreciated most gratefully the kindness of Captain Naylor, who sent me out, two days ago, a wondrous plaid, the thickness and warmth of which is of the greatest service to me. Tried to find a pair of muffetees for poor Lord Killeen, whose fingers, like mine, are chilled to the bone.

Tuesday, January 16th.—We changed our anchorage today,

and moved to a berth nearer the mouth of the harbour. Ingress and egress to the ship is now much more difficult, as we are much further from shore.

Thus we shall lose many of our most frequent visitors, and be made almost prisoners on board the ship, which is a nuisance that we resent in true English fashion, by grumbling all day long.

A large augmentation of the Russian army arrived yesterday near Inkermann. Our (English) force consists now of 11,000 bayonets. The leaders of the *Times* have, I see, taken up the subject warmly enough, and by so doing have cheered and refreshed many a heart that was well nigh tired of

The trouble and the pain of living.

Friday, 19th.—Captain Sayer, who has been so long a resident on board the *Star of the South*, left us early and suddenly this morning, fearing he should not be able to reach England by the expiration of his leave. When going ashore this afternoon, I discovered that, not satisfied with the ten dead horses and three camels already rotting on the shore, they make a practice of goading all the dying commissariat animals to this corner, to add to the congregation already assembled.

Saturday, 20th.—For two days we have had alongside our ship a Turkish steamer, so close as to chafe our ship's side very considerably. She took up a position in the harbour pointed out to her by the authorities; and soon after she had anchored, she began blowing off her steam, and emptying the burning cinders overboard between her own side and ours. Henry and Captain Frain were both on deck; but it was not until after many and frantic efforts that they at last made the captain of the steamer understand that we had powder on board.

Today 360 plague-stricken Turks have been put into her; but one becomes so indifferent and callous that nothing dismays one now. Henry and I tried to go out fishing this morning, but we got the net foul of the rocks, and caught nothing. The band of the 14th regiment was playing on board the *Emeu* all the time.

They have just arrived in harbour.

The 39th, on board the *Golden Fleece*, are suffering terribly from sickness, and have lost so many men that a portion of them are to be disembarked and sent ashore today, so as to render her less crowded and more fit for the accommodation of the sick. The *Arabia*, steam-ship, which succeeded the Turkish steamer in the occupation of the berth alongside us, was discovered to be very extensively on fire this morning about five o'clock. I look upon the preservation of our lives, entrusted as they are to such inefficient and unprincipled hands as those who have the management of ships in this harbour, to be a perpetual miracle.

Wednesday, 24th.—Riding to the camp today I met Lord Raglan coming down to Balaklava, and I took the opportunity of asking his lordship whether I might not live in any house, however small, on shore. My request was not acceded to.

Saturday, 27th.—250 sick embarked today.

Sunday, 28th.—130 sick embarked today.

Monday, 29th.—295 sick embarked today.

Truly our army is in a lamentable state. I have grieved until I have no power of grieving left. I think that if I knew I was going to die myself, I should merely shrug my shoulders and lie down quietly.

We have no ambulance wagons; they are nearly all broken down, or the mules are dead, or the drivers are dead or dead drunk: as well one as the other, as far as usefulness goes. Our poor cavalry horses, as we know full well, are all unequal to the task of carrying down the sick; and the French have provided transports for us for some time.

They were complaisant enough about it at first, but now (the men I mean) begin to grumble, and to do their work cruelly. One poor fellow, wounded and frostbitten in the hands and feet, was taken roughly from his mule and huddled down in the mud, despite his agonised screams and cries. Another Frenchman drove his empty mule so carelessly past one that was still laden as to cut the poor sufferer's legs with the iron bar, and cause him cruel pain.

Why can we not tend our own sick? Why are we so helpless and so broken down?

Oh, England! England! blot out the lion and the unicorn: let the supporters of your arms henceforth be, Imbecility and Death!

A cargo of "navvies" came out today in the *Lady Alice Lambton*. Their arrival makes a great sensation. Some of them immediately went ashore, and set out for a walk "to see if they could see e'er a — Roosshian."

The 39th, who have been hitherto employed as working parties on the road, yield their work to the navvies, after having given the greatest satisfaction at it themselves.

Henry and I dined in camp with Captain Portal, of the 4th Light Dragoons, who gave us a dinner that contrasted wonderfully with our hard fare on board ship, and whose hospitable and cheerful welcome we shall always remember with pleasure.

Tuesday, 30th.—Captain Hillyar, who came in last night in the *Malacca*, called on me this morning with his brother, and asked us to dinner tonight.

Wednesday, 31st.—Eight nurses, under the direction of a "Lady Eldress" and Miss Shaw Stewart, came up today from Scutari to the Balaklava hospital.

We lunched on board the *Malacca*, and met Captain Lushington, who engaged us to luncheon on Tuesday next.

The report is that the Grand Dukes are again in Sebastopol.

Monday, February 5th.—Dined with Major Peel.

Oh! what terrible work it is to ride over these wretched roads! You flounder along in the most helpless manner; and coming back in the dark, I put the reins on the old horse's neck, and exhorted him in this wise:—"Remember, 'Bob,' that any fool of a horse can tumble down here, so pray recollect what a much cleverer horse you are than any other of your species."

I conclude the admonition had the desired effect; at any rate, we got safely home.

Tuesday, 6th.—A beautiful morning, but blowing very heavily. We started about twelve for the naval camp, and ten minutes after down came the rain! We persevered, and arriving at last like drowned rats, were most hospitably entertained. Captain Lushington appeared sufficiently amused at my determined indifference to the rain. The weather cleared about four; and we had a delightful ride home along the high land, and then down to Kadekoi, by the brook in the valley, and over the dykes. I hardly know whose heart laughed the most, the brave old horse's or mine, as he laid his slender ears back, and, bearing on the bit, flung himself along, as though the starvation and the cruel suffering were all a myth, and he was once more in the merry hunting field at home.

Thursday, 8th.—Roused in the middle of the night by a report that the Russians were coming down in force, and that the crews of the transports must all turn out armed. What an order! What could such a disorganised rabble do in the midst of regular troops? They would most probably fire away at whatever came first, and cause endless worry and confusion.

Saturday, 10th.—Exchanged the *Star of the South* for the *Herefordshire*, a fine old East Indiaman, and a most comfortable ship; a most desirable change in every way as far as comfort and good living go.

Monday, 12th.—What a soft and pleasant day. The sun was so hot as to make it impossible to walk uphill. We sat in the valley and thoroughly enjoyed the genial day, and, then descending to the shore, watched the varying colours on the rocks and sea.

At night came on a hurricane of wind and rain.

Tuesday, 13th.—Blowing terrific squalls. Captain Lushington, however, came on board, at great risk, to call on me. Some of the sick officers, who are on board the *Herefordshire*, left today for Scutari, and others came in their places. Amongst them Colonel D—, of the 90th, who had wounded himself this morning while playing with a revolver.

Friday, 16th.—Henry, Mr. Foster, Mr. Carr, Captain Lushington, and I rode over to the monastery, and I was as much pleased with it the second time of seeing it as the first. They report an attack on Inkermann this morning, but, although the firing was very heavy, I believe nothing extraordinary occurred.

Lord Lucan sailed for England today.

Tuesday, 20th.—A reconnaissance in force started this morning at four o'clock, to endeavour to surprise and take the outlying army over the hills. The snow began to fall immediately that the men were under arms, and presently came down with such hearty good-will as to render it impossible to proceed

The English infantry who turned out were the 14th, 17th, 42nd, 71st, 79th, 93rd. The Light Cavalry, also, made a contribution of about thirty-five or thirty-eight men and horses. But after groping about in the intense cold and utter darkness, till every man was saturated and chilled to the bone, they were all ordered to turn in again.

On board our ship, the *Herefordshire*, we have a most painful scene. One of the chaplains (Mr. Wyatt), who has long been ill of fever, is now delirious and in the utmost danger. He lies in a cabin separated from us by only a Venetian shutter; his incoherent ravings and frantic efforts to escape intrude themselves above the hushed voices of all who occupy the cabin. Fortunately, we none of us have a dread of infection.

Poor Mr. Taylor, too, another chaplain, whose exertions have been most unremitting and most noble, lies also on board another ship in the shadow of death. I know that Mr. Taylor has spent day after day in these pestilential hospitals, never giving himself rest or purer air.

Saturday, 24th.—Lunched in camp with Colonel Doherty, and afterwards went to see one of the women of our regiment, who is suffering from fever. I found her lying on a bed on the wet ground; she had lain there, in cold and rain, wind and snow, for twelve days. By her side, in the wet mud, was a piece of ration biscuit, a piece of salt pork, some cheese, and a tin pot with some rum! Nice fever diet! She, having failed to make herself popular among the women during her health, was left by them when she was sick; and not a soul had offered to assist the poor helpless, half-delirious creature, except her husband, and a former mate of his when he was a sailor.

Thursday, March 1st. —It being reported that all the transports are to be ordered out of Balaklava Harbour, Captain Lushington rode down from the Naval Brigade, and most kindly, and with great consideration, offered to put up a hut for us in the camp- it being too cold for me to think of living in a tent. Captain Lushington, who is a very old friend of Henry's family, could not have given them a greater proof of friendship: he has offered to furnish men to put up the hut, dig the cooking-house, stables, &c.

Sunday, March 4th. —The *Herefordshire*, which Admiral Boxer had long been threatening, was duly turned out of Balaklava harbour at eight o'clock this morning. We had been cried "wolf" to so often, that when the order really did arrive it took us all by surprise. The hurry and confusion was most absurd; and, after all, we were obliged to go out to sea in her, and return in the tug. But it was a lovely day, and we enjoyed the sail. Every one left the *Herefordshire* with regret; and we took leave of kind, cordial, hospitable Captain Stevenson with many expressions of hope that we should soon meet again. We returned to the *Star of the South*.

Monday, 5th. —Started on horseback at one o'clock, to attend the "First Spring Meeting," the first race of the season. Wonderful, that men who have been starved with cold and hunger, drowned in rain and mud, wounded in action, and torn with sickness, should on the third warm, balmy day start into fresh life like butterflies, and be as eager and fresh for the rare old English sport, as if they were in the ring at Newmarket, or watching the colours coming round "the corner."

There were four races: the first I was not in time to see. Just as the riders were going to the starting-post for the second race, somebody called out, "The picquets are coming in; the Russians must be advancing!"

Away we all hurried to the camp, but found out it was a false alarm, caused by two Russian deserters whom our picquet had taken. It did not take long to return to the race-ground: and the transition struck me as equally abrupt—from the racecourse to the battlefield, from the camp to the course. Two pony races were won by sheer good riding, by Captain Thomas, R. H. A.; and after the "Consolation Stakes," as the sun was still high, the meeting dispersed for a dog-hunt. I rode with them as far as Karani, and then turned back. I could not join in or countenance in any way a sport that appears to me so unsportsmanlike, so cruel, so contrary to all good feeling, as hunting a dog.

I must mention that our hut progresses wonderfully; it is nearly finished, and the carpenters are making me a table. We are indebted to the kindness of Captain Franklyn, master of the *Columba*, for a large sheet of plate glass, which makes a magnificent window.

Tuesday, 6th.—The *Canadian* went down to Constantinople today full of sick. What a serene and balmy day!

Wednesday, 7th.—In spite of a fog, which hung like a pall over the summits of the hills, I resolved to join a riding party we had made to the Monastery of St. George. I thought that I could fight with a Crimean fog, and get the best of it; but I very soon found out my mistake. Oh, the fever, lassitude, aches, and pains of this evening!

Wednesday, 14th.—The warm sun drew me out of the cheerless cabin, and tempted me to try and walk on deck, though so weak as to be unable to do so without help.

Thursday, 15th.—A brilliant day for our Second Meeting. The horses are improving wonderfully; and in the hurdle race for English horses which had wintered in the Crimea, they went at the fences as if they liked the fun. Men of every regiment,

English and French, were on the course. Amongst the latter, a Comte Bertrand, who amused me by the eloquence with which he descanted on his own powers of equitation, his "hotel" in the country, his ten English horses, and English coachman called "Johnson." He spent the evening on board the *Star of the South*, and showed us that, whatever his equestrianism might be, he could play at *ecarté*.

Sunday, 18th.—Walked up to camp with Colonel Somerset and Mr. Foster; found the house so far advanced that we settled to come into it on Tuesday.

Nothing reaches us from the front, except reports that the French attack, and fail nightly in taking, the rifle-pits of the Russians. The French can beat us in their commissariat and general management, but the Englishman retains his wondrous power of fighting that nothing can rob him of but death.

CHAPTER 5

The Camp

Three hosts combine to offer sacrifice,—
Three tongues prefer strange orisons on high,—
Three gaudy standards flout the pale blue sky.
Byron.

Tuesday, March, 20th.—Left the *Star of the South,* and once more resumed our life in camp. A gleaming day, with lovely lights and shadows. Thanks to the kindness of Captain Buckley, of the Scots' Fusilier Guards, and Colonel Somerset, who lent us means of conveyance for our *impedimenta*, I was able to move up in one day. Major Peel and Captain Cook, of the 11th Hussars, saved us from starving by most hospitably inviting us to dine. The dinner was enlivened by a perfect storm of musketry, which made us fancy something unusual was going on in front; but perhaps my being unaccustomed to be disturbed by musketry at night makes me fancy it worse than it is. I am writing at one o'clock, and am, oh, so tired!

Wednesday, March 21st.—In our saddles by half-past ten, riding towards Kamiesh. We were to have been joined by Colonel Somerset, who kindly undertook to be our guide; but by some fatality we missed him, and reached Kamiesh at last by a very circuitous route. Here we made purchases of chickens, carrots, *petits pois verts*, and various other necessaries of life; all of which we packed upon our saddles, and then cantered home. Henry decorated the pommel of his saddle with six fowls, slung three on each side, and "Bob," who had never been turned into a market-horse before, was alike frightened at their screams, and disgusted at the way they scratched him with their claws; so he wisely took the shortest and quickest way home, hardly breaking from his hand gallop the whole way. Poor chickens!

Thursday, 22nd.—The chickens are all walking about as if nothing had happened, except that one or two go a little stiff.

Colonel Shewell, Lord Killeen, Colonel Doherty, Major Peel, and Captain Cook called on me today. The French took, and held, four rifle-pits last night, which accounts for the tremendous firing that shook the hut. We hear that the loss was very great: they report here, 300 French, and eight English officers, names at present unknown.

Friday, March 23rd.—Our 93rd battery firing this morning, we ran to see what was the cause. A shell burst just at the foot of Canrobert's Hill; and with our glasses we saw two deserters running in, while three or four of our men went to meet them. Lord George Paget and Colonel Douglas called on us today. The former has promised to give me a little smooth terrier. The establishment only wants a dog to be complete; and I, who have never before been without a dog, look forward with great pleasure to having this little terrier to make a pet of.

Saturday, 24th.—Can this be a *journal of a campaign*? I think I must change its name to a new edition of the *Racing Calendar*.

The French races today were very amusing. The course was crowded, the sun shone, and French officers were riding at full gallop everywhere, and making their horses go through all the tricks of the *manege*. The "steeple-chase" course, "*avec huit obstacles*," was delightful: the hurdles were not sufficiently high to puzzle an intelligent and active poodle; the ditches were like the trenches in a celery bed; and the wall about two feet and a half high.

But it was a very merry meeting. We rode up with Captain Lushington, Colonel Douglas, Colonel Somerset, Mr. Vansittart, and Major Peel, and afterwards lunched with le Comte Bertrand, on game pie and champagne.

Sunday, 25th.—A day reminding one of the great heats in Bulgaria. The men fell out in all directions from church parade. Late in the afternoon Henry and I rode up to hear the band of the 27*ième de la ligne*.

Monday, 26th.—Races at the Fourth Division; chiefly remarkable for the difference between the Englishman's and Frenchman's idea of a fence. Today we had a formidable wall of four foot, built as firmly as possible, while the ground on either side was hard enough to make it anything but a tempting jump.

Wednesday, March 28th.—More races. Count Bertrand, Mr. Foster, Captain Lushington, Colonel Somerset, and Mr. Vansittart came to luncheon, and we rode afterwards to the course. "Goodboy," ridden by Captain Thomas, came in an easy winner. The day was most lovely, but too hot for enjoyment. We fancied that summer was come, and that we had done with the cold weather.

Saturday, 31st.—Winter has returned. The very hills are blue with cold. A hard, frozen-looking haze covers the landscape, whilst a cruel north-east wind searches one throughout, filling the bones with rheumatism, and the lungs with cold. I did not move from my stove till evening, when we were engaged to dine with Major Peel. We did not return until rather late, which was fortunate, as, hearing groans coming from the stable as we passed, Henry went to see what was the matter, and found that my chestnut horse had had a kicking fit on him, and had kicked away at the principal post till he brought the whole roof, rafters and all, down about his ears. The weight fell on all the horses' backs, but chiefly on the poor pony, "Whisker," who was supporting all the heaviest rafters, and groaning with disgust. Luckily, none of the horses were hurt.

Tuesday, April 3rd.—Went over with a large party to Kamiesh. We hear it is the general opinion that the fire on Sebastopol will recommence in a few days. The number of guns that it is supposed will be at work on that day, English, French, and Russian, are computed at between 1600 and 1700. Meanwhile our hut is shaken every night by the explosions of the heavy guns, and we ourselves are roused by the incessant rain of musketry. Some few are sanguine as to the result of this bombardment.

I heard one person assert that in his opinion the place could not stand twenty-four hours against such a fire. The ships are to make a demonstration, as though they were going to attack the forts on the north side, but it is doubtful whether they will attack. War, horrid war! Why can we not ride in peace over this lovely country, abounding in flowers and coloured with tints, which, by their freshness and beauty, remind me perpetually of Copley Fielding's pictures.

It is strange that, to express my admiration for nature, I am obliged to compare it with art; but I never saw elsewhere scenery so clear, so wondrously coloured, looking so warm, yet actually so cold. It impresses me as a picture would. I admire it, but it does not affect me. Perhaps the absence of trees takes away from the "home" feeling; and, by making the landscape appear like a picture, fails to excite any sympathetic feelings of admiration. The scenery and I may get on better when these cruel cold winds have passed, and the glorious sun throws some of his magnificent heat into it.

Saturday, 7th.—Light Division races. The day was perfect; the races well attended; and, had it not been for an accident, the sight of which seemed to stun me, and stop every pulse in my body, we should have had an enjoyable day. In the steeple-chase course they had built a wall, over four foot, and as firm as it could be built, turfed over at the top, and as solid as an alderman's wit. Captain Thomas, R. H. A., and Captain Shiffner, two of our best riders, were in the race. The crowd collected round the wall to see the jump, and I shoved my horse in as close as I could. After a moment's suspense, they are off—three noble horses, all well ridden. Mr. Wilkins's horse takes the wall easily, and rushes on; Captain Shiffner's horse strikes it with his chest, and, after one effort, rolls over headlong, falling on his rider;

Captain Thomas's horse clears the wall, but lands on the man and horse already down.

At first, neither was supposed to have survived; but at last Captain Thomas moved, and presently they found that poor Captain Shiffner was not dead; but the doctors pronounced him so much injured internally as to leave no hope of his surviving the night. They were both carried from the ground. About an hour after we rode to inquire for Captain Thomas, who was lying in a hut close by, and found that he was conscious. His first words were, "Who won the race?" Of poor Captain Shiffner we hear there is no hope. I think this has rather made me lose my liking for steeple-chasing.

Sunday, 8th.—I heard this morning that poor Captain Shiffner died during the night. What little comfort for the mourners at home to reflect that his life was lost in such a way!—with neither glory nor honour to assuage the bitterness of death. Such an accident, coming in the midst of strong excitement, seems to make a pause, stillness, in one's own life. I am so shocked, so nervous by what I have seen, that I am fit for nothing; and yet, if he had been shot in the trenches, he would have had, most probably, no other requiem than, "Poor Shiffner was killed last night."

"Dear me! Was he? Poor fellow!" instead of forming the subject for thought and conversation to all.

Six o'clock.—Colonel Somerset has just called, and tells me the report of Shiffner's death is false; that he lives, and they have hopes of him.

Monday, 9th.—Torrents of rain; incessant, soaking, unrelenting rain, in the midst of which the roar of the sullen guns came down to us with a sort of muffled sound; and no wonder, coming through so dense and sodden an atmosphere. Of course, everybody who was not absolutely on duty in the trenches staid at home, except, I believe, one or two soldiers, too red hot to be affected by the rain. We hear that our opening fire took the Russians so much by surprise, that each of our guns fired seven rounds before they returned a single shot.

The report is (as usual) that our fire is doing great damage to the enemy's works; but we hear that always, as a matter of course.

Tuesday, 10th.—Rode up ourselves to the front to watch the firing. We saw it to great advantage (it being a very clear day) from a point opposite to Sir Richard England's division. I have not been to the front for some time; not, at least, far enough to observe the works before the town; they therefore strike me as being about twice as extended as when I saw them last, in, I think, December. The Mamelon and Malakoff batteries, both new, have opened a most formidable fire; while the Redan appears, to my eyes, much better furnished with guns in and about it than before. We did not remain long in the quarry, but went to the Mortar Battery, on our right, to watch the practice of the Sea-service mortars. Somehow I never felt less interested in any transaction of the war. I cannot believe that this bombardment will be productive of the slightest effect on a position which we have allowed to become so strong.

When Sir Richard England asked me, whilst we were watching from the quarries, whether I was interested, I gave him two answers, equally truthful—"Yes," and "No." If we could see any point on which to build a hope—any gun dismounted—any embrasure knocked in, we could find something upon which to fasten and feed an interest; but it seems to me very like a bombardment in a picture—blue sky overhead, a town, and innumerable puffs of smoke all round it.

Wednesday, 11th.—Rode up again, but this time to the French left attack, and took up our position near the *Maison d'Eau*. I was much pleased by obtaining a better view of the town than I had hitherto been able to discover. We were almost over the harbour. We saw steamers and little boats pulling between the forts. We saw people moving in the town. The sea and the sky, all God's part of the picture, looked so blue and calm; while all man's part of the picture was noise, smoke, and confusion. I could not but reflect, though perhaps such thoughts are inappropriate here, upon the vastness of that Rest, which enwraps, as with an infinite mantle, all the fretfulness and vain effort of this world; and I must confess, that instead of attending to the statistics of my companions, I lost myself in a wondrous reverie, inspired by the contrasts of the scene before me, on that most blessed of all theories—*There remaineth, therefore, a rest.*

Sunday, 15th.—Captain Lushington called, and seemed in despair.

It appears that his battery [4] had knocked a breach in some particular spot at which they had been hammering with that wonderful energy and inconceivably careless courage which has characterised them so especially throughout the war, and had made an opening sufficiently wide for troops to storm, but "the French were not ready." Captain Lushington's brigade has suffered severely during this last bombardment, both in guns and men; above a hundred of the latter are killed and wounded.

We endeavoured to "administer to the mind diseased" a little of the tonic wherewith we have often refreshed ourselves during the last twelvemonth, and which we have found most serviceable. It is composed chiefly of one ingredient—namely, the contents of an old proverb:—*Blessed are they who expect nothing, for they will not be disappointed.* Leaving Captain Lushington to try the efficacy of my cure, Henry and I rode up to the French band playing on the hill.

Tuesday, 17th.—Put up a large Turkish tent outside the hut, to serve as a drawing-room, and later as a dining-room; for we find it inconvenient to have only a room of twelve foot square in which to eat, sleep, and receive company.

This tent, large, hexagonal, double lined with dark blue, and open at both ends, is a great addition to one's comfort. We have it matted, carpeted, and furnished with a table and an armchair-luxuries which were to us, when in Bulgaria, but a dream of our youth. There is a great stir in Balaklava, owing to the arrival

---

4. That of the Naval Brigade.

and disembarkation of the 10th Hussars, who have come from India, and are reported to be 680 strong, and mounted on the finest Arabs in the world (at least, so says Colonel Parlby, who commands them).

Everyone is anxious to see this new regiment; and it is most amusing to hear the various speculations regarding these same horses—some declaring that there is nothing like an Arab horse; he is up to any weight, can endure any fatigue, live without food, and never sleeps: whereas others remember the mud of last winter, and how the vast thews and sinews of the most powerful English horses were only strong enough to pull them *into* it- and then leave them there to die.

Wednesday, 18th.—We rode up—Henry, Colonel Somerset, Mr. Calvert, and I—to look at such of these *wondrous winged steeds with manes of gold* as had landed. We found them perfect in shape, so purely bred that each horse might have been a crowned king; clothed in coats of sheeny satin, that seemed defiant even of the rays of the blessed sun himself when he looked at them; their small heads never resting, and their eyes like outlets for the burning fire within. But I will write down my first impression, and then see if time proves it correct. These horses are not in one respect suited for their work here, and they will fail at the commencement of winter—too small, too light, too excitable. This is merely what strikes me, and I merely write it as a specu- lation, knowing of this country what I do.

Thursday, April 19th.—A strong reconnaissance went out this morning, commanded by Omar Pasha, to Kamara, to inspect the Russian force, and with the intention of ultimately pushing forward, and allowing the Turks to occupy their old position in the plain from which they ran with such a cheerful alacrity at "Balaklava." Omar Pasha is very anxious to impress us favour- ably with the Turkish force that he has brought with him from Eupatoria, and which is composed of the same men who fought so well at Silistria. We hear, also, that the soldiers themselves are most anxious to give proof of their courage and steadiness under fire. They assert that the Turks who formed part of our force in the winter were only militia, and not regular troops; and I should fancy that by this time all those poor creatures had died of the plague.

I had arranged to accompany the reconnaissance, but Henry was unfortunately so far from well as to be unable to go, and of course I remained also.

I seldom like writing from report; and as I was not present, am unwilling to say anything about this reconnaissance, save that the Russian force appears to be by no means numerous.

Saturday, April 21st.—Rode with Henry and Colonel Poulett Somerset to the head-quarters of the Turkish force, as Omar Pasha had done us the honour to ask us to luncheon. We found him sitting in a small but very light and convenient tent, which opened towards Sebastopol; and being on high ground, we had a very good bird's-eye view of the position of the English and French armies. The band, a remarkably good one, was soon after sent for, and played for some time with a great deal of precision. They played, amongst other *morceaux*, "*Il Rigoletto*," and some marches composed by *Madame*, the wife of Omar Pasha, for His Highness's band.

Madame is, I believe, either German or Wallachian, and evidently possesses a knowledge both of the science and *esprit de la musique*. The pieces played by the band, and written by her, evinced both taste and power.

Luncheon, consisting of champagne and sweetmeats, was going on at the same time as the music; and when both were finished, His Highness ordered his horse, and we accompanied him to General Bosquet's, and afterwards to the brow of a hill opposite the Russian camp, where one of the mountain guns used in the Turkish army was placed and fired, to show General Bosquet its enormous range.

These guns are small—made precisely like the barrel of a Minié rifle, about five feet in length, and firing a conical leaden ball of four and a half pounds' weight. It is mounted on a very small carriage, and drawn by a single mule. Omar Pasha said it would carry 4000 yards. This fact, however, I am unable to vouch for from personal observation, as I never saw the ball after it was put in at the muzzle of the gun—I mean to say, my eyes were too much unaccustomed to follow the shot, nor did we see it strike. But, like true believers, we admitted that it struck wherever we were told it had done so; and, as far as I was concerned, I was quite satisfied. We then remounted, and returned to General Bosquet's tent. Our order of march was somewhat as follows:—

Omar Pasha, on a chestnut Arab, which he made go through every evolution that a horse's brain was capable of remembering, or his legs of executing; a group of attendant pashas and effendis, amongst whom we were mixed up; Lieutenant-Colonel Simmonds, English engineer, attached to the Turkish staff; General Bosquet, and one or two French officers belonging to his staff; and an escort of Turkish lancers on small horses, very dirty, very slovenly, and diffusing a fragrance of onions which made one's eyes fill with tears.

We took leave of our host at General Bosquet's camp, and rode slowly home in the dusk.

Omar Pasha impressed me as being shrewd, decided, energetic, as well as an amusing companion, and a man capable of appreciating more of the refinements of life than I should have thought he would have found amongst the Turks; though he tells me he hopes, after the war is over, to be made Minister of War at Constantinople, and,—very probably, be bowstrung!

May 1st.—Captain Christie died this day at Kamiesh, where he was awaiting a court-martial, to consider his conduct with reference to the ships left outside Balaklava Harbour on the 14th November. The decision of trying him by court martial, the worry and grief consequent upon so cruel an interpretation having been put upon the conduct of a man distinguished for gentleness, kindly feeling; and a desire to act rightly towards all parties, doubtless caused his illness and his death.

Captain Christie was beloved and regretted by all over whom he had control. The masters of transports, I think eighty-three in number, had subscribed for the purpose of presenting him with a testimonial of their affectionate esteem. I hear many of them have determined on going over to Kamiesh, to show a last mark of their respect for him by attending his funeral.

May 3rd.—Expedition started to Kertch—7,000 French, and about 2,600 English, with a few cavalry; the object being to take and destroy Kertch, and to intercept the conveyance of provisions and stores into Sebastopol. We had ridden over to Kamiesh in the morning, and when we returned, we saw from over the hills the ships silently stretching out from Kamiesh and Kasatch to sea. We all hope much from this expedition.

May 6th.—The expedition to Kertch is returned, and, at the moment that I write, it is off Balaklava Harbour. It was recalled by an express messenger. I suppose we shall hear more about this tomorrow,—at present, the simple fact is as much as we can digest.

The sun is come to visit us once more in all his magnificence; and we should be able to give ourselves up to perfect enjoyment of the, to me, delicious warmth, were it not for the violent gusts of wind, which deprive us of all comfort and all satisfaction in our otherwise delightful Turkish tent, which is always, except when the wind blows hard, a charming place of refuge from the sun.

Yesterday, Henry and I rode into the plain as far as the Woronzow Road,—the extreme limit that prudence would allow. We let our horses graze for an hour on the thick, rich grass, which covers these most marvellously fertile valleys and plains, and then covered the dear old horse's head with branches of white May and dog roses, with a wreath of mignonette and larkspur. The mignonette grows in these plains in far finer specimens than are usually found in English gardens.

Monday, May 7th.—Stretched out again into the plain; this time, underneath the hill occupied by our Rifles. We crept up the green ravine between the Rifle hill and the hill in occupation of the enemy. But the Rifles were amusing themselves with target-practice far over our heads; and the whistle of the balls, as they flew over us, made us remember that we were very much in the position of a brace of partridges on the 1st of September; so we turned, and reached home just in time to change horses, and canter over to the Guards' encampment, where we dined with Lord Adolphus Vane.

Tuesday, Wednesday, Thursday—Three days of incessant rain.

Oh, how miserable everybody was! the ground ankle-deep in swamp,—a slippery, sticky sort of wet clay, which sends you sliding as though you walked on ice; while, at every step, it closes over your horse's fetlock-joint. Added to this, towards nightfall came occasional gleams of rheumatism glancing through the bones.

I feel myself like St. Simeon of the Pillar, as Tennyson describes him,—

> *While I spake then*
> *A pang of shrewdest pain ran shrivelling thro' me.*

And all this cold, damp, rain; wind, and sleet have come to make memorable this tenth day of May, 1855.

Saturday, 12th.—Rode up the hill to see how the 10th and 12th had prospered during the wet weather. Poor little brilliant Arab horses, they looked like rats that had been drawn through wet mud and hung up in the sun to dry. They were living cakes of mud; their long tails reminded us of ropes of sea sand. Poor little gay creatures, all draggled and besmirched! Vicious to a degree beyond words are these fairy horses; and if they once get loose, they fly at, fasten on to, and tear each other with a tenacity and venom that I should have supposed only to have existed amongst women.

Saturday, 19th.—The first arrival of the Sardinian troops in Balaklava harbour.

Sunday, 20th.—Omar Pasha, who has returned from Eupatoria, whither he took flight the day after the one I have previously described, in consequence of a reported augmentation of the Russian force before that town, called on me this morning.

He gave us a very pressing invitation to accompany him to Eupatoria, where he intends to go on Tuesday, and offered us accommodation on board the *Valorous*.

Monday, 21st.—A match for 50*l.*, between Colonel Poulett Somerset's chestnut, "Goodboy," and General Barnard's brown horse, "Coxcomb"—"Goodboy," ridden by Captain Townley, who had the reputation of being the best race-rider in India (he came over with the 10th Hussars, to which regiment he belongs), and who certainly rides like a professional jockey, and looks like a gentleman rider; and "Coxcomb," ridden by Mr. Morgan, of the Rifle Brigade, son of Sir Charles Morgan, of Tredegar. "Coxcomb" was an easy winner—at least, so I was told; for the match I was not destined to see, as General Airey had very kindly lent me a very pretty horse of his own to ride; and which horse, never having been accustomed to a habit, fancied that by dint of galloping he could run away from it. This he found was a fallacy; but I could not bring him to the course until after the race had been run.

Tuesday, 22nd.—Leave refused to Henry to go to Eupatoria. 500 cavalry horses went over from our camp to Kamiesh, to bring back convalescents, who had arrived there from Scutari.

The Sardinians were disembarked in great numbers today; and, as we rode towards Kadikoi in the evening, we met two or three regiments marching up. Omar Pasha took a considerable Turkish force away with him today to Eupatoria; and those who were left behind, near Kadikoi, were changing their ground, and marching, with their frightful and discordant music, at the same time that the Sardinian troops were coming up the road. The dust, noise, confusion, and heat may be imagined, but I cannot describe it.

The appearance of the Sardinian troops gives general satisfaction. The Rifle corps, which we met today, is most picturesque. They are dressed in a dark tunic and trousers, with a broad-brimmed glazed hat, with a bugle stamped in gold on the front, and long massive plumes of black and green cock's hackle flowing over the left side of the hat, reaching to the shoulder. Their baggage transport is also well arranged. They are large covered carts, on two wheels, made entirely of wood, and painted light-blue, drawn by one, or sometimes two or three, magnificent mules.

Wednesday, 23rd.—A day entirely occupied with receiving morning visitors. Whilst we were at dinner, we heard some of the heaviest firing that we have listened to for months. Captain Lushington, who was with us, was at first anxious to go to his own battery, being alarmed lest the firing should be on the English, but after listening some time, we found that it came entirely from the French on the left.

Thursday, 24th.—The morning, till five o'clock, spent in the same busy idleness; but at five o'clock we ordered the horses, and rode down to our old grazing ground, near the Woronzow Road. As we were sauntering home, flower-laden, we met a second regiment of Sardinian Rides, and rode by the side of the regiment until we reached our camp. As soon as they came in sight of the cavalry camp the men began to cheer them; and as they passed, regiment after regiment took it up, and such a storm of shouts filled the air as must have frightened the pale young crescent moon looking shyly down from the serene, calm, evening sky—such cheers as only Englishmen know how to give.

I have been much amused today by hearing of the theatre which the Zouaves have established at the front, and where they perform, greatly to their own satisfaction, "*Les Anglais pour rire.*"

This morning brought us news. Twelve hundred French were killed and wounded, besides many officers. One company went in hundred men, and came back—three. They had attempted to storm and take the Flagstaff Battery, and had failed. General Pelissier, who has succeeded to General Canrobert in the command of the French army, will doubtless fight it out again, as his chief characteristic seems to be most resolute determination, and disregard of all that interferes between him and his object. I think that General Canrobert's resignation of his post as commander-in-chief has given rise to many an expression of respect and kindly feeling, which would most necessarily have been withheld from him so long as he continued to hold a position for which it was obvious to himself and others that he was incompetent.

This evening we made up a party, and rode to Karani, to hear the band of the Sardinian Guards. There was a crowd of Englishmen and Frenchmen already assembled. Perhaps it was because one fancies that every Italian must necessarily be a musician; but I certainly waited for the commencement of the music with an impatient interest with which no military band ever inspired me before.

But today at least I was disappointed. Beautifully they played, each instrument weaving its own peculiar harmony, with a truth and expression, such as could only be produced by genuine artists; but for today they contented themselves by looking round at their audience, and—playing to them Valse and Polka, Galop and Quadrille. I fancied, as I watched the handsome swarthy faces of the band, that there was a proud look of concealed scorn as they regarded the waggling heads and beating hands of the admiring crowd. To me it seemed a derision, a mockery of music. We left early.

While we were listening to the Sardinian music, the French were repairing their last night's work: they succeeded tonight in driving back the Russians, and there is nothing now between them and the town.

Today has been kept as the Queen's birthday, with a cavalry review, at which Lord Raglan, General Pelissier, and Omar Pasha were present, with a very brilliant staff.

Omar Pasha's dress was to my idea perfection. His dark-blue frock-coat, magnificently embroidered in gold, was fastened at the waist by a sword belt, the buckle of which, as well as the hilt of his sword, blazed with diamonds; a crimson ribbon across the shoulder bore the French order of Napoleon, while his crimson fez, instead of the usual tassel, was embroidered in front with diamonds and gold. The review was satisfactory enough. It was very hot, and rather dusty. The staff in scarlet must have paid dearly in discomfort for the brilliancy they gave to the "*tout ensemble.*" The 10th Hussars and 12th Lancers made a numerous, but I cannot think an imposing, show. The remains of our Heavy Cavalry looked to my eyes far more soldierlike, more English, more solid.

Declining an invitation from Omar Pasha to take luncheon in his tent, we rode straight to head quarters, where Henry saw, tried, and purchased a horse; and then we went to the plain below Kamara, where the Guards had games and footraces, and Lord Adolphus Vane an illumination in the evening, in honour of the day. We remained until about eleven o'clock; and then, to quote the words of the famous Mr. Pepys, *with great content, but much weariness, home to bed.*

Friday, 25th.—In our saddles by five, ready to accompany the Sardinian and Turkish armies, together with a strong force of French and some English cavalry, who were to take Tchergoum, a village on the banks of the Tchernaya, and to establish themselves in the plain lately occupied by the Russians.

The troops began to march at midnight; and consequently, when we reached the foot of Canrobert's Hill, we found the French cavalry returning from Tchergoum, from which, after some sharp firing, the Russians had fled.

The French destroyed some of the houses, and plundered others, and then left the village. Seeing that it was useless to go to Tchergoum until later in the day, we followed some French artillery until we came to a very handsome stone bridge over the Tchernaya. Here the Russians opened fire on us from a battery on the Inkermann heights; but though they fired several shots, it was at long range, and they did no damage.

One or two passed over our heads as we were watering our horses in the clear stream of the Tchernaya; and several more annoyed the French, who were destroying an earth-work from

125

which the Russians had removed their guns. We ascended the hill, and had a good view of the valley and ruins of Inkermann; and soon after, finding the heat on the hillside becoming intolerable, we turned our horses, and proceeded, a party of five, along the winding banks of the Tchernaya.

To us, who had not seen a river, and scarcely a tree, since our arrival in the Crimea, the shady windings of the Tchernaya appeared to possess greater beauty than, perhaps, actually belonged to them; though none but ourselves can know the wondrous luxury of riding through the tall and flowering grass, under the shade of oak and ash, creeping clematis, and climbing vine. We crossed the ford, and let our horses graze, while we sat underneath a spreading tree.

Some more adventurous members of the party found two fish-traps, full of fish, which we carefully put into a haversack, and then rode over the hill and along a lane, until we carne to the height overlooking Tchergoum. Here we found various parties of English officers, all exploring, like ourselves. We descended into the valley, but were presently warned that the Cossacks were behind us, and we must lose no time in getting away, which we did in as dignified a manner as we could. A few shots followed us, but not sufficiently near to excite any apprehension; and, clambering up a perpendicular hill, through thick masses of underwood, we got once more into our own country, and rode home in peace.

Saturday, May 26th.—This evening must always keep its place in my memory. We rode to hear the Sardinian band. Owing to a large number of their army having arrived, their audience was mostly composed of their own people. Then they played!

Amongst other pieces selected for our enjoyment, was one with solos on the *cornet-à-piston*, which the maestro played himself. I listened with closed eyes, to shut out all this outer world of camps and trumpet-calls, round-shot, dust, and noise, that I might be alone with the clear voice now speaking to my heart. The music was so sad! it rose and fell like the sighs and aspirations of a soul shut out from Paradise, yet striving to enter in.

Now there was an agony of wild, impassioned anguish;—now the notes fell soft, low, clear, and calm, as though angels had come to minister to the distracted soul. Each tone spoke,—not to my ears, or to my heart, but to the innermost depths of my soul;—those depths that lie far down, as much out of human knowledge as the depths of the deep, deep sea!

Sunday, May 27th.—Rode this evening all over the valley of the Balaklava charge,—*The valley of death,* as Tennyson calls it; but it reminded me more of another expression of his, *Oh, death in life!* The ground lay gaudy with flowers, and warm and golden in the rays of the setting sun. It was literally covered with flowers; there was hardly any grass,—in places, none,—nothing but dwarf-roses, mignonette, larkspur, and forgetmenots.

Here and there we passed the carcass of a horse;—we saw five, with 8. H. on the hoof. Six-pound shot lay strewn about thickly enough, and pieces of shell. I did not see it, but was told that a skull had been found quite blanched and clean, with most wonderfully beautiful and regular teeth. We saw today no traces of unburied human bodies,—the horses had all been lightly covered over, but many of them were half-exposed.

We gathered handfuls of flowers, and thought,—oh, how sadly!—of the flowers of English chivalry that had there been reaped and mown away!

News came this morning of the expedition to Kertch. It was put into general orders, and read to the troops. Kertch was taken, without difficulty, the moment the allies appeared before it, as the Russians blew up their forts and retired. We also became possessed of sixty guns of large calibre, and many ships of transport, laden with grain and stores. The Russian steam gun-boats attempted some resistance, but the *Snake* went at them in the most gallant manner, and very soon drove them back. General orders went on to say, that the Russians had sunk several steamships, and that our fleet is in possession of the Sea of Azov. The plunder, we hear, has been enormous. No casualty up to this time had occurred in the allied force.

We hear most distressing reports of the sickness among the

Russians. Fifteen thousand are supposed to have been sent from Sebastopol to Kertch, Yenicali, &c. These, of course, are now (such as were not blown up with the forts at Kertch) distributed amongst the various villages, to be abandoned again as we advance.

Sunday, June 3rd.—Chiefly remarkable for a proposed ride to the Baidar Valley, which did not come off, and for a delightful *diner à la belle étoile*, which did. We sat on the summit of a rock, so perpendicular that one dreaded looking down its giddy height upon the quiet sea below. At length the glimmering twilight died away, and, one by one, the stars came out. As far as nature was concerned in it, never was a fitter evening to conclude a Sabbath day.

Wednesday, June 6th.—I was extremely unwell; overpowered with the terrible heat, and weak and languid to a degree that compelled me, as I thought, to remain perfectly quiet and still. We intended to give our saddles a rest-day, when suddenly, at three o'clock, the guns pealed out from the front, and announced, with their tremendous voices, that the third bombardment had begun.

We knew that this time the guns would not play an overture for another farce; so we ordered our horses, "Bob" and the pony, for I was unequal to riding any other horse than my "sweet pony," and we galloped to the front. The first point of observation was opposite Sir George Cathcart's grave; our second at the quarries, further on. At neither of these places could we see the least what was doing, owing to the dense smoke which hung over town and battery. Lady George Paget was sitting on the rock-work of the quarry, vainly endeavouring, as were many more, to trace the operations through the fog.

We, who came up at so much cost to ourselves, were determined to see if possible, and rode along the front until we came to a post of observation opposite the *Maison d'Eau*. Here we saw very well, as the breeze had risen, and left the French attack clear from smoke. Altogether, our observations today were very unsatisfactory, as the principal firing was on the *Mamelon vert*, which stands to the right of the Redan and Malakoff batteries. We were told that the storming of the *Mamelon vert* would take place tomorrow; and as we were determined to see as much as possible of the working of the guns on that battery before the assault, we left the *Maison d'Eau* at seven o'clock, and, dining about eight, went to sleep earlier than usual.

Thursday, June 7th.—Rose at three. Started at four for the front, where we established ourselves in the piquet-house, exactly opposite the *Mamelon vert*. The firing at that time was tremendous. Gun after gun, shell after shell, pitched into, on, or near the fated battery. Most of the embrasures were knocked in, nearly every gun dismounted. The Russians, who had already begun to fire very wild, only replied with two guns, one at each corner of the battery. These guns worked till the last.

Presently a shot came bobbing up the hill, like a hare, to where we stood, though we were not in the line of any of our batteries; but it seems that, whenever the Russians saw a group of people, they fired into them.

The heat, for we had watched (I confess to having fallen asleep in the middle—but then I was very tired and weak) from half-past four till ten o'clock, was getting intolerable, so we mounted and rode home by the Fourth Division. On our way home we met a French officer, who told us on no account to omit being at the front by four o'clock this afternoon.

By three o'clock we ordered fresh horses and started once more. As we approached the French lines of General Bosquet's division we saw the storming party forming up—five-and-twenty thousand French. They stood a dense and silent mass, looking, in their dark blue coats, grim and sombre enough. Presently we heard the clatter of horses behind us, and General Bosquet and staff galloped up. General Bosquet addressed them in companies; and as he finished each speech, he was responded to by cheers, shouts, and bursts of song.

The men had more the air and animation of a party invited to a marriage than of a party going to fight for life or death. To me how sad a sight it seemed! The divisions begin to move and to file down the narrow ravine, past the French battery, opposite the Mamelon. General Bosquet turns to me, his eyes full of tears—my own I cannot restrain, as he says, "*Madame, à Paris on a toujours l'Exposition, les bals, les fêtes; et—dans une heure et demie la moitié de ces braves seront morts!*" But let us ride up the hill to the piquet-house and watch from thence for the third rocket—the signal of assault.

Our stay at the piquet-house is short, for shots are coming up there fast. A navvy just below us has had his head taken off; and, besides, there is a place a little further back commanding a much better view. Here we can seat ourselves on the grass, and let our horses graze.

What a vehement fire! and all directed on the one spot. Two rockets in quick succession are gone up, and a moment after comes the third. Presently the slope of the Mamelon is covered with men, ascending separately and rapidly; not marching up in line, as our infantry would have done, but scattered like a flock of sheep. Two guns, hitherto masked, in the Mamelon open quickly upon them; but they rush up, and form when they reach the entrenchment.

For a time we can see nothing but clouds of smoke. The guns are all silent now,—nothing but the volley and file firing of musketry. The Russians, standing on the fort, fire down on the advancing French; but presently some men are seen leaving the Mamelon and rushing towards the Malakoff. They are Russians, and the *Mamelon vert* is now in possession of the French. A momentary silence which succeeds enable us to distinguish musketry on our left. It is the English, who are attacking the quarries in front of the Redan; and an artilleryman, who comes up soon after, informs us that the English have taken the quarries with but little loss, and, if let, will take the Redan.

But the noise in front commences again, and I see men in hundreds rushing from the Mamelon to the Malakoff. *Per Dio!* they are not satisfied with what they have gained, but are going to try for the Malakoff, with all its bristling guns. Under what a storm of fire they advance, supported by that impenetrable red line, which marks our own infantry! The fire from the Malakoff is tremendous—terrible; but all admit that the steadiness of the French under it is magnificent.

On our left the sun is setting in all his glory, but looking lurid and angry through the smoky atmosphere, that is becoming dense and oppressive from perpetual firing. Presently the twilight deepens, and the light of rocket, mortar, and shell falls over the beleaguered town.

We cannot hope to hear any accurate report of what has been done tonight; and as it is now ten o'clock, and too dark to see anything, we catch our horses and ride slowly away.

Meantime cholera is come among us, and at Balaklava has asserted itself by stopping a career of much energy and usefulness. Poor Admiral Boxer has fallen a victim to its remorseless gripe, and is buried at the head of the harbour, where he worked so hard, early and late, to endeavour to rescue Balaklava from the plague-stricken wretchedness in which he found it a few months before.

Friday, June 8th.—The French are in the Mamelon, where they found seven big guns, They have thrown up an 18 lb. battery, from which I saw them throw the first shot at the Malakoff. We should have taken the Malakoff but for a deep trench twenty feet wide and eighteen deep; and there was no reserve with trusses of hay to throw in, so the French could not cross it. We have nearly silenced the Malakoff guns with our fire today. They were burying in all directions. We lost thirty-three officers killed and wounded. I have not heard of anyone I know being killed. No words can do justice to the gallant conduct of the 49th Regiment; and all are full of admiration of the French, and the way they rushed at the forts. A strong sortie is expected tonight.

Saturday, 9th.—Was again at the front, though the fire had considerably slackened, and there was nothing doing.

But who could keep away from a place where so many interests were at stake? Not I.

Monday, 11th.—Took such a lovely, quiet ride to the Sardinian outposts, through a country of massive foliage, green hedges, and deep mountain gorges, to where a little village peeped out at us from beneath its heavy crown of verdure. The little village looked gay and smiling enough at a distance; nearer, it was all deserted and desolate. The houses had been plundered, and terribly knocked about. I found a deer's foot, which I carried away as a memento of our pleasant ride, and which I shall have mounted as a riding-whip if I ever live to return.

Thursday, 14th.—The Kertch expedition has returned, and is in Balaklava Harbour.

The destruction of Anapa appears to afford the principal topic of camp conversation. We hear that the "Kertch heroes" have brought home lots of plunder, and we are rather curious for their disembarkation. The success attendant on the expedition seems to have put everybody in good spirits; and "We must have a try for Sebastopol now" is the cry from the general to the newly-arrived ensign.

I was occupied principally with a private grievance of my own, which, although to me a cause of very great annoyance and inconvenience, put me much in mind of the Old Lady in *Albert Smith's ascent of Mont Blanc*, who lost her favourite black box. This box (of mine) has been coming out to me ever since the latter end of February, and it is now the 14th of June! Disgusted by the delay which at first attended the delivery of goods *viâ* Hayter and Howell, this immortal box was sent out to me by what was to have been a shorter route; and after an expensive correspondence, an incalculable quantity of ill temper on my part, and a most vexatious delay, we heard this day that the ship in which this *bête noire* left England had arrived in Balaklava and had discharged her cargo.

We sent down a man and pack horse to the agents of the ship, but received a message in reply denying all knowledge of the box. Next morning the same man and horse went down to

Balaklava to the Parcels' Office. No box. Immediately on their return we sent them down a third time; this time desiring the servant to see the ship-master, and to go on board the *Odin* himself. He did so, and returned with a note saying that, in consequence of a stupid mistake on the address of the box, it had been left at Scutari, where it had been delivered on the 7th of May!! It contains my summer clothing.

Friday, 15th.—Breakfasted with Général Féray, who commands the Light Brigade (Chasseurs d'Afrique), and afterwards rode, accompanied by his staff and an escort of *chasseurs*, to the Château Periouski, a Russian hunting-box about a mile from Baidar. The ride was through a country absolutely lovely—a country of hills and valleys, green trees, and fountains bright, clear, and cold. The *château* is evidently only just completed. It consists of a large dining room, with a beautiful *parquet*, and several smaller rooms on the ground floor, and a turret and gallery. Except near the stables, where were two large rooms, there seemed no accommodation for servants. There was a granary, a coach-house, a four-stalled stable—such narrow stalls!—and a cow-house, carefully floored with boards, but looking clean and comfortable nevertheless.

A garden all run to waste, and a perfect wilderness of trees, completed the inventory of the place. After we had thoroughly explored it, we returned to the camp of French Heavy Cavalry, at a village about two miles in the rear (Vernutka), where *le* Marquis de Forton, the general commanding the Heavy Brigade of French cavalry, gave us a most hospitable invitation to a *déjeûner à la fourchette*, arranged under large spreading trees, the branches of which had been interlaced to form an arbour, and ornamented with masses of flowers.

In this delicious shade we remained chatting as gaily as if we had all been old friends, until the sun went down behind the cliffs on the sea shore, when Général Forton and some of his officers accompanied our party back to the tent of *le* Général Féray, which we did not leave until near midnight, after having passed one of the most agreeable days of our Crimean experience.

Saturday, 16th.—The Brigade of Guards marched up to the front, to be in readiness for the storming, taking, and destruction of Sebastopol, which is announced to come off on Monday next.

Sunday, 17th.—The guns opened fire in their usual rattling style, and had a magnificent burst of about half an hour without a check. They then slackened for a little while, but soon recovered speed, and went on at best pace till the afternoon, when they got very slack. But people seemed everywhere in the highest spirits about tomorrow.

We remained at home till late in the evening, as several friends came down to see us, to say and to hear kind words, and to be wished good luck for tomorrow.

About six o'clock Henry and I rode up to the front, not so much to see the fire as to shake hands with many who we knew were going in tomorrow morning. A few amongst these were, Captain Agar, Colonel Wyndham, Major Hamilton, Captain Hume, and Lord Adolphus Vane. It was eleven o'clock before we reached home, and at that hour we found *le* Capitaine Léon Müel awaiting us in the tent.

We sent our horses to have a double feed of corn. I am sorry to say we have two horses out of four useless; "Bob" having hurt his heel, and the other, "Chestnut," his back. Ordered some tea for ourselves, and then, having listened as long as my weariness would permit to an elaborate account of the wonders about to be performed by the French cavalry and Chasseurs d'Afrique tomorrow, I crawled into the hut, and lay down for two hours without taking off my habit.

Monday, 18th.—At two, a.m., we were drinking some coffee, and at three o'clock we were at the front, seated on the ground as far forward as the Light Cavalry (who have been made into special constables!) would permit. We were a few minutes late for the opening fire, but in time for such a storm of shot, grape, shell, and musketry as had never before annoyed the ears of Heaven. We could see no troops. The Malakoff is firing gun after gun, though as many as five of our shells burst in it at one moment.

The answering fire of the Malakoff is tremendous, and they have run up an enormous flag. The heavy guns of the Redan play away like so much file firing: the whole western horizon is dense with their smoke. So long as these guns fire, it is evident these forts are in possession of the Russians. But the French sent down 25,000 men, and what with all our men told off for the storming party, such pertinacious resistance cannot last long; and if once we get in, the Russians will pay dearly for their obstinacy. The firing, however, grows less: there are no guns from the Malakoff now.

The great flag which they hoisted there is hauled down; and the Mamelon has been silent for some time. They fire a stray gun or two from the Redan; and we, who are looking on and wondering, inquire, "What next?" Alas! we are soon told. The supports are seen moving. We fancy they are going down to the quarries to strengthen the force already there, for they disappear for moment in a ravine—but no, they are advancing towards us: they are coming away. The firing is over; ambulance mules are going down. So, then, we have been beaten back.

The Brigade of Guards and Highlanders who have been waiting on our right are forming in column, and marching back to camp. We too turn away—blind with watching, and stupefied with the intense heat of the sun. We meet countless wounded coming down. Sir John Campbell is dead, Colonel Yea dead, and Colonel Shadforth; while many that we know are cruelly wounded: there seems no end to the ghastly train. Colonel Mundy, of the 33rd, shot through the thigh with a Minié rifle ball, walked into the mess hut of the 23rd, where we were sitting, as gaily as though he were untouched. Many soldiers, shot through arms and legs, walked up from the trenches, self-supported and alone; nor would anyone have perceived their wounds but for the small hole in the coat or trousers.

How magnificent is such defiant courage!

Tuesday Evening.—We heard that poor Captain Agar is also

dead! He was mortally wounded, and expired from exhaustion soon after he was carried back to camp. Poor Shiffner, who so nearly lost his life some time ago, is also killed.

Thursday, 21st.—The 10th Hussars are moved out into the plain with the Turkish and Sardinian force. The French talk of storming the Malakoff again in about twelve days; meantime, they are making regular approaches to it as to a town.

Friday, 22nd.—General Estcourt is taken ill with cholera. What a suppressed feeling of disgust and discontent runs through this army! It is no part of my business to enter on such a discussion, and I have hitherto carefully avoided doing so; but I cannot help sharing in the general interest and anticipation of a great and speedy change: men feel that their lives have been trifled with too long.

Saturday, 23rd.—General Estcourt is still alive, and the account today is more hopeful.

We rode to the monastery, and returned in one of the most tremendous thunderstorms I ever remember The lightning was continuous and dazzlingly vivid, while the rain poured down in such torrents as to detach pieces of rock of half-a-ton weight from the cliff, and send them headlong into the road. The waters too rose so rapidly that tents, saddles, and kits were all washed away; while near Balaklava eight Turks were this morning found drowned.

Sunday, 24th.—Poor General Estcourt died this morning. It strikes us that Death has taken the recall of those in authority into his own stern hands.

Thursday, June 28th.—We had heard that Lord Raglan was prevented by indisposition from attending General Estcourt's funeral, which was a strictly private one; and we heard yesterday that Lord Raglan's health was improving, and that nothing serious was apprehended. Our consternation was great, when one of his staff, who was with us at the monastery, received a hasty message that Lord Raglan was rapidly becoming worse.

I can hardly imagine a greater misfortune to the army than his death at such a moment as the present. Now, when we may be about to lose them, we remember how valuable and necessary are his diplomatic powers in an army composed of so many nations. We are almost tempted to lose sight of the inefficient general, in the recollection of the kind-hearted, gentlemanly man, who had so hard a task, which he fulfilled so well, of keeping together and in check the heads of so many armies.

Friday Morning, June 29th.—Lord Raglan died last night!

It seems as though some pulse in this vast body had ceased to beat, the army is so quiet. Men speak in low voices words of regret. The body is to be conveyed to England for burial. There is a report that Baraguay D'Hilliers is coming out with 40,000 men to land at Eupatoria, and invest the north side of Sebastopol.

A day or two ago, this might have caused some interest; now, for today at least, the thoughts of all meet in one darkened room, where lies he who a few hours ago was commander-in-chief.

Saturday, 30th.—The Russians, always aware of our movements almost before we are so ourselves, having heard of our loss, made an attack on our trenches last night, and were driven back with some loss on our side. I hear that thirteen of the Naval Brigade were killed, and sixteen of the Guards.

General Scarlett and Colonel Lawrenson arrived in Balaklava yesterday; the former takes command of the cavalry division, and Colonel Lawrenson of the Light Brigade. We are all glad to have General Scarlett in command of the division, instead of the senior colonel, himself commanding a regiment, which is always objectionable, and indeed in the French service is not permitted.

I have been ill for some days, as, indeed, who has not? and would gladly avail myself of Captain King's kind offer of his cabins on board the *Rodney*, in Kamiesh Bay; but Henry dares not apply for leave, as the troops have no money. The officers' field allowances are all due today, and for the last ten days there has not been any money in the Commissariat chest!

The report in camp is that Commissary General Filder has signified his inability to provide forage for the number of horses now in the Crimea.

Sunday, July 1st.—As we were riding yesterday along the banks of the Tchernaya, we could not but remark the vast herds of cattle grazing by the stream, and we compared them with our own starved, over-driven, cruelly used beasts, with broken tails, and bleeding from hard knocks and blows. The Transport Corps some days ago reported that they would not be in an efficient state until they had 22,000 baggage animals. At present they have between 8,000 and 9,000. If Commissary General Filder's report is correct, the poor horses already here, and the hundreds that are coming out, may look forward to a cheerful winter! The very idea of such another winter fills me with pain and dread.

July 2nd.—It is in orders this morning that the cavalry division moves out to the plain, in the direction of Baidar, on Wednesday next, to strengthen the position at the outposts held by the Sardinians, as two divisions of the Russian army have marched down within the last few days to the Crimea. This will disarrange us all very much, we have become so settled in our old camp. As for me, when I look at the number of things with which I have become surrounded in hut and tent, I confess I can only sit down and shrug my shoulders, for it is absurd to think of packing in this tremendous heat.

Lord Raglan's body is, I understand, to be escorted by ten squadrons of cavalry tomorrow to Kamiesh, where it will be put on board the *Caradoc*, and so taken to England. Meanwhile General Simpson reigns in his stead.

CHAPTER 6

The Fall of Sebastopol

Giace l' alta Cartago, appena I segni
De l' alte sue ruine il do serba.—Tasso.

Sebastopol est prise!—Napoleon III., Oct. 1. 1854

Lord Raglan's funeral procession from head quarters to Kasatch, where the body was embarked on board the *Caradoc*, to be conveyed to England, took place on Tuesday, the 3rd of July. It was escorted by several squadrons of English cavalry, and the melancholy procession left head quarters after a salute of nineteen guns. Vast bodies of French troops, with Sardinian cavalry, lined the road the whole length of the journey, whilst the mournful notes of the "Dead March in Saul" were taken up at intervals.

I describe this from hearsay, as all those who were not actually engaged in the ceremony were confined to camp; in consequence of which order we were unable to witness a sight which I have since been told was "too fine to be described;" and also, that "the Duke of Wellington's funeral was nothing in comparison." From head quarters to Kasatch Bay is between seven and eight miles, and such a distance lined with the armies of three nations must in itself have been a magnificent sight.

July 6th.—Anniversary of my mother's death. For some days past I have been very far from well, and am now reduced to such a state of weakness that I am desired to procure change of air, if possible, and without delay. To this innumerable difficulties oppose themselves. There is the difficulty of Henry's obtaining leave, the difficulty of my getting over to Kamiesh, for I fear it will be many days before I can ride so far. I have written to Captain King, of the *Rodney*, to ask his permission to go on board for a week; but, with an ill-luck peculiarly mine, he is on the point of leaving that ship for the *St. Jean D'Acre*; and of course, in the confusion consequent on such a change, I should only be in the way.

Meantime I must endure the mighty heat of this breathless valley as best I may, knowing that if I am to live, I shall do so in spite of everything; and if I am to die, so it has been ordered by One who cannot err. I cannot understand that inordinate fear of death, which possesses the souls of many. He who sees not as man seeth, and who can do no evil, will surely do with us what is best.

July 7th.—A draught of men and horses came out yesterday for the 5th Dragoon Guards. We had a great deal of thunder in the air, and one or two heavy showers, followed by bright hot sunshine. Several people, hearing that I was ill, kindly came to inquire for me today, as well as yesterday. How many friends has this break-up at head quarters caused us to lose! I shall feel, as I ride about the camp in future, almost as though I were in a land of strangers. Poor deserted head quarters!—the ravens always used to croak up there: they will croak twice as much now.

The chestnut pony, sole survivor of the *aide-de-camp's*, came down to us yesterday, and, like another sleek and well-conditioned pony that he knows, he bears the name of "*Poulett Pasha.*"—Poor pony! I think he had a presentiment that head quarters, and its comfortable stable and litter, was lost to him forever—for he tried his utmost to conciliate us, his new masters, by licking our hands, and cramming his nose into all the pockets he could see, in search of bread.

July 10th.—The chances of my being able to get away, at any rate for some time, are getting less and less. Everybody seems to be going home. I sent the first part of my journal to England by an officer going home sick; another, who has been out here about a fortnight, returns immediately from the same cause. Colonel Steele merely remains to wind up his affairs, and then he too sets sail for England. General Airey and Colonel Blane are alone left at head quarters of all my old friends. Mr. Calvert and Vico are there still, I believe. In fact, who would not get away if they could from the flaming sword of the pestilence?

Omar Pasha has withdrawn himself and 20,000 men from Baidar, much to the dissatisfaction of the French, who reckoned on his remaining there until they had cut the magnificent grass of the valley and made it—oh, English memories!—into fragrant hay.

Canrobert and 10,000 men have left the plain, and are gone up to the front before Sebastopol. From this it is augured that we shall, before long, have another try for the Malakoff. In Canrobert's division are included the Premier Zouaves, one of whom I overheard saying to a comrade, the other day, when they were both sitting fishing on the banks of the Tchernaya—"*Ah, mon enfant, mais, quand il n'y aura plus de Zouaves, l'armée Française sera finie!*"

Thanks to the kindness of Mr. Vansittart, who lent me a very quiet pony, I was able this afternoon to leave the shadow of my tent, with which I was getting sorely discontented, and to reach once more the cliffs overlooking the sea. I know of hardly any more lovely spot than the one we chose as our resting-place this afternoon. Before us lay the sea, blue, serene, and quiet—

Like beauty newly dead.

To our right and left rose the magnificent outlines of a coast naturally stern and terrible, but now bathed in a flood of rose-coloured light, with which the setting sun soothed the landscape, all flushed and scorched before from the power of his great heat; while round us, and underneath our feet, grass, leaves, and flowers looked up with pale, exhausted faces, thirsting for the evening dew.

July 11th.—Spent the morning in bewailing the hard fate which bereft us of our cook—a Maltese, who for some time had officiated in that capacity, having gone out one morning, and left us, as a legacy, the delightful intimation, that "he was gone away, and warn't coming back any more!"

We soon fell in with a real Samaritan in Captain King, then commanding the *Rodney*, who lent us his own invaluable servant; but Captain King's subsequent removal to the *St. Jean D'Acre* obliged him to take his cook with him, and we are once more left servantless, helpless, and dinnerless.

Feeling that we were doing no good by sitting at home, we ordered the horses, and rode to hear the Sardinian band. I had heard no sound of music for nearly two months, and when I pulled up in the crowd round the band I was in a state of mind that jarred with everything save annoyance, impatience, and disgust. ("Bob" had refused to jump a gutter, and eventually dropped his hind legs into it, though all the Sardinians were looking at him,—"Bob," who is the best water jumper out of Ireland.)

In fact, I was as much out of temper as out of health; but presently a voice, to which no one not utterly devoid of soul could listen unmoved, speaks to me in low and trembling tones. Ah, where is the petty gall that "wrung my withers" not a moment ago? It is down below me, in the mire and mud of my daily life; while I am carried away far beyond this material world of trial and annoyance, and am walking side by side with angels— dreaming that I have caught the commencement of a harmony such as *ear hath not heard, neither hath it entered into the heart of man to conceive.*

Returned at half-past eight, or rather, I should say, fell crashing down from the top of Mount Olympus, where I had been conversing with the gods, into a soup tureen, and dish of fried fish more disgusting than anything ever produced in the annals of cookery.

July 12th.—I think I have a cook! We rode up first of all to General Bosquet, and afterwards to General Féray. We found him at dinner with *le* Colonel Polles, who commands a regiment of Zouaves, and who took pity on my distress.

The French made a reconnaissance beyond Baidar yesterday—met a few Cossacks, and saw a body of regular troops in the distance. A large Russian force is supposed to be hovering about somewhere in the neighbourhood.

Lord Ward's sale took place today, as he is returning to England immediately. I was shocked to hear of the death, by cholera, of Mr. Calvert, who at head quarters filled the office of Chief of the Secret Intelligence Department. He had been consul at Kertch for some years, and was a man of great information, as well as a universal favourite with all who knew him. A few hours later we heard that Vico was also dead. How the plague festers at head quarters! The perpetual presence of death is enough to make the strongest of us quail.

July 14th.—News reached the camp that a new commander-in-chief is to be appointed in place of General Simpson. Vico's sale at the English head quarters.

Tuesday, July 19th.—A heavy cannonade was opened tonight by the Russians on the French left attack. General Luders is supposed to be in Sebastopol now; and we imagine that he ordered a sortie, as nearly at the same moment the Russians made an attempt on our quarries. But they could not bring their men on; and as we opened our heavy guns on them, they soon retreated, with loss. For some time after this they kept up a cannonade, apparently for the purpose of making a noise, as they fired very wild, and did not aim at any special point. They succeeded in disturbing everybody. We fancied that it was the opening of another fire. They kept it up from seven, p. m. on Tuesday, to about the same hour on Wednesday morning, and since then there has been hardly a gun fired by anybody.

July 20th.—Sat once more by the seashore in the quiet evening, saying over to myself the last words of Spenser's *Fairy Queen*, at which the poet himself paused, and was silent evermore:—

Then gin I thinke on that which Nature said
Of that same time when no more change shall be,
But stedfast rest of all things, firmly stay'd
Upon the Pillars of Eternity,
That is contraire to mutability;
But thenceforth all shall rest eternally
With him that is 'The God of Sabaoth' hight—
Oh, Thou great Sabaoth God, grant me that Sabath's sight!

July 22nd.—I have had today the pain of bidding *adieu* to nearly the last of my kind old friends in the Crimea. Captain Lushington, now Rear Admiral Sir Stephen Lushington, K.C.B., who was promoted a few days ago, returns tomorrow, laden with honours, to England. And well deserved honours they are, and must be, for this reason, that not one man out in the campaign has made a single observation implying that his distinctions were cheaply earned, or that he had been rewarded above his merit; and as such observations are very rife in the camp on like occasions, I think that their absence now is the surest sign that "his honours do become him well."

I am writing late at night, amid a storm of heavy musketry. Occasionally a huge gun flings forth its volume of death, shaking our hut and the table at which I write. All the Guards, and Sir Colin Campbell, are in the trenches tonight; Sir Colin going down as a volunteer, to give a little novelty and spirit to men who—God help them!—after being shot at every third night for ten months, like rabbits in a warren, require a little stimulus, not to give them courage, but to keep them from the heavy sleep induced by the overwhelming heat and the monotonous voices of the guns.

The heavy guns are silent now, but the musketry is pouring on, making ghastly *music in the ear of night*. I heard today of two atrocities committed in the army, and I think it strange we should have so few to record.

One was a tragedy which took place two nights ago. Some Greeks—two men and two women—lived in a hut near the railroad, and also within a couple of hundred yards of a troop of artillery. The people were honest and quiet enough, taking in washing, and earning money by various kinds of work. Two nights since, some Turkish soldiers went down to the hut, murdered the two men, after a vehement struggle, and clove the head of one of the women open to her throat; the other woman they stabbed in three places, and left for dead. They then ransacked the house, and found 100*l.* in money—what enormous sums are made by the hangers-on of the camp!—and escaped.

All next day the mutilated woman lay, the only living thing amid such ghastly death, and the day after it occurred to her neighbours to inquire why none of them had been seen on the previous day. The survivor is now in hospital, and has intimated that the murderers were Turkish soldiers, and that she could identify them. Only a week ago Henry and I took shelter under the eaves of that very house during a thunderstorm.

The second story is shorter, and occurred some little time since. A man attached in some way to the army, Commissariat or otherwise, was walking late from Balaklava to the front, having about him 120*l.* Some Greeks, who knew that he had money with him, had tracked and followed him until he reached a sequestered spot in the road, when they fell upon him. He called out lustily, "*Au secours! au secours!*"

Whereupon a French soldier of artillery ran to his aid; but the Frenchman's eye detected the glitter of the coin, and, with a presence of mind truly admirable, he rapped the howling wretch over the head with the butt end of his carbine, seized the money-bag, and sped away before the astonished Greeks could at all recover their wits, either to cry out or to give chase. So the Frenchman got the money, and escaped, while the Greeks were discovered standing, open mouthed, beside the corpse, and were carried off forthwith. Four squadrons of Light Cavalry—one of the 8th Hussars, one of the 11th Hussars, one of the 4th Light Dragoons, and one of the 19th Lancers—went out this morning to Baidar, ostensibly to collect forage, but really to keep the peace between the Frenchmen and the Turks.

July 24th.—On the 12th of this month I was credulous

145

enough to believe the asseverations of a French general, and a Colonel of Zouaves, who, with many protestations, promised me a cook. I might as well, at any rate, have saved myself the trouble of believing them, for no cook, or servant of any description, has made his appearance, and the consequent discomfort of our lives must be felt to be appreciated.

The cause of the heavy firing on the night of the 22nd was a smart attack made by the Russians on the French, and on our left attack. We hear the Russians were not repulsed until they had suffered severe loss.

A messenger came over to me this evening from the squadrons at Baidar, telling me that they would start for a reconnaissance tomorrow morning, about fifteen miles further up the country. They kindly offered us the accommodation of a tent if we wished to ride up overnight and join them; but the letter found us smitten down beneath the fierce strokes of the mighty sun, far too weak and oppressed to think of undertaking so long and fatiguing a ride.

The report is that 300,000 Russians have just arrived in the Crimea; and as they are perfectly aware that they cannot be provisioned, they intend to seize on our stores, and drive us into the sea! This report is balanced by a fact that I happen to know—namely, that the quartermaster-general has telegraphed for enormous supplies of wood, boards, and huts, to quarter us and our horses for the winter months.

July 30th.—A stronger will than my own,—one which the most resolute and powerful among us are obliged to obey, has kept me silent these few days. I have been ill: and to be ill in the Crimea is no light matter, as many beside me can testify. Poor Lord Killeen, too, is gone away to Therapia. In my distress I wrote to Captain Moorsom, of the Naval Brigade, to implore him to make arrangements so that I also might go on board ship. My position here is unfortunate. If my husband were ill—which God forbid!—he could obtain leave to go at once; whereas I am wholly dependent on the kindness of such as have not had all human feelings knocked out of their hearts.

My appeal to the Naval Brigade was answered in a way that I must ever remember with gratitude. Captain Moorsom and Captain Keppel, who now commands the Naval Brigade, rode down to our camp, although the latter was quite unknown to us, and with the former we had but a very slight acquaintance; and in a few minutes they had arranged everything for my going either on board the *Rodney* or the *St. Jean D'Acre*, as soon as I am able to be moved. It seems as though I could never speak gratefully enough of the kind hospitality of these two sailors. Now, the only difficulty is, whether the soldiers will have humanity enough to permit Henry to accompany me. If they do not, I must go quite alone.

The dearth of any active proceedings at the front gives me time to remark on a little circumstance which rather edified me the other day, as I was riding home from an afternoon spent among the cliffs on the seashore.

At a little distance from us were riding three officers belonging to the English cavalry, when we suddenly heard shouts and cries, and saw a Tartar running with all speed towards the three, holding up his hands, and apparently appealing for protection. The three rode on, until at last the Tartar, by dint of running, overtook them and tried to speak. With frantic gestures he endeavoured to induce them to listen, and with what success?

Two endeavoured to ride over him, and I believe I am right in saying that one of the two struck him with his hunting-whip; at any rate, the arm was raised. As we rode homewards, I reflected on the vast superiority that exists in the civilised over the uncivilised part of the world: the latter, true to the old world instincts implanted by nature, appeals from the weak to the strong for protection—from ignorance to education and Christianity; civilisation (perhaps because he has not been introduced) rides over the man who is defenceless and wronged, or rids himself of him with the thong of his hunting-whip. Let us sing "*Te Deum*" for civilisation, Christianity, and the Golden Rule.

July 31st.—Heavy mortar practice all last night, with what result I have not heard.

My husband has succeeded in obtaining leave to accompany me to Kasatch, on condition that he returns twice a-week to camp. This permission is kindly given him by Colonel Shewell, Acting Brigadier in the absence on leave of Lord George Paget, and confirmed by General Scarlett

Monday, August 6th—We have now been since Thursday on board the *Rodney*, in Kasatch Bay. The first evening that we arrived, Captain Charles Hillyar came on board, but only to say "goodbye," as he left the next morning in the *Gladiator* for Corfu, where he was sent to fetch up troops and guns. It is reported here that General Simpson intends opening fire this autumn, and with 400 fresh mortars!

Ah! what a sound will rise, how wild and dreary,
When the death-angel touches these swift keys!
What loud lament and dismal miserere
Will mingle with their awful symphonies!
I hear even now the infinite fierce chorus,
The cries of agony, the endless groan,
Which thro' the ages that have gone before us,
In lost reverberations, reach our own.
The tumult of each sack'd and burning village;
The shout that every prayer for mercy drowns;
The soldier's revel in the midst of pillage;
The wail of famine in beleaguer'd towns.
The bursting shell, the gateway wrench'd asunder;
The rattling musketry, the clashing blade,
And ever and anon, in tones of thunder,
The diapason of the cannonade.

One would fancy Longfellow had been himself an actor in the weary tragedy that is dragging on around us, so faithful are his descriptive lines.

During the cool evenings we sit in the stern walk of the ship, and watch the shells bursting over the "beleaguered" town. Last night there was a very extensive fire in Sebastopol, which shot its fitful gleams far up into the sky. The French must have made it doubly hazardous to extinguish, as they poured in rockets and shells as fast as possible, producing to us lookers-on a beautiful effect—a large sheet of light in the back-ground radiating on all sides with exploding fire-works. The *Terrible* steamed away yesterday afternoon to Gibraltar for heavy guns and ammunition. We envied her the trip, for she will catch the cool sea breezes; while we, lying in harbour, surrounded by shipping, can with difficulty induce a single wandering zephyr to waft himself past our vessel.

Captain Drummond, who is appointed to the *Albion*, but is at present commanding the *Tribune* here, called on us during the afternoon of yesterday, and rowed us out as far as the *St. Jean D'Acre* and the *Algiers*. Captain King, of the *Acre*, called on me the day before yesterday, and has promised to send me a pianoforte, which was taken from Kertch, and which is now on board the *Princess Royal*. I think there must be something in the profession of a sailor that makes him less selfish and more considerate for others than men of any other class.

The Duke of Newcastle is on board the *Royal Albert* with the admiral, who has changed his position, and moved out, together with the *Hannibal*, the *Queen*, and one or two other ships, off Sebastopol. The Duke is reported to be suffering from the effects of the climate; and I have not heard anybody say they were sorry to hear it. If Cinderella's good fairy would but reappear .and turn him into a private soldier in the trenches, in the depth of winter, I still do not think that many would be very sorry for him. Poor man! perhaps he was misled by false information after all.

A large American transport came in yesterday filled with French infantry. The French have constructed a series of earthworks and redoubts, so as to fortify the harbours of Kamiesh and Kasatch, and also to take up a position (and a very strong one) on the rising ground inland, in case they should ever be driven back from their trenches.

A French steamer, with heavy guns, went today round Strelitzka Point, and occupied herself for some five hours in firing mortars at the enemy, with what success we in the harbour were unable to determine; but at seven o'clock she returned to Kamiesh, bringing with her a smaller steamer in tow.

About four days since Captain Baillie, Lord Rokeby's *aide-de-camp*, came on board the *Rodney*, suffering extremely from an attack of one of our prevalent diseases. Mr. Layard, brother to the member of Parliament (who, with a noble cause, and with half England at his back, contrived to ruin it), has died within the last two days, also on board a man-of-war.

I was interested today in listening to anecdotes of the trenches. Amongst them was the following:—The Guards have been engaged in trench work since the 17th of June, and have of course taken their fair share of the work. A few days ago Lord Rokeby was going the round of the hospitals of his division, to see that the men wanted for nothing, when he recognised among the recent admissions a young man who had distinguished himself for steadiness in the camp and gallantry in the trenches. On being asked what was the matter, the poor fellow said, "I've lost a leg, my Lord. I and my two brothers came out with the old regiment: the first one died at the battle of the Alma; the second one had both his feet frozen off when we were up in the front, soon after Inkermann, and died in hospital; and now I've lost my leg. 'Tis not much to boast of,—six legs came out, and only one goes home again."

Profoundly touched, Lord Rokeby asked him whether they three were the only sons. "Oh no, my Lord, we are seven brothers in all; but we three preferred soldiering, and enlisted at the same time."

The *Arrow* gun-boat went away last night to Perekop, and the *Harpy* is under orders for the Sea of Azof tonight.

Our hopes of a servant are small indeed. we have written to Constantinople, Malta, and England; and today I hear that General V—, the greatest gourmet of the French army, is at his wits' end to find a cook.

August 12th.—Went on shore yesterday afternoon, and inspected the dockyard, which is rapidly approaching its completion. It consists of several huts, two of them very lofty and very large; one occupied as a foundry, the other containing machinery of every description, worked by a steam engine in a building adjoining; machinery for turning wood, cutting and finishing iron, and performing all the work required for the ships. The energy and resources displayed, the use that was found for every bit of old wood or iron, the ingenuity which turned every material to account, made the inspection doubly interesting. Here were three forges, built of stone work brought from Kertch, of fire bricks taken from various of our own steam ships, a pair of bellows from somewhere on the coast of the Sea of Azof, and the anvils from the ships in harbour, or else supplied from England. A part of the machinery was of French manufacture, and taken from Kertch.

Saw-pits are being dug, pipes are laid down, bringing a constant supply of water from the sea, and the little row of store huts are each provided with a couple of buckets hung outside, and a large cask, half sunk in the earth, and filled with water, close to the door; so that there need not be the delay of a moment in case of fire breaking out. From the dockyard we went on to examine the stables and horses. The stables are models of ingenuity and good workmanship.

In some cases the walls are built of stone, with a wooden roof, the building divided into stalls, and the floor pitched with small stones, as neatly as we are accustomed to see our own stables in England. Where damaged hay or straw cannot be procured for litter, the stones are thickly covered with sand, so that the horse cannot injure the foot when stamping, as he does all day at countless hordes of flies. The admiral's stud consists of six Arab and Turkish horses.

One flea-bitten grey was a gift from Omar Pasha; but his favourite horse, and the one Sir Edmund usually rides, is a dark chestnut, very small, but well bred, active, and clean limbed. I recognised in one of the stalls a dun-coloured pony, which formed one of Lord Raglan's stud some months ago. We were shown, too, a wonderful proof of the efficacy of a little kindness and care in the case of a mule, which came to Balaklava in the baggage train of the Sardinian army, and having been terribly knocked about, and very severely hurt on board ship, during a rough passage, was left by them for dead on the sea shore.

The boatswain of H. M. S. *Rodney* happened to pass where the wretched animal lay bleeding but still alive, and with the blessed instinct of humanity, he stopped to help the sufferer. He raised the dying head, and gave the parched throat some water, and by-and-bye he brought some food. In a day or two the mule was able to crawl, and, to make a long story short, when I saw him yesterday he was fat, and strong, and sleek; still covered with sores, which are in a fair way to heal, and following his friend, Mr. Collins, the boatswain, precisely like a dog. In and out into the huts, among the workmen, wherever his business on shore calls him, may be seen the boatswain and the attendant mule; and when he recovers from his scars, he will be one of the finest and handsomest mules that we have out here. Such instances as these of kind-heartedness and humanity on the one hand, and gratitude on the other, are doubly pleasing in the midst of a life where we must, necessarily I suppose, see so much that is distressing and painful of suffering and indifference.

Monday, August 13th.—We dined last night on board the *St. Jean D'Acre*; and amongst the guests was Lord Rokeby, who is staying on board the *Tribune*, to be near his *aide-de-camp*, who is still in a critical state on board the *Rodney*. Just before the party were thinking of dispersing, Captain Wellesley, also one of Lord Rokeby's *aides-de-camp*, came on board, and reported that the Russians were advancing on all sides, and that the whole of the allied army was turned out.

The night, however, passed off quietly, and the enemy did not appear, and at daylight the forces were turned in once more. The reason assigned for the postponement of the attack by the Russians is, that a man of the 21st Fusiliers deserted early in the evening, and is supposed to have given such information to the Russians as would make them aware of our being in readiness for them at all points. I went this morning for a short cruise in the *Danube*, which, as tender to the flag ship, runs from Kasatch Bay to the *Royal Albert* some four or five times daily; and during the run homewards was extremely interested in conversing with an English officer, Captain Montague, of the Engineers, who has just returned from Russia, where he has been a prisoner since March.

He appeared to speak very fairly of the Russians, mentioned gratefully the kindness he had received from Osten Sacken, and the hospitality which he had met with generally. Soon after he was taken, he travelled for more than a month in the wretched post *Talega*, going only eleven or twelve *versts* a day. He was detained for three days at Fort St. Nicholas, in Sebastopol, and one or two more in a house in the north side of the town. I was the more glad to have seen Captain Montague, as he had spent some time with Mr. Clowes and Mr. Chadwick, both taken prisoners in the disastrous Light Cavalry charge, the former belonging to our own regiment, the latter to our brigade. He was able to give us favourable news of them.

Thursday, August 16th.—A grand fête-day with the French army and navy. All the ships of the united fleets were decorated, and at noon a tremendous salute was fired. About three o'clock, three of our smallest mortar-boats left their anchorage, and took up a position before the harbour of Sebastopol, for the purpose of shelling the camp and barracks on the north side, and the town behind Fort Alexander on the south side. We went out in the *Danube*, and had an admirable view of the practice. The shells from the little mortar-vessels pitched with great precision, and must have caused no little consternation in the camp and barracks, as we saw many people running about in haste, and making for Fort Constantine. Presently a flag of truce was hoisted from the top of this fort. Our fire, however, continued, although it was principally directed on Fort Alexander. We remarked that, with a single exception, all the answering shots of the Russians fell short.

There was nothing but feasting and gaiety on board the French ships. Sir Edmund Lyons and Sir Houston Stewart both dined on board the *Montebello* with Admiral Bruat, and before sunset the French flag ship fired a second salute.

The medical inspector of the fleet pronounced sentence on me yesterday—namely, that I retrograde instead of improve as far as my health goes, and I am to go, if possible, for ten days to Therapia for further change of air.

Of sixty shots fired by the mortar-boats yesterday afternoon, twenty pitched into the Quarantine Fort, but those fired at Fort Alexander were at too long a range, and all fell short.

News has this moment come in as I write, of an engagement on the banks of the Tchernaya. The Russians came down in force (I give merely the first reports as they have this instant reached me), and the French and Sardinians gave them a tremendous repulse, took their floating bridges, and drove them back, with a loss on the side of the Allies of 500 men. Up to this time I cannot hear that the English cavalry were engaged.

Five o'clock.—Henry has just ridden over from Balaklava, and tells me that the cavalry turned out at daybreak. The Russian army amounted to about 50,000; and they attacked the exceedingly strong position of the French Zouaves and Sardinians in a most gallant manner. The French, by whom the attack was quite unexpected, were very weak, as to numbers, on this point; the position itself being so strong. The Sardinians, also, had to collect themselves after their outposts were driven in. The Russians crossed the river with determination and gallantry, and ascended the hill side of the French position.

By this time French reinforcements had come down, and the Zouaves, leaving their camp, charged downhill upon the enemy with their bayonets, repulsing them with fearful slaughter. They were also beaten back by the Sardinians on their left attack, materially assisted by our new heavy field battery (Captain Moubray's 32-pound howitzers), which ranged far beyond all others, and blew up nearly all the Russian ammunition wagons, dismounted their guns, and killed their artillery horses. The loss of the French and Sardinians was not heavy. It was a brilliant day for our Allies. The English cavalry was not under fire, except the

12th Lancers, who crossed the river, but were recalled immediately by Lieutenant-General Morris, who observed that "*ces diables d'Anglais* were never satisfied unless they were trying to get annihilated." The Russians were all gaunt and hungry men, who had evidently been driven to death by forced marches. The enemy fired on the French while they were charitably engaged in removing the wounded Russians.

Sunday, August 19th.—Went to church on board *The Royal Albert*, by invitation from Sir Edmund Lyons. We remained to dine; and as it came on to blow so hard that it would have been difficult for us to reach the *Rodney*, we stayed in our most hospitable quarters all night.

During the afternoon. Admiral Bruat came on board; and I had an opportunity of seeing, for the first time, the French naval commander-in-chief. He struck me as being shrewd, and I was going to write false, but perhaps my meaning may hardly be understood; his manner was certainly polished enough. The two admirals sat in conversation, side by side, and the contrast struck me with such force, that I was obliged to lie awake at night to try and analyse it.

Monday, August 20th.—The sea going down slightly, enabled us to leave for the *Rodney* in the *Danube* at ten o'clock, after we had listened to the band playing on board the *Royal Albert*, and gathered a more distinct acquaintance with the Russian works of defence than before. They are now busily employed in constructing a bridge across the harbour, so as to form a retreat from the Malakoff and Redan when we take triumphant possession of those two forts.

The sunlight shone full on the face of the town, showing us long lines of windowless houses riddled with shot; and yet, standing in the centre of the town, one or two houses still intact; one a fine house, with a light green roof (I fancied it was only their sacred buildings that are green-roofed), and another house, solid, handsome, and large.

Sir Richard Airey, who received an official notification of his promotion to the rank of lieutenant-general, is also on board the flagship, endeavouring to shake off an attack of fever which, like every disease in this country, however slight, leaves you weakened in a wonderful degree. There were two explosions in the Russian batteries this morning, but I fancy neither were of much importance.

Wednesday, August 22nd.—The *Gladiator* came up from Balaklava yesterday, where she had discharged the products of her trip to Corfu; she brought, in addition to eight mortars, 2200 shells and a couple of hundred artillerymen. I dined on board with Captain Hillyar, and there was a report that the French intended opening fire from their new work on the extreme left this afternoon, and that our little mortar boats were to go in, and throw mortars at the same time; but this did not take place. The mortar battery did not open, and although our pretty little boats got under weigh, they dropped anchor again almost as soon as they got outside.

There was a telegraph made from the flagship to headquarters about twelve o'clock, to the effect that "large bodies of troops were assembled outside the loopholed wall;" but they did nothing unusual this afternoon, although just before sunset a very heavy fire was opened all down the line of the right attack on the town. It was a lovely afternoon, and I walked along the shore towards the lighthouse of Khersonnese. Here, driven almost on to the beach, I found the remains of a French or Austrian brig, which had been cast ashore. She was mostly broken up, and so close in that I could easily climb about among her rotting timbers.

She had been laden with bullocks; their bones lay white and glistening all around; polished skulls, white as plaster of Paris casts, many with a bleached rope still wound about the horns, and several with the rusty shoe and large-headed nails adhering to the shrivelled hoof. I brought away a bone or two, more than usually polished, and a few parts of the fittings of the ship; and then, feeling that the sea was shaking the drift wood on which I stood, I carefully collected my relics, and scrambled to the shore.

Friday, 24th.—Went to stay on board the *St. Jean D'Acre,* anchored off Sebastopol, and remained on board some days. During my stay I had frequent opportunities of inspecting, through powerful glasses, the works, guns, and actual movements of the inhabitants. The bridge across the harbour, in front of the men-of-war moored at the entrance, which they commenced a week or two ago, is now complete. The traffic over it is perpetual both of men and horses.

For two days, the stream set principally from the south to the north, we fancied that the Russians were removing their goods, previous to evacuating the south side; and this appeared more probable, as they were busily employed in erecting fresh earthworks on the north side; but lately opinion has changed on the subject. It is universally believed that the Russians in the town are suffering cruelly from short rations and over-work. All deserters agree in the same sad story of sickness, privation, and distress. Meantime the town looks outwardly fair enough.

On Monday we heard that the Highland division has been sent down to the Tchernaya, to strengthen the position of the Sardinians, as another attack is expected. The English cavalry turns out every morning at four o'clock, and takes up a position in the plain, ready, in case of another attack from the hungry Russians. The reason of this daily turn out is obvious enough. There are only two outlets from Balaklava to the open plain, and a large force would necessarily be detained some time in filing through.

I could not but be struck on Tuesday evening, as I was watching the moon rise from the deck of the *St. Jean D'Acre,* by the wonderful and glorious difference between God's work and man's. It was a picture composed by two artists. It might have been fitly called "Peace and War." Shining over the central forts of the town was the full moon, looking with calm and steadfast face out of the serene sky, in whose "deep heaven of blue" star after star trembled into life and light; whilst down upon the placid waters gleamed the pale broad pathway reflected from her beams.

The distant hills wrapped in light haze were visible to the eye; but, immediately before us, no object save the grim corner of a fort could be discerned from the heavy, heavy weight of smoke that clung to and covered the city like a shroud. Here and there across it shot the lurid glare of the guns, darting across the palpable atmosphere like a flying ball of fire. Who cannot see in this a representation of what has often filled his own mind? The wrathful stir of passion raging within, until calmed and softened by the blessed influence of the Holy Spirit of God.

Last night and this morning two explosions occurred. The one at half-past one a.m. I am sorry to say was in the Mamelon, where a shell blew up the magazine. This did, of course, immense damage; not so much to the battery, as to the soldiers. There were, I hear, above 200 killed and wounded. The explosion about nine a.m. was in the Russian works, but was not nearly so extensive.

Lord Stratford de Redcliffe has been up here to invest the G.C.B.s and K.C.B.s. On his arrival and departure, he was saluted by the English and French ships. Being on board ship and away from the horses, I had no opportunity of going to witness the ceremony, which, I believe, was as imposing as uniforms, decorations, forms, and ceremonies, could make it.

I cannot refrain from mentioning a brilliant little work entitled *The Roving Englishman in Turkey*, and from thanking the author for the pleasure he has afforded me in its perusal. It was put into my hands a short time ago, and since then it has sparkled on my table like a gem.

September 5th.—For the last three mornings in succession we have been kept on the *qui vive*, turning out the whole cavalry at two a.m. and marching them down beneath the hill which hides the Traktir Bridge, as, from information received from spies and deserters, the Russians have been meditating a second effort for the repossession of the Balaklava Plains.

They have been augmented by a large reinforcement of Imperial Guards and other soldiers, it is said, to the amount of 90,000 men. The attack, for which we have now been waiting patiently for three days, was to have been made by the whole of this force; 50,000 were to endeavour to take the Traktir Bridge by storm, while the other 40,000 were to attack the French and Sardinians on the right and left.

Rumours relative to the non-appearance of this army are rife. Some say that in marching down they met the wounded from the Tchernaya going to Bachsi-serai, and were so horrified at their number and their ghastly wounds, that they refused to advance, and more than 100 of these wretched soldiers were shot forthwith. Now, it appears that the whole force are either sent into Sebastopol, or dispersed on the plain of the Belbec, where they can get water. Meanwhile, we have opened a very heavy cannonade upon the town. The traffic over the bridge is incessant, and the Russians appear to be carrying all their valuables, goods, furniture, and pianofortes over to the north side, as we suppose previous to evacuating the south side entirely.

Last night we dined with General Féray, and when we arrived we found him just returning from the front, where he had been inspecting the works of the *Mamelon Vert* and the *Ouvrages Blancs*. During dinner, he told me that a Tartar deserter had come into General Bosquet's division during the day, and had told them of the agonies of thirst suffered by the army which fought at the Tchernaya on their march. Some little distance before they reached the Belbec, they passed some wells. Order of march was at an end; the foremost threw themselves down headlong; the rest, struggling to get at the water, and impatient of those before them, drew their bayonets, and presently the wells were filled with upwards of 150 dead and dying bodies!

I remember our own sufferings while marching, for short distances, in the hot weather in Turkey, and especially the frantic horses at Jeni-bazar, so that I can, in some slight degree, .understand the torments of the Russians. As we rode home from General Féray's [5], our way was absolutely illumined by the light of a fire which seemed to set all heaven in a blaze. We could not see the fire itself for the hills which intervened; but, from the bril-

5. General Féray commands three regiments of Chasseurs D'Afriques.

liancy of its light, we fancied the whole of the south side must be in a blaze. Not that Sebastopol would ever burn; the houses are too detached, and built so much of stone, that they would never keep alight for any length of time.

The cannonade was densely heavy, and the light of the guns radiated off from the brilliant centre of the vast fire, and seemed like perpetual lightning.

The French are supposed to have opened their new battery, by which they are to reach the ships. I am now on the point of mounting, to ride up and ascertain for myself what the light of the fire meant.

Ten o'clock.—The blaze of last night was caused by the firing of a two-decker, one of the ships in the harbour. Captain Keppel, to whom I went for information, tells me he fancies it was set on fire by a French rocket. However that may be, she burned away famously; the outline of mast, spar, and rigging showing with terrible distinctness in the lurid light.

We reached Cathcart's Hill this afternoon in time to see a perfect explosion of guns from the French line of attack. Every gun and mortar appeared to fire at once; those that did not go off at the precise moment following with the rapidity of file firing. It was, indeed, "a noble salvo shot," and was loudly cheered by the English soldiers who were looking on. Presently we met the brigade of Guards marching down into the trenches. The whole brigade goes down now every third night.

We were fortunate enough to see General Markham just starting for a ride, as we passed his quarters. His reputation as the most rising man in the army, and likely to succeed to General Simpson's command, made me very anxious to see him. General Markham was formerly colonel of the 32nd, to which regiment Henry belonged. He is slight and wiry, with long grey beard, and eyes which, though ambushed behind a frightful pair of spectacles, I could tell were piercing and keen beyond most others in this vast camp. Having an engagement at the moment, he was prevented saying more than a few courteous words, and left us, with a promise to call upon us at his earliest leisure. The fire from the French lines still continues fast and heavy.

September 8th.—We rode up to the front again yesterday afternoon, although the north-east wind was blowing a hurricane; and for half the distance I trotted with my hat in my lap, and my left hand gathering up my habit to prevent its acting like a mainsail, and blowing me completely off my balance. We passed General Bosquet's division, and struck out the shortest track to Cathcart's Hill. A party of fusilier guards were marching slowly towards us, and close behind them followed a chestnut horse I knew but too well.

Poor Captain Buckley, who yesterday was so full of strength and life, is being borne to the resting-place of many brave hearts, and will sleep on Cathcart's Hill. I begin to grow superstitious. I fancy that every man to whom I speak just before any great danger, is sure to fall a victim to it. Last night, on his way to the trenches, I met Captain Buckley, and he stayed a few moments to talk to me.

Within two hours after I saw the last of him, spurring his pony round a corner of the ravine to overtake his men, he was lying on his face, shot through the heart! I cannot watch that sad procession. I cannot picture to myself the frame so full of life and vigour yesterday, now a mouldering heap of dust. I show him what respect I can, although a black habit, and handkerchief, and a strip of crape round my arm, is all. He said he would "live and die a soldier," and right well he kept his word.

But I must turn away from the melancholy funeral on my right, and look forward at the siege. There is a huge blaze in the centre of the harbour, and Colonel Norcott, of the Rifles, tells me it is a frigate set on fire by French shells. How bravely it burns! bright and clear as a wood fire in the vast home-grates at Christmas time. Presently General Markham rides up, and says, "Mrs. Duberly, we shall have a fight tomorrow. You must be up here on Cathcart's Hill by twelve o'clock."

And then we ride briskly home, for the evenings are chilly, and the horses' coats begin to stare. As we lay our horses into their long, striding gallop, we talk of the prospects of tomorrow, and the chances of our friends—how much their number is reduced! Of Major Daubeny; of the boy Deane, who only joined last week, and will make his first entry into the trenches tomorrow; of Mr. Glynn, who exchanged only a day or two ago from the 8th Hussars to the Rifle Brigade; of Colonel Handcock, whose wife is with him at the front; of Lord Adolphus Vane; of General Markham, and many others.

September 9th.—Last night I was overcome with the shock of poor Buckley's death, and felt so unhinged that I did not start for the front until eleven this morning. The cannonade was terrific, exceeding anything that had previously occurred during the siege. After some difficulty in "dodging" the sentries, which General Simpson, with his most unpopular and unnecessary policy, insists on placing everywhere, we reached the Fourth Division just as the Guards were marching down to their places in reserve.

The Highlanders were the first reserve, and then the Guards. Here, I am glad to say, we overtook Lord A. Vane, and he promised to come down to us the first moment that he could get away, after the fight was over. I remembered poor Captain Agar's like promise, and my heart grew still as I listened; but we were advancing on the batteries, so we turned our horses' heads across the ravine, and rode up to the front of Cathcart's Hill, where we found the cavalry at their usual ungracious work of special constables, to prevent amateurs from getting within shot. Now, in the first place, amateurs have no business within range; and in the next place, their heads are their own; and if they like to get them shot off, it is clearly nobody's business but theirs.

The cold of today has been intense. Two days ago I was riding in a linen habit; and today, with a flannel wrapper, a cloth habit body, and an extra jacket, I was chilled to my very bones. If hospitable Mr. Russell, the *Times* correspondent, had not kindly sent me down to his hut, and told me where I should find the key of the tap of the sherry cask, I think I must have collapsed with cold.

Meanwhile in the front nothing was to be heard or seen

but incessant firing and masses of smoke. The perpetual roll of musketry and the heavy voices of the guns continued without intermission, and the anxious faces of all were strained towards the Malakoff and Redan. By-and-bye wounded soldiers come up from the trenches, but their stories differ, and we can place in them no faith. "I was in the Redan when I was wounded," said the first, "and our fellows are in there now."

"We have been three times driven out of the Redan," said a second; so we found that we could depend on nothing that we heard, and must wait in faith and patience. We left at about half-past six o'clock, thoroughly tired, and chilled to our very hearts. Since then, within the last half hour, I have heard that Colonel Handcock is dead; and that poor Deane, the young boy, just entering into life and hope, lies in the hospital of his regiment, laid out ready for burial.

As he was standing on the parapet of the Redan, waving his sword and urging his men to follow him, a bullet struck him in the eye, and taking an upward direction, passed through the brain. His fearless courage, although for the first time under fire, has been several times remarked. I fear this is but too authentic, as our assistant-surgeon, who was working in the hospital of the 30th, assures me that he saw him brought in dead. The firing is just as continuous,—just as rapid,—just as heavy. I am told the Guards are not yet gone down. Oh! who can tell, save those who are on the spot, in whose ears the guns roar incessantly, what it is to see friends one hour in youth, and health, and strength, and the next hour to hear of them, not as ill, or dying, but as dead,- absolutely dead? Ah! these are things that make life terrible.

Colonel Norcott, of the Rifles, is a prisoner, and I hear un-wounded. He sprang first into the Redan with his usual courage and recklessness; and the two men who followed immediately behind him were instantly shot, and he was taken prisoner before he had time to turn round to look for fresh supports. He will soon be exchanged we hope.

Meantime who will buy and keep that pretty, prancing, chestnut pony he was riding last night when he took his way with his battalion to the trenches?

Wednesday, 12th.—Since writing the foregoing I have been three or four times to the front. On Monday we endeavoured to ride as far as the Redan and Malakoff, but were stopped by the cavalry, who were posted as sentries just this side of the twenty-one gun battery. On Sunday Henry rode up at eleven, a.m., and after making such inquiries after our friends as might tend to relieve our anxieties on their account, he went on to the Redan. He described it to me as a heap of ruins, with wonderfully constructed defences, and with bomb-proof niches and corners, where the Russian officers on duty in the battery lived, and where were found pictures, books, cards, and glass and china for dinner services.

Le Capitaine Müel called on me on Sunday, and told me the French loss was seventeen general officers killed and wounded, and about 12,000 men. This I have since heard reduced, I think correctly, to 10,000.

On Sunday evening as it grew dusk I ordered the pony "Charley," and rode up to the Turkish Heights. From thence I could see distinctly the south side in flames. I counted ten separate fires. It was a magnificent sight, and one which afforded me, in common I fancy with many more, greater satisfaction than pain. I could not think at such a moment of the destruction and desolation of war. I could only remember that the long-coveted prize was ours at last, and I felt no more compunction for town or for Russian than the hound whose lips are red with blood does for the fox which he has chased through a hard run. It was a lawful prize, purchased, God knows! dearly enough, and I felt glad that we had got it.

On Monday I rode to see Major Daubeny, 62nd Regiment, Colonel Windham, and General Markham. Whilst calling on Colonel Windham, I heard of poor Colonel Eman's mortal wound. Our loss in officers has been heavy enough, I believe 149. In the 62nd Regiment 180 men went into attack, and 105 were killed or wounded. There can be no doubt that the assault was unexpected, and the Malakoff taken by surprise. The Malakoff was the key to the whole fortress; the Malakoff once taken and held by the French, the Redan became untenable by the Russians. We assaulted it after a curiously ill-managed fashion, and we were driven back. About that there exists no doubt. Nor should we ever have forced the Redan, unless the plan of attack had been entirely reorganised.

Two hundred, a hundred and fifty, or three hundred men out of every regiment in the division formed the storming party. Men who had been fighting behind batteries and gabions for nearly a twelvemonth, could not be brought to march steadily under fire from which they could get no cover. As Colonel Windham said, in speaking of the assault, "The men, the moment they saw a gabion, ran to it as they would to their wives, and would not leave its shelter." Why not have taken all this into consideration, and ordered the newly-arrived regiments to lead the assault?—the 13th Light Infantry and the 56th.

By daybreak on Sunday morning, just as we were preparing to "go at" the Redan again, it was discovered to have been evacuated during the night. Malakoff gone—all was gone; and by night on Sunday all that remained in Sebastopol were burning houses, mines, and some wounded men, prisoners. The English until today have been denied admission to the town, except with a pass provided by Sir R. Airey.

The French, on the contrary, have been plundering and destroying everything they saw. The town was mined, and these mines, going off perpetually, made it very unsafe for amateurs. Nothing, however, deters the French. Five officers were blown up today; and a Zouave came out driving a pig, carrying a dead sheep, a cloak, and a samovar, and wearing a helmet, like those which were taken at Alma, and brought on board the *Danube*.

It is exceedingly difficult to gain admission into the Redan and the town. Until today orders were only procured through the quartermaster-general; but I see it is in general orders now, that any general officer can give a pass; and Colonel Windham, who commanded the storming party, and distinguished himself by his magnificent conduct, and his frantic efforts to rally and lead on the men, while standing himself inside the Redan, and on the parapet, is made governor of that quarter of the south side appropriated to the English. I need scarcely say, the English quarter is the worst, containing all the public buildings round the dock-yard, the custom-house, hospital, &c., but no dwelling-houses that are not reduced to the merest heap of ruins.

Thursday, September 13th.—A memorable day of my life, for on it I rode into the English batteries, into the Redan, the Malakoff, the Little Redan, and all over our quarter of Sebastopol. Such a day merits a detailed description.

Eight consecutive hours spent in sightseeing under a blazing sun is no light and ladylike *délassement* at any time, but when the absorbing interest, the horrible associations and excitement of the whole, is added to the account, I cannot wonder at my fatigue of last night, or my headache of today.

So many descriptions, pictorial and otherwise, have gone home of our own batteries, that I need not stop to describe them in their present half-dismantled state; so, clambering down (how wonderfully the Turkish ponies can climb!) the stony front of our advanced parallel, we canter across the open space, and ride at a gallop over the steep parapet of the salient angle of the Redan. "Look down," said Henry, "into the trench immediately beneath you; there, where it is partly filled up, our men are buried. I stood by Mr. Wright, on Sunday morning, when he read the funeral service over 700 at once."

What wonderful engineering! What ingenuity in the thick rope-work which is woven before the guns, leaving only a little hole through which the man laying the gun can take his aim, and which is thoroughly impervious to rifle shot! The Redan is a succession of little batteries, each containing two or three guns, with traverses behind each division; and hidden away under gabions, sand-bags, and earth, are little huts in which the officers and men used to live.

Walking down amongst these (for we were obliged to dismount) we found that tradesmen had lived in some of them. Henry picked up a pair of lady's lasts the precise size of my own foot. Coats, caps, bayonets lay about, with black bread and broken guns. The centre, the open space between the Redan and the second line of defence, was completely ploughed by our thirteen-inch shells, fragments of which, together with round shot, quite paved the ground. We collected a few relics, such as I could stow away in my habit and saddle-pockets, and then rode down into the town.

Actually in Sebastopol! No longer looking at it through a glass, or even going down to it, but riding amongst its ruins and through its streets. We had fancied the town was almost uninjured—so calm, and white, and fair did it look from a distance; but the ruined walls, the riddled roofs, the green cupola of the church, split and splintered to ribands, told a very different tale.

Here were wide streets leading past one or two large handsome detached houses built of stone; a little further on, standing in a handsome open space, are the barracks, with large windows, a fine stone façade of great length, several of the lower windows having carronades run out of them, pointing their grim muzzles towards our batteries. Whilst I am gazing at these, a sudden exclamation from Henry, and a violent shy from the pony, nearly start me from my saddle. It is two dead Russians lying, almost in a state of decomposition, at an angle of the building; while in the corner a man is sitting up, with his hands in his lap, and eyes open looking at us. We turn to see if he is only wounded, so lifelike are his attitude and face; no, he has been dead for days.

A little further on we came to the harbour, and by the many mast-heads we count the number of ships. Here, too, are fragments of the bridge which I had watched the Russians building, and across which I had seen them so often pass and repass. There is a kind of terrace, with a strong wooden railing, overlooking the sea, and underneath us is a level grass-plat, going down with handsome stone steps to the water's edge. Following the wooden railing, we overlooked what had evidently been a foundry, and a workshop for the dockyard; Russian jackets, tools and wheelbarrows, were lying about, and hunting among the ruins was a solitary dog.

But all this time we are trying to find our way to Brigadier General Windham's office near the custom house. To get there we must ride round to the head of the dry docks, as the bridges are either broken or unsafe. What is it that makes the air so pestilential at the head of the dry docks? Anything so putrid, so nauseating, so terrible, never assailed us before. There is nothing but three or four land transport carts, covered with tarpaulin, and waiting at the corner. For Heaven's sake, ride faster, for the stench is intolerable.

We go on towards the custom house, still followed by this atmosphere: there must be decaying cattle and horses behind the houses; and yet they do not smell like this! Admiral Sir Edmund Lyons and Admiral Bruat are riding by, so we stop in a tolerably sweet place to congratulate each other on meeting in Sebastopol. We then continue our road to the custom house. What is it? It cannot surely be—oh, horror!—a heap, a piled-up heap of human bodies in every stage of putrid decomposition, flung out into the street, and being carted away for burial.

As soon as we gained possession of the town, a hospital was discovered in the barracks, to which the attention of our men was first attracted by screams and cries. Entering, they found a large number of wounded and dying; but underneath a heap of dead men, who, as he lay on the floor, fell over him and died, was an English officer of the 90th Regiment, who being badly wounded, and taken prisoner, was put into this foul place, and left, as in the case of the hospital near the custom house, to perish at his leisure of hunger and pain.

He had had no food for three days, and the fever of his wound, together with the ghastly horrors round him, had driven this poor Englishman to raving madness; and so he was found, yelling and naked. I think the impression made upon me by the sight of that foul heap of green and black, glazed and shrivelled flesh I never shall be able to throw entirely away. To think that each individual portion of that corruption was once perhaps the life and world of some loving woman's heart—that human living hands had touched, and living lips had pressed with clinging and tenderest affection, forms which in a week could become, oh, so loathsome, so putrescent!

At the moment, however, and I think it a wise ordinance, no sight such as war produces strikes deeply on the mind. We turned quickly back from this terrible sight, and soon after left the town. Riding up towards the Little Redan, we saw where the slaughter of the Russians had principally been. The ground was covered with patches and half-dried pools of blood, caps soaked in blood and brains, broken bayonets, and shot and shell; four or five dead horses, shot as they brought up ammunition for the last defence of the Malakoff. Here we met Colonel Norcott, of the Rifles, who had been reported a prisoner, riding the same chestnut pony which has had honourable mention before.

Our congratulations on his escape, when we fancied him marching with the retreating Russians, were neither few nor insincere. The Malakoff lay just before us. I am told that it is, and it struck me as being, one of the most wonderful examples of engineering work possible. It is so constructed, that unless a shot fell precisely on the right spot, it could do no harm. What with gabions, sand-bags, traverses, counter-traverses, and various other means of defence, it seemed to me that a residence in the Malakoff was far safer and more desirable than a residence in the town.

Buried underground were officers' huts, men's huts, and a place used as a sort of mess room, with glass lamps, and packs of cards. We are not allowed to carry any outward and visible signs of plunder, but I filled my habit pockets and saddle pockets with various small items, as relics of these famous batteries and the famous town—lasts, buttons, and grape shot from the Redan; cards, a glass saltcellar, an English fuzee, and the screw of a gun from the Malakoff; a broken bayonet from the Little Redan; and rifle bullets from the workshop in the town.

Then, as it was growing late, we rode back to camp by the Woronzow Road, and down the French heights on to the Balaklava plain. On these heights are still retained a few guns in position, which are, and have been ever since the 25th of October, worked by Turkish artillerymen. They are famous for their artillery practice; and when the heights were reinforced after the Balaklava charge, they were placed at these guns, with a French regiment close behind them in case they should run. With these Turks I have made quite a pleasant little speaking acquaintance, as we are constantly scrambling either up or down their heights. "*Bono Jeanna*," "*Bono atla*," "*Bono, bono*," being generally the extent of our conversation, varied sometimes by "*Bono Cavallo*," according to the province from which "Johnny" comes.

September 17th.—I went again last Saturday, provided with a permit from the French Head-Quarters, to see that part of Sebastopol, and the French works which lie to the left—the French parallels running to almost within a stone's throw of the opposing battery, the "*Bastion du Mât*", the Garden Battery, and the fortifications of the town itself. The French have by far the most extensive quarter, but I begin to doubt whether they have the best. We have such fine ranges of buildings for barracks; while they have streets of ruined dwelling houses, with the addition, however, of the Court of Justice, a very handsome building, and two churches.

I was not much interested with what we saw in our expedition; indeed, we could not well be, for we were scarcely permitted to enter any of the houses without producing our pass, and making more fuss and chatter than it was worth. Many French and English soldiers had evidently been drinking "success to the war," for they lay about in all directions hopelessly drunk. One French *sous-officier* professed himself so astonished and delighted at seeing an English lady in Sebastopol, that he induced us to turn back half a street's length, in order to present me with some "loot."

I fancied, of course, it was something that I could carry in my saddle-pockets; fancy, then, our dismay, when he approached with the solid leg of a large worktable, with a handsome claw, about three feet high, and proportionably heavy. He tried to fasten it to my saddle, but "Bob" would none of it, and snorted and backed. We all, with many protestations of gratitude, declined the leg, and accepted a piece of Russian black bread instead,- more portable and more valuable.

We heard last night that the artillery are under orders to be inspected tomorrow morning; and we also hear a rumour that all the cavalry are to march up towards Simpheropol. It has been much commented on, that no movement was made by the army immediately on the evacuation of the town; and, on discussing the matter with one of the authorities, I was told that at one time we were under orders for Eupatoria, but next day they were countermanded. The cavalry have done nothing since the 25th of October.

We are now nearly 4000 strong, with an enormous amount of artillery. Our horses are in good condition, our men very fairly healthy; and if they do not keep us out too long, and the Commissariat can be urged into acquitting itself with anything like decency for once, we may have a very brilliant little campaign of about three weeks in comparative comfort.

At the end of three weeks the weather will become such that we must pack up, and be off to winter quarters. These are to be upon the Bosphorus. Oh! how we had hoped they would have been in sunny Egypt instead of on the shores of the draughty, miry Bosphorus, with its "Devil's Currents" both of sea and wind!

The Naval Brigade, now that there is no longer need for the Sailors' Battery, are all ordered on board their respective ships. I think there are very few but are sorry to leave their comparatively free life on shore for the imprisonment and strict discipline of a man-of-war. They would be (if we were to remain the winter) a very serious loss to us, as there were no workmen, carpenters, joiners, builders, half so handy or so willing to assist as those in the Naval Brigade. There certainly was no camp in which more kind consideration for others, more real active help, has been afforded to all than in that of the sailors; and their cheerfulness and willingness to labour encouraged and comforted all through the difficulties and sufferings of last winter.

I rode down to Balaklava a day or two since; and while the

memory of the miseries of that terrible time are fresh in my mind, I may as well say how much, in common with everything else, Balaklava has changed. It is no longer a heap of dirty lazar houses, infested with vermin, and reeking with every kind of filth. Its principal street is no longer crowded with ragged, starving soldiers, hauling along dying horses by the head, and making the houses echo back their curses and blows until one's very heart grew cold. Balaklava was then filthy, naked, and starved. Balaklava is now washed, and dressed, and fed. Balaklava was ugly and loathsome to see; Balaklava now is fresh, healthy, and even pretty. Neat rows of store huts have replaced the wretched houses of the Russians.

The navvies have their stable at the entrance, and in the midst of the town is an open space; walls are pulled down, the road is raised, and a strong railing runs along its outer side; rows of trees are planted, and down the centre street the railway runs, giving dignity and importance to the place. Admiral Boxer did wonders towards facilitating the arrangements for embarkation and disembarkation, by the construction of his admirable quays, as well as by reclaiming the shallow water and marshy ground at the head of the harbour, which was generally covered last winter with the half-imbedded carcases of bullocks, and was always emitting a malaria most foul and deleterious.

I think the thanks of the army, or a handsome national testimonial, ought to be presented to Mr. Russell, the eloquent and truthful correspondent of the *Times*, as being the mainspring of all this happy change. That it was effected through the agency of the Press there can be no doubt; and the principal informant of the Press was "Our own Correspondent," whose letters produced the leaders in the *Times*, the perusal of which, in many a sodden and snow-covered tent, cheered the hearts that were well nigh failing, and gave animation, hope, and courage to all.

More than once, when I have been fireless and shivering, the arrival of the then often delayed mail would bring me a copy of the *Times*; and its hot indignation, its hearty sympathy, and the mutterings of its wrathful anger have warmed me, and revived me, and made me feel for the moment almost like my former self. [6]

We are still in a state of uncertainty whether we move or not.

September 18th.—Nearly opposite the loopholed walls of Sebastopol, and about half a mile distant from it, lies a ravine with a church and graveyard, behind the French advanced works, and within easy range of the Russian shot. The tall spire of the church is covered, in common with all their sacred buildings that I have seen, with lead painted green; and it is only when you are close to the church that you discern the ravages of shot and shell. We turned our horses' heads down the precipitous side of the hill, and tied them to the churchyard gate. Trees of various growths filled the enclosure, and flowering shrubs, laburnums, and acacias, with clumps of lilac. Struck by the shots of their own people, the monuments and gravestones lay scattered and broken all around, while the sun, glancing through the thick green leaves, played upon broken pillar and shattered cross.

How I lingered under the shadow of the trees! How the repose of the place and scene diffused itself over my heart, which never felt so travel-stained with the dusty road of life as now! My life seemed to stand still, and be wrapped for the moment in a repose as deep as that of the slumberers around me, whom shot or shell could not waken, nor bugle-call arouse. At last I heard myself repeating those exquisite lines by some author whose name I cannot remember—

---

6. The evil done by the *Times* to the Crimean army predominated greatly over the good. The *Times* spread the news that Sebastopol had fallen, and when this turned out to be untrue, continued to predict its immediate capture, thus preventing private speculators from carrying supplies to the Crimea. The *Times* had previously softened the horrors and blunders of Devno and Varna, and it again for weeks concealed the sufferings and wants of the army before Sebastopol, and suppressed the accounts given by Mr. Russell of the mismanagement and inefficiency which prevailed in almost all departments. It was by means of private letters, handed from man to man and read with the greatest eagerness, that the true state of the case became known; and it was only when starvation and cold had done their work, and concealment was no longer possible, that the *Times* broke silence, and endeavoured to gain credit as the mouthpiece of public indignation.—Ed.

Give me the soft green turf, the fresh wild flowers,
A quiet grave in some lone churchyard's shade,
With the free winds to breathe a requiem, where,
Imploring rest, the restless heart is laid.

"Why Mrs. Duberly, you are a living representation of Hervey's *Meditations amongst the Tombs!* For heaven's sake come away from the churchyard, or you will not be amusing any more all day." So I mounted, and we speedily got into the hard clattering road again. Returning home from this long ride, we were sensible of a sudden and keen change in the atmosphere of this always variable climate. The wind veered to the north, a cold deep purple haze covered the distant hills, clouds from the sea came up full of promise, not of a good hard soaking rain, but of that penetrating cold mist than which nothing is so chilling and depressing. We lost no time in hurrying through the gathering darkness, back to the camp; and, having arrived there, lighted our stove for the first time this autumn. How comfortable and pleasant the hut looked in the warm firelight!

Thanks to the kindness of many contributors, I have been supplied with sufficient copies of the *Illustrated London News* to paper the walls entirely. This has afforded employment to my ingenuity. But the walls when covered looked too black and white for my fastidious ideas; they wanted warmth, colour, and effect. I delight in colours. They give me almost as much pleasure as music. I like gorgeous music and gorgeous colour. I would have all my surroundings formed for the gratification of this taste if I could.

I have therefore tried to colour those pictures which appeared most to require it, and the effect on the walls of our hut is now, I flatter myself, good; at any rate they look home-like and *soigné*, which is a great point. We both confess to an incipient affection for this little wooden room, where we have lived so many months; and we shall be quite sorry to leave it, never to see it any more, when we go down to the Bosphorus for our winter quarters in November.

The facility of attaching oneself is a great misfortune. If it adds a little to the enjoyment of life at times, it increases the pain of it, I think, in a double proportion. My anxieties, for instance, when my dear friend and companion the chestnut horse embarks for the Bosphorus, will be positively painful to myself, and very probably a nuisance to my husband.

September 23rd.—The evil done by the *Times* to the Crimean army predominated greatly over the good. The *Times* spread the news that Sebastopol had fallen, and when this turned out to be untrue, continued to predict its immediate capture, thus preventing private speculators from carrying supplies to the Crimea. The *Times* had previously softened the horrors and blunders of Devno and Varna, and it again for weeks concealed the sufferings and wants of the army before Sebastopol, and suppressed the accounts given by Mr. Russell of the mismanagement and inefficiency which prevailed in almost all departments.

It was by means of private letters, handed from man to man and read with the greatest eagerness, that the true state of the case became known; and it was only when starvation and cold had done their work, and concealment was no longer possible, that the *Times* broke silence, and endeavoured to gain credit as the mouthpiece of public indignation.—Ed.

After some days of cold and wet, mud and discomfort, the sun blazed out again in all his strength. Nature, washed and refreshed, looked red, green, and golden, in the warm autumn tints. We came out like the lizards; and although there were still heavy thunderclouds about, we disregarded them, and at three o'clock on the 20th started to join a party of twelve who were to meet at Kamiesh, and dine at the "Luxembourg." We were unpunctual, and started late; but made up for it on the road, or rather along the track of the ravine from Karani to Kamiesh. It was well we lost no time, as a thunder-shower came pouring down just as we reached the shelter of the stables.

The dinner really deserves a place amongst the annals of the war, and is worthy of description by an abler pen than mine. But I most enjoyed the exciting ride home by moonlight, galloping along the narrow track, by furze and bush, past carcasses of

French bullocks left unburied, and lying ghastly in the moon-light, a terror to all ponies, and a horror to our own noses. Every now and then a clink underneath an iron shoe tells of fragments of a broken bottle, but it is too dark to see; and a Turkish pony never stumbles or puts his foot down in a wrong place by any accident: and so on we go, our ponies leaning on the bit, till they reach the watering troughs of Karani, where they plunge their heads in to their eyes, and then walk steadily along the slippery slope of the hill side down into the hollow where the cavalry is encamped.

The certainty that we are to leave the Crimea for winter quarters makes us anxious to revisit every part of its known world once more before we go; and yesterday we rode to the Sardinian observatory, a building erected on the summit of their highest hill, and from which a wonderful view is obtained of all the surrounding English, French, and Russian camps. We left this observatory behind us, passing to the right of it, and soon after came upon the tents which form the French depôt for General D'Allonville's cavalry at Baidar. Beyond these again, on the extreme outpost, were Turkish cavalry, and Turkish guns in position, overlooking a deep and precipitous hollow closed in with rocks.

This was the neutral ground, across which Russian and Turks could glare at each other to their hearts' content. A dignified wave of the hand from the Turkish sentry warned us that we could not pass; so we rounded the base of the hill, and, by a judicious turn into a vineyard, came up with the "*avante poste*," also Turkish, and were able to look down the dizzy height into the deep hollow.

On every side the rocks rose perpendicular, stern, and bare, while far down beneath our feet lay the valley, clothed with trees and shrubs, appearing such a mass of verdure that the Tchernaya, which ran swiftly through it, foaming like a mountain torrent, looked but a silver thread wound in and out amongst the over-hanging trees. A mill and a lane, scarcely perceptible through the trees, but running—the lane I mean, not the mill—close alongside the river, were all that occupied this profound valley. The only music to which that mill-wheel ever could have turned,- the only song the miller ever could have sung,—must have been the "*De profundis clamavi.*"

The Turkish sentry close to us suddenly began to jabber away with a face of unmistakable delight. He had evidently discovered something, for his small, keen eyes were twinkling with excitement. The Turkish officer of the picket soon joined him, and, after some little conversation, turned to us, and said, pointing with his finger to the side of the opposite rock, "*Russes.*" We could not find them, even with our glasses, though we saw Cossack horsemen further on.

The "*Russes*" whom he saw were probably tending a large herd of cattle, which was grazing on the opposite hill-top, not 1000 yards from us. He took the glasses, and appeared much pleased with them. He then pointed out the Turkish cavalry picket; and having remarked on the number of fires which blazed last night on all the Russian hills, we exchanged bows, and rode away; for the sun was set, and the moon looking at us over the shoulder of the hill. Nor could we stay to listen to the Sardinian band, which was playing on the plateau near Kamara, but had to make the best of our road to reach the camp.

Thunder-showers have not failed us these last three days. Yesterday morning the Highlanders at Kamara were deluged, and the watering places at Kadekoi were fetlock deep in mud—a faint foreshadowing of what the roads would have been after two or three months' rain, had not the siege been stopped, and all the army turned into road-makers. Beautiful roads are now being constructed: one runs by the side of the railroad from Kadekoi, joining that made by the French last year, and lately put in thorough repair by the Army Works' Corps; another runs from the Woronzow Road to the French position on the heights; while one railway is to be constructed from Balaklava to Kamara to bring provisions for the Sardinian army, and another to Kamiesh to transport food and forage for the French.

The little stream which runs from Kadekoi into the sea at

Balaklava, instead of being in a shallow bed, and deluging the plain after every two hours' rain, flows now between two high banks, so that it cannot easily overflow. It is really a pity—except, of course, on account of the trenches—that the siege is over; for if we remained here another year or two, we should be as comfortably established as if we were at home.

September 25th.—Yesterday, to everybody's infinite surprise and pleasure, Mr. Clowes, who was wounded and taken prisoner at Balaklava, walked up into camp in a shooting coat and wide-awake, looking precisely as if he had never been absent, and answering everyone's greetings with much the same sort of dignified composure that a very big dog exhibits in noticing a little one.

I had taken an opportunity afforded by a flag of truce, to send him in a letter about a month ago; but he was then travelling down to Odessa, and did not receive it. He gives a most painful account of his adventures on the 25th of October, and afterwards in his march up the country. He was wounded in the back by a grape shot, which took him across both shoulders; but he rode on until his horse was shot, when he, of course, fell to the ground.

Seeing our brigade returning from the charge, he tried to run after them, but soon fell down from loss of blood. His first thought was to lie quiet, and pretend to be dead, so that he might have a chance of escaping after dark; but he very soon saw parties of Cossacks coming down, who ran their lances into everyone of the English lying on the ground.

Perceiving that the really dead were stabbed as well as those who pretended to be so, he rose, as well as his wound would allow, and throwing down his sword, gave himself up to a Russian officer of lancers. He took him and Mr. Chadwick, of the 17th Lancers, before the general, who asked them several questions, all of which they declined to answer.

They were then sent to Simpheropol, and soon after they began their march to Perekop. They marched on foot in company with prisoners and convicts, and at night were locked up with them. They remonstrated, but were told that there were no horses or means of conveyance to be had, and that there was no other way of transporting them. Their sufferings during this severe march were very great; aggravated, of course, by the utter want of consideration shown them. The last part of the time during which Mr. Clowes was a prisoner appears to have passed pleasantly enough. He went into society, and travelled post. I think his case is a hard one, as he cannot get a month's leave to return to England, if only to provide himself with clothes. He has no uniforms, no kit, and has been obliged to buy back his own horse.

Yesterday we rode up the heights till we overlooked Vernutka, and then returned by the good and even road made by Sir Colin Campbell along the summit of the heights, through his own camp down to Balaklava. After all, Englishmen are not so helpless, so hopeless, and so foolish, as they tried hard last year to make themselves out to be. I think they rested so entirely on the prestige that attached itself to the name of a British soldier, that they thought the very stars would come out of their courses to sustain the lustre of their name. Alas! their name was very literally dragged through the mud, during the miry winter months.

Upon the strength of the evacuation of the south side of Sebastopol, the fleet made a demonstration in their turn. They all got up their steam and their anchors, and sailed away, some to Balaklava, some towards Eupatoria. One of the first-rates crowded her forecastle with marines, dressed in their uniforms, and made as if for Eupatoria. This was merely a ruse, to persuade the Russians that she was transporting regular troops.

The Tchernaya outposts are still vigorously watched. The French have it that 125,000 men are encamped on the plateau and about the Belbec, with the intention of making a rush upon our position should we weaken it by sending any considerable force to harass the retreating garrison. The Russians in that case aim at burning Balaklava and Kamiesh; but their murderous designs do not prevent our sleeping just as soundly in the neighbourhood of Balaklava, or enjoying the triumphs of art in the shape of the "Luxembourg" dinners at Kamiesh.

The Indian summer is come to us, and we are again almost complaining of heat at midday; whilst the clear sky and brilliant moonlight show us how enjoyable autumn would be in this climate, if we had all the advantages of the fertile soil, and could live in peace and plenty. The Russians, however, appear determined that we shall not have much peace. They have begun to throw shot and shell into the town from the earthworks on the north. One of these round shot came through the roof of Brigadier General Windham's house, and fortunately struck without doing any injury to the inmates.

Could not the fleet have so annoyed the Russians with their mortar boats as to prevent the construction of these works?—and if so, why did they not do so?

A French woman, riding in the French quarter of the town yesterday, is reported to have had her horse struck by a shell. For the truth of this I cannot vouch; but it is not improbable, as on the day I was last in the town, the firing was very heavy, and the riding consequently dangerous. It has also been said by General Morris that none of the French cavalry will move into winter quarters, as the object of the large Russian force on the plateau, and by the Belbec, is to make a rush upon Balaklava, as soon as they find the army sufficiently weakened to admit of their doing so with a chance of success.

We called today upon General Bosquet, who was very severely wounded at the assault on the Malakoff, and to our surprise and pleasure, he was sufficiently recovered to be able to admit us. We were shown into his room, which forms one of the compartments of a large wooden hut, and found him reclining in an armchair, having been able to sit up only within the last two days. He was struck by a piece of a 13-inch shell under the right arm and on the right side; it had completely smashed all the muscles and sinews, and his arm is as yet powerless above the elbow-joint. He showed us the piece of shell by which he was struck; it could not weigh less than four pounds. It is astonishing how he escaped with life, from a wound inflicted by so terrible an implement of war.

He appeared cheerful enough, and glad to "*causer un peu;*" said he was ordered away for change of air, but did not wish to leave his post here, and fully coincided in my quotation, pointing to his wounded side, "*On ne marche pas à la gloire par le bonheur.*" In his room was a *fauteuil* taken from Sebastopol, and which he had very appropriately covered with the green turbans worn by the Zouaves of his division.

September 27th.—News reached us today of two "*affaires de Cavalerie:*" one with General D'Allonville's division, at Eupatoria; the other with the 10th Hussars, at Kertch These reports require, of course, official confirmation; but, as the engagement at Eupatoria appears to receive credence from one or two French generals whom I have seen today, it must be tolerably authentic.

We rode this afternoon to the Sardinian observatory, and, after admiring, as all must do, the neatness of fortification as well as its strength, we ascended to the telescope, which in placed at the summit of a high *tour d'observation.* By its aid we could discern huts in the course of erection, and the plateau by the Spur Battery, and could even see the Russians sending their horses down to water—one man riding and leading a horse.

The Russian huts are wooden and like ours; while the Sardinians are digging out and covering with earth huts, that will not only be waterproof, but absolutely warm, from the solidity and closeness with which they are built. There never was such a pretty little army sent into the field as that of the Sardinians. Had they not established their reputation by repulsing the Russians on the 16th of August, they would be still considered in the light of the prettiest "toy army" that ever was sent to fight, each department is so pretty and so perfect—their artillery, their cavalry, their guards, and, above all, their band.

Today is my birthday, and in consideration of it, I was allowed to choose my own horse to ride, and my own country to ride over. I chose the celebrated "*Café au lait,*" that prince of pretty Indian horses, and rode him to the observatory, and back by the

Sardinian band. Here we met several officers of the Highland Brigade, and heard that General Markham, on whom we had all built such magnificent hopes of British achievement under British *generalship*, was going on board ship ill; I am sorry to say, very ill, and it is said he must return to England. Coming out with all the prestige which surrounded his name, I think this sudden sinking into ill-health, and the abandonment of the army, will have its bad effect.

We want good generals; we want men who are in a position to lead, not brigades, for we have good brigadiers enough, but divisions, or even the whole army; we want men with youth, energy, and courage to fight against and pull through any adverse fortune that may assail them. Our best general, our most unflinching leader, has been the Press. To the columns of the *Times* the army owes a "National Debt;" and so long as every incident of this war is laid before the public at home, so long as every man is familiarised, as it were, with the life of the soldier, so long will this war be a popular war, and so long will the sympathies of all England be enlisted on our side.

We suppose that the campaign for this year is over. The cavalry, we understand, are to go into winter quarters on the Bosphorus. It is now becoming late in autumn, and the nights, and even days, are chilly enough. No orders have been issued, nothing official is known. Should it be at last decided that we really embark for the Bosphorus, I trust we may find ourselves transferred to proper accommodation for man and horse; but, if not moved before many days, to say nothing of weeks, are over, we shall be much worse off on the Bosphorus than we should have been, had we been allowed to remain on our old ground and permitted to prepare ourselves, from our own resources, for a second winter in the Crimea.

Campaigning Experiences
in Rajpootana and
Central India

Contents

Tis I who here attempt unusual strains,
Of hosts unsung and unfrequent plains,
Where India reddens to the early dawn.

BEATTIE.

In brief, a braver choice of dauntless spirits
Than now the English bottoms have waft o'er,
Did never float upon the swelling tide,
To do offence or scath to heathendom.

SHAKESPEARE

DEDICATION

As one who, walking in the twilight gloom
Hears round about him voices as it darkens
And seeing not the forms from which they come,
Pauses from time to time, and turns and hearkens;

So, waiting here in twilight, oh! my friends,
I hear your voices, softened by the distance,
And pause, and turn to listen as each sends
His words of friendship, kindness, and assistance

Perhaps on earth I never shall behold
With eye of sense your outward form and semblance:
Therefore to me ye never will grow old,
But live forever young in my remembrance.

Never grow old, nor change, nor pass away!
Your gentle voices will flow on forever,
When life grows bare and leafless with decay,
As through a leafless landscape flows a river.

Therefore I hope, as no unwelcome guest,
At your warm firesides, when the lamps are lighted,
To have my place reserved among the rest,
Nor stand as one unsought, or uninvited.

Longfellow.

Preface

As little can be gathered from the letters published in the newspapers of the daily adventures and occupations of soldiers engaged in an active campaign in India, I venture to put before the public a faithful record of the services and sufferings of one portion of the army occupied in the suppression of the mutiny; and I trust that I shall be pardoned if occasionally I am tempted to touch upon points which may seem beyond a woman s province.

That which struck me most in India was the great distance which still seems to separate that country from England, and the necessity for drawing them closer together. We frequently met with persons high in rank, both civil and military, who said, "I have not been home for twenty years: it is now nearly thirty years I was in England." To these men, English thoughts and English ways are a sealed book; they have remained in India until they have almost ceased to be Englishmen; and should they eventually go "home, they will find themselves as it were in a foreign land, without friends, and without an object to live for.

Surely, if some arrangement were made by which our country-men in India could escape for a tune to their native air, without losing by the indulgence, the Government would benefit by the additional energy they would throw into their work after being invigorated by the life-giving breezes of Scotch Highlands and English Downs. Brigadier General Jacob, in his pamphlet on *The Native Army of India, its Organization and Discipline*, suggests a means by which the number of sick furloughs might be materially reduced, if not done away with.

"Let us, he says, "have recourse to a principle as old as the history of man the institution of the Sabbath."

My proposal is to give every officer every seventh year to himself, if he wishes to avail himself of the indulgence; to allow him, during that period, to go wherever it might please him to go, whether in India, or any other part of the world. To allow him, during that year, to receive his full Indian pay and allowances, to retain his staff appointment, if he held one; but, during his absence, not to receive the start salary, winch would go to the officer who might officiate until his return.

If an officer chose to allow his Sabbath to pass by and to wait until he had served twelve years, he should be allowed two years' rest on furlough; after eighteen years' uninterrupted work, three years should be allowed, and so on.

The amount of vigour infused into India by this means would be incredible. The continual return to England, and reflux into India of the tide of Europeans, would be to the body moral and politic exactly what the circulation of the blood would be to the animal body. England would be our lungs, the old blood would be there aerated, and new life, health, and strength thereby sent flowing vigorously to every corner of our Empire. Energy and health would take the place of languor and disease."

How many prematurely old men with cadaverous faces, sunken eyes, and hollow cheeks have we seen to whom the sabbatical year would have been a boon indeed!

Before any real good can be effected in India, that country must be brought nearer to England. The officers must have more frequent furloughs on advantageous terms. Able men from England must be induced to travel through the country and to accept some of the higher appointments, by reduced terms of service. The Company's rule has done many good things, although not as many as it might have done; nor was their system free from grave faults: but as for civilising, and educating, and converting the natives of India, we must first set an example of consistent Christianity ourselves, We must show them that Englishmen, being Christians, cannot he, deceive, bully, or oppress.

And when we throw our Christianity, and consequent superiority, in their teeth on every occasion, we must recollect that we are dealing with a people whose religious faith actuates them every hour of the day.

India presents a magnificent field for work, with a prospect of vast and noble results; and it is impossible not to feel the deepest interest in everything connected with it; but if we desire to maintain our supremacy, it will not be enough to vindicate our mastership by force of arms: we must also prove our moral superiority, and make that superiority an evident and incontrovertible fact.

CHAPTER 1

Arrival at Bombay

Look not mournfully into the past: it cometh not again.
Wisely improve the present; it is thine. Go forth to meet
the shadowy future, without fear, and with a manly heart
Longfellow.

The mighty wind arises, roaring seaward,
And I go.

Tennyson

On the 11th May, 1856, the 8th K. R. I. Hussars disembarked at Portsmouth, to be inspected by Queen, on their return from the Crimea, and on the 8th October, 1857, the magnificent steam-ship *Great Britain*, John Gray, captain, left Cork Harbour for Bombay, having on board the 8th Hussars, 17th, Lancers, and fifty men and several officers of the 56th regiment The wind, which had blown a hurricane on the 7th, was still raging in our teeth as we steamed out of Queenstown, and the heavy, confused sea made the ship labour hard to keep her way, and sent us all to our cabins.

The violent rolling continued until we had passed the current running through the Gut of Gibraltar. But as we followed our southern course the sea became tranquil, and the manifold beauties of tropical days and nights gradually unfolded themselves—days all gold and nights all silver. Our ship spread her white wings and sailed slowly and gracefully over the foam-flecked, sparkling waves.

Each cavalry regiment had brought its band, refreshed with new instruments since their return from the Crimea; and from half-past two until four o'clock their music completed the luxury of the day. Life on board ship becomes so listless and so objectless, that those who have been accustomed to exercise and activity usually suffer both in health and temper. Fortunately for us there was no lack of books, for the East India Company, with praiseworthy liberality, had sent on board five hundred volumes for the use of the troops, and the officers of each regiment had previously provided themselves with a goodly store.

When the *Great Britain* had been ten days at sea we came in sight of the Islands of the Gape de Verde, where we stopped for two days and a half to take in coals. Noah from the windows of the ark did not look forward to being on land again with greater eagerness than we; and like Noah we stood upon a rock. St. Vincent is of volcanic formation; no vegetation clothes it, no flowers bloom on it. Save where the mists fold the rugged hills in gauzy drapery they stand scorched and bare, as though blasted by a curse. The island is a large coal depôt for steamships, and the few inhabitants were all at work upon the wharf.

The English consul, sole European and judging from his appearance he is contented with the station in which Providence has placed him. An American sloop-of-war was lying in the centre of the picturesque harbour, and a Sardinian merchant steamer bound for Genoa came in from Rio Janeiro; she had on board one of the Princes Buonaparte, mortally sick of consumption, who sent a message to the *Great Britain* requesting medical aid. A deputation of doctors, of whom we had eight, waited on him, and enforced his prayers to be put ashore. The Sardinian skipper, doubtless with an eye to his effects, resisted his removal to the utmost of his power, but nevertheless the poor sufferer was committed to the goodness of the English consul. The relief, however, was too late; for next morning, as we left the harbour, the consular flag was floating half-mast high.

For the next fortnight one bright day wore away as its predecessor had done, with sunshine, monotony, and music, when suddenly as we were sitting dreaming on the after part of the deck, and the men forward were amusing themselves with games and songs, the cry of "A man overboard!" was taken up from mouth to mouth, till, in an instant, it surged from end to end of the ship. Rushing to the side, we saw him flash by underneath the stern, and drift away almost before thought could suggest a life buoy.

Colonel Morris sprang to one, cut it loose, and flung it over: but could the poor struggling wretch see it? or seeing, could he reach it? The captain now strode up the deck, and with him came hope. His enormous voice soared above the surging noise. "Cram down the helm!"

"Lower away the gig!" and down the boat went from her davits, like a live thing, and manned by five hands soon reached the drowning man. Soon in reality, but it appeared long to us. The poor man was found floating on the life buoy, and was hauled alive, but insensible, into the boat, and brought on board in safety. He was a soldier of the 14th Light Dragoons going out to join his regiment, and having climbed into the rigging to overlook the amusements on deck, he had missed his footing, and so fell overboard.

Our captain had no intention of stopping at the Cape of Good Hope, but wished, by standing away towards the American coast, to fall in with the trade winds and so to pass some three or four hundred miles south of the Cape. We did, in fact, stand over until we neared the island of Trinidad, but the winds would do nothing but coquette. One day they blew shyly—the next day not at all—then they blew all round our sails, filling them one moment and backing them the nest: so that the heavy consumption of coal rendered it imperative to take in a fresh supply, and the ship s head was turned, with much grumbling on the part of her officers, and. great joy on that of the troops, towards Table Bay, where we cast anchor on the 17th November, thirty-eight days from England.

We had heard so much of the heavy seas that run into this anchorage, and of the difficulty of getting to and from the shore, that our anticipations were a good deal damped when on the evening before our arrival the wind blew stiffly from the north-west.

But the next morning neither wind nor swell ruined. the calm surface of the sea, and every one of the officers, except the few detained on duty, went ashore. Cape Town was the first English colony I had ever seen, and I was agreeably surprised at the half-foreign, half-English aspect of the place. There were Dutch-built houses surrounded by English railings, and pretty gardens with pomegranate hedgerows. The streets looked painfully new and unfinished, but the trees planted before the houses gave a pleasant aspect to the town.

There were hotels kept on English principles by Dutch landlords, Hansom cabs driven by Caffres, with their heads tied up in pocket-handkerchiefs, or dressed in wide-awakes with plumes of ostrich feathers—while coming in from the country were the teams of mules, and the famous spans of bullocks, often twenty in a span driven with the stock-whip, which—long and lithe as a salmon-rod—rarely touches its victim without leaving a crimson trace—Caffre women with receding foreheads and projecting mouths English settlers riding into town like gentlemen-farmers on a market day, or driving in *shegrums* with a pair of horses harnessed *curricle* fashion. As we wished to see something of the country, riding and driving parties were quickly organized.

We selected a nice-looking *barouche*, with four fresh, well-matched little Cape horses, and were soon flying through clouds of dust along a broad and sandy road, with an English turnpike (toll one shilling), and so away into the country, our pretty leaders playing and biting at each other as they sprang along. We shot past hedgerows of cactus, some bearing a pink and others a yellow flower past pomegranates with their scarlet bells past stilt and stately aloes, and little wax-like heather—past English houses buried in deep foliage—past little fair-haired, blue-eyed children, playing with little natives black as coals—past a poor, blind, black beggar, sitting with uncovered head like blind Bartimeus by the wayside—and at last going up one sharp hill at a gallop and down another at a trot, we came to the level plain and. the smooth, lawns on which stand. Mr. Cloëte's house and the vineyard of Constantia,

We inspected the large vats ranged round rooms on the ground floor, tasted and bought some wine, and wandered into the garden to gather the magnificent oranges from the overloaded trees. We afterwards proceeded to "Deep River," where we found a large and comfortable country hotel, and saw a famous old Cape horse, formerly the wender of his time, and even now a beautiful animal, and also one or two foxhounds, part of the pack which the Irish stable-keeper told us was farmed out during the summer months.

It was difficult, on the 17th November, to take in the idea of hounds being farmed out for the summer, but at the Cape, Christmas Day is often the hottest of the year. I filled my hands with oleanders, lilies, pomegranates, arums, and roses, and twined a wreath of passion-flowers amongst the feathers of my hat We then resumed our places in the carriage, and as it was verging towards evening we returned to Cape Town, not forgetting "Bartimeus" as we passed. Our driver did not bait his horses the whole day, nor even wash out their mouths. I suggested it to him, but he said it was not the custom; and however long the journey, the horse was never refreshed until it was over.

At the *table d'hôte* at Parke's Hotel, where we dined, we met some officers of the 98th, bound to Kurrachee, landed from on board the steamship *Ireland*, which had been fifty-four days out. We spent two whole days on shore, and the second we devoted to riding round the Table Mountain, and enjoying, as much as the intolerable dust would permit, the lovely and extensive view of sea and land.

In the harbour was every imaginable; species of craft, from the *Himalaya* to the light fishing barque of Cape Town. The *Great Britain* and *Himalaya* had never been side by side before, and owing to the tremendous spars and heavy rigging of the *Great Britain*, she, although in reality some few feet shorter, appeared the larger of the two.

Oh how yon argosies, with portly sail,
Like signiors and rich burghers of the flood—
Or, as it were, the pageants of the sea,
Did overpeer the petty traffickers
That curtsied to them reverence,
As they flew by them with their woven wings.

The inland view, when we could clear out our eyes to see it, was extensive and fine, and the flowers most fragrant and refreshing; but the strong wind and storms of dust made us glad to hasten to our inn, where I found, on consulting my glass, that my hair and face were of a uniform brick red.

We afterwards went to the stables of Mr. Kaien Meyer, from which our horses of this and the previous day had. been furnished. He showed us a fine three-year old bright bay horse, over fifteen hands, and very powerful. We were half inclined to purchase, but considering the risk of transport to Bombay and the long price asked, we thought it, more prudent to decline—a decision we had afterwards no cause to regret.

The next morning we were awakened by the rain beating heavily against our windows. As the *Great Britain*, was to go out of Table Bay at twelve o'clock, it was important to lose no time in engaging a large and sea-worthy boat, for me waves often rise to such an extent as to render it impossible to leave the shore. Many a captain of a vessel has stood on the pier and seen his ship standing out to sea, to avoid being driven on the rocks, while he has offered 100*l*. or even 200*l*. to the boatmen to put him on board; and offered it in vain.

The wind and the sea were both much. rougher than was pleasant; but we fortunately fell in with some of our friends who had engaged a large sailing-boat, and we secured two places in her. We sprang into the boat, from the pier-head, as she rose on the waves, and after some little confusion, got under weigh. We went on very well for those who like boating in a storm, which I confess I do not, until we neared the ship, when the danger of keeping the boat alongside the gangway ladder, and the difficulty of springing from the gunwale of the boat to the ladder, called into requisition all ones self-control. However, at last all were safely re-embarked, though not without some very narrow escapes; and we then hove anchor, and put out into a rough and disagreeable sea.

The *Himalaya* which had been sent to the Cape from Bombay for a cargo of horses for the use of the troops, brought the tidings of the fall of Delhi. We had been so long unable to obtain Indian news, that we felt inclined to overrate the value of what now reached us. We fancied that with the taking of Delhi the chief part of the mutiny was crushed, and that the rebels would never attempt resistance any more. To the seekers for military distinction, the news was unwelcome, as they feared the work would be over before they arrived.

One officer, especially, to whom the smoke of the cannon was as the breath of life, would chafe at the tardy motion of the ship that held him back from the tented field; little knowing that she was bearing him, the strong, the gentle, the bravest of the brave, true Christian, true soldier, and true friend, not into the pomp and circumstance of war, not to contested fields, and the thunder of the guns, but to long and weary sickness—to a wasting of energy, and strength, and hope, and to his death and burial! So mercifully does a good Providence veil the future from our eyes.

The first few days after leaving the Cape were disagreeable, and cold, and rough; and the *Great Britain* rolled about, as if she had uneasy dreams, although from her great size and breadth of beam, she went through the seas more easily than a smaller craft. This was the most uncomfortable part of our voyage. By and by the sky cleared, and the waves became blue, and the Indian Ocean opened out before as—an expanse of unutterable calm.

All round the ship the languid air did swoon,
Breathing like one that hath a weary dream.

Scarcely a ripple moved the surface of the lake-like sea, Mr.

Chapman, our chief mate, who had been attacked by sickness, and whose absence was regretted both as an amusing companion and as an admirable seaman, now resumed his place on deck, to the especial delectation of "Toby," a little spaniel which had come on board with the 17th Lancers.

We began to suffer very much from the heat of the weather, which made it almost impossible to remain in the saloon or the cabin. The thermometer hanging in our cabin (which being nearly always on the weather side, was one of the coolest in the ship) ranged, from the 3rd December to the 16th, at from 74° to 88°; but it was remarked that on each occasion of our crossing the line, the day was unusually cool and agreeable.

At length our voyage began to draw near its completion. It had been a weary time for all of us, though perhaps less so for me than for others, as I could occasionally find occupation in needlework. But it was with feelings of regret that I thought of leaving the ship, where so much consideration and kindness had been shown me. I had begun the voyage in much unhappiness at having so soon again to leave England, and to separate myself not only from my relations, but from all my household gods. The parting from attached servants, from horses, which one learns to love so much—from the pet dog, gift of one now lying beneath the rose-coloured plain of Balaklava, had each a separate pain.

The beauties of tropical sea and sky, however, had turned my thoughts from the past to the present: the contemplation of the present braced my spirits, and I gradually learnt to unwind my heart from England, to which it had for a second time begun to cling, and to allow it to anticipate its Indian future. To England shall I ever again return? Was my last short *sojourn* there but the opening chord of a *nunc dimittis*, bidding me depart in peace from it forever? My house there is set in order: the rest is at the ordering of Him who holdeth our lives in His hand.

In spite of the sunshine, three days before our arrival at Bombay, a gloom fell upon us, owing to the death of one of the men of the 17th Lancers from rheumatism affecting the heart. Up to a late hour on the previous evening, the doctors entertained a hope that he would recover, or, at any rate, linger for some time; but at five o'clock the following morning he expired, and was buried between ten and eleven o'clock the same day. The quiet of the calm and shining sea robbed his grave of its horror. This was the first and only casualty of our otherwise prosperous voyage. Throughout his burial day the wind was calm and the sea at rest.

Next morning, a very strong breeze sprang up from the north-east, dead ahead of the ship, retarding her way so much that all hope of saving the Bombay mail, which we believed left on the 17th, was at an end. The captain was extremely desirous to reach Bombay before its departure, in order that his ship might be reported at Lloyds as having arrived. In that event, she would have made her outward voyage in seventy days, winch she was bound under heavy penalties to do.

On Tuesday evening, after we had abandoned all expectation of reaching Bombay on the Thursday, the wind dropped, and the sea grew calm. Every furnace (eighteen, I believe) was alight; the ship throbbed from stem to stern, like an over-driven horse; her waste pipes gasped and sobbed, and every yard was braced up, so as to otter least resistance to the air. After dinner, the health of Captain Gray was given with many just expressions of regard, and the cheers from the saloon were taken up by the men on deck.

The ship still strained and panted forwards, making such good way during the night, that at breakfast next morning, we were greeted with the cheerful news, "We shall drop anchor in Bombay Harbour this afternoon at four o'clock; completing our voyage in seventy days from England, and sixty-four under steam." The Indian shore lay on our starboard side—red, arid, parched, and bare. We traced, it with interest all the morning, following its outlines on the chart. About half-past two, we came in sight of Bombay, and also of the ship *Arabia*, Captain Forrest, an old Crimean friend, which was lying becalmed, with her head towards Bombay. About three o'clock, we took a pilot on board, and soon after four were at anchor in the harbour, and learnt to our great joy that the mail did not leave until the 18th, so that plenty of time remained for the ship to be reported, and for letters to be posted to our friends. The ship rested.

The colonels of the 8th Hussars and 17th Lancers came on board, and from them we heard that the interior of India was still very gravely disturbed; and that so far from being stationed in cantonments, one if not both of the regiments would have to march immediately. Early on the following day, the 8th disembarked, and encamped on the esplanade; and on the next morning, the 17th landed, and proceeded at once by railway towards Kirkee.

CHAPTER 2

A Native Entertainment

In a strange land,
Strange things, however trivial, reach the heart,
And through the heart the head; clearing away
The narrow notions that grow up at home.

Rogers.

That day we gave
To pleasure, and, unconscious of their flight,
Another and another.

Ibid.

On Saturday, 19th December, my husband and I left the *Great Britain* and established ourselves in a large tent in the garden of the Hope Hall Hotel at Mazagon, near Bombay, preferring the open air and sunshine to the close rooms of a crowded house. On landing at the Apollo Bunder, we found no other conveyance was to be got, so I satisfied some clamorous natives by allowing them to carry me in a *palki*. The motion was easy, and the attitude luxurious; but the idea of transforming my fellow-creatures into beasts of burden was repugnant to me, and at the first halting-place I dismissed the *palki* and waited until a carriage was procured.

I could not believe that the time would come, when I should gladly travel in a *palanquin* for miles; being too much prostrated with pain and weakness to sit in my saddle, or to endure the motion of a carriage. My first impression on entering .Bombay was one of disappointment One saw nothing but native houses with, wooden fronts and. deep projecting roofs leaning over unpaved streets; and open shops, as in a Turkish bazaar, with here and there the funniest Parsee names, written in English characters. Nearly all the English residents live outside the town, on Malabar Hill, in bungalows, more or less capacious and handsome.

The part of .Bombay near the sea is strongly fortified; and immediately outside the fort is the esplanade where the 8th Hussars, and the 95th Regiment, were encamped. This is the place of fashionable resort, where from half-past four until seven o'clock may be seen every equipage and horse in Bombay, and some of the latter are magnificent. Near the esplanade is a large native quarter, densely populated and very squalid. In the country just beyond are the Byculla Club, the church, the racecourse, and the houses of the wealthy merchants, both English and Parsee.

The officers of the 17th Lancers, during the few hours which they spent in Bombay previous to their departure for Kirkee, endeavoured at any cost to provide themselves with horses. Never had the native dealers such a golden harvest. "A thousand *rupees*," "two thousand *rupees*," were words familiar to their mouths; so much so, that they forgot all intermediate numerals. The enormous demand, and the very inadequate supply, enabled them to obtain almost any price they liked to ask.

The soldiers encamped on the esplanade are loud in their praises of Indian life. The large roomy tents, and numerous native servants, contrast pleasantly enough with their Crimean experiences. The officers' tents, double-walled, and roofed, with a bathroom adjoining and grass or wire-woven doors, appear to possess every means of comfort, and at this present season, the 28th December, the climate is absolutely perfect. The mornings and evenings are cool and breezy, noonday is excessively hot; and during the few days we have as yet passed in India, I have not seen a cloud.

The glory of the sunsets fills the mind with wonder and admiration; nor can I feel astonished at the Parsee who prostrates himself on the sea-shore, with his face towards the declining sun. The number of servants requisite to form a moderate Indian establishment diners very materially from English notions. We found it necessary to engage a head servant or butler, who is in fact the house-steward, and. provides for the household and horses; a second, servant or bearer, who attends to the master as personal servant, and waits at table with the butler; a cook; a *mapaul*, who cleans lamps, plates, knives and forks; a *bheestie*, or water-carrier: a *dhobie*, or washerman; a *dirsee*, or tailor, to repair the ruthless damages done by the *dhobie*; a tent lascar, to pitch the tent; a *gari-wallah*, to drive the covered bullock *shegrum*, which it is necessary to have for going out in the sun; and, lastly, a *ghorawallah* for each horse. I could not understand at first how so large an establishment would be transported on the march, but time, which teaches many things, showed me that without each and every man of them, it was next to impossible to move at all: and in India an army of 10,000 men is reckoned to have not less than 30,000 camp followers—a number which would have astonished Julius Caesar.

A. thermometer showing 80° at noon made us almost doubt the possibility of its being New Year's Day, with which our associations are of clear frosty atmosphere and ice-bound ponds and fields. Every bell on shore and in harbour kept up a merry peal, and the guns of the fort saluted at daybreak. How little we thought as the last new year dawned upon us through clouds and nipping wind, that before another came we should be basking beneath an Indian sun.

But—

All that moveth doth, in change delight.

And now that the voyage is over, I cannot but be glad that this new phase of life opens before me. We are at present established in the lines of the regiment on the esplanade, in a large double-walled and double-roofed tent, sixteen feet long by fourteen wide, which, with carpets, arm-chairs, tables, lamps, and a pianoforte, is comfortable enough. Opening from this is a *baychuba*, or tent without a pole, fitted up as a sleeping–room, while beyond the *baychuba* and also opening into it, is the bathroom. The servants tents are pitched in the rear, and the horses are picketted close by.

Each horse has his own *ghorawallah*, or *syce* (Anglicè groom), sitting near his head all day and sleeping close to him at night. The Arab horses are, with few exceptions, as tame as English pet dogs: they never start back from the hand, as do English horses reared in stalls and badly treated by their grooms, nor do they object to the handling of their hind legs, by which they are hobbled,

In our search for horses we have had to visit the various dealers yards. We went first to Mahomet Bouker's stables, where upwards of a thousand horses were ranged under open sheds. These, however, were of inferior caste, and had already been selected for the ranks of various regiments. A large-boned chesnut horse hid in a dark corner caught our attention.

"His price is a thousand *rupees*, said the courteous Mahomet; "shall I have him run out for you?"

He appeared accordingly, and was such a veteran that we could not refrain from laughing at the estimate placed on our knowledge of horseflesh; so we bowed, and walked out of the yard.

Our next visit was to Dhady, whose horses, fewer in number, were mostly new arrivals from shipboard, and in very poor condition. Of him we purchased "The Pearl." Fukergee's stables consisting of rows of loose boxes, next claimed our attention, and several horses were examined and. tried, without success, until one day he brought "The Rajah" down to camp.

My husband's stud, which is now complete, consists of "The Rajah," his first charger, a very handsome mottled Arab four-year old, with black mane and tail, as full of tricks as a monkey, and. half inclined, if not well managed, to become vicious; his second charger, a strong white Arab, which speedily became a great favourite—a powerful dark iron grey, with large, black, good-tempered eyes, and the sweetest disposition in the world, which soon learnt to know his name of "Prince," and of which I immediately took possession for my own riding; and lastly, my little nutmeg grey, deservedly called "The Pearl,"—slight, wiry, active, showy, full of life and fire, of which I am the more proud, as I broke him in myself, and no one else has ever been upon his back.

A few nights after our arrival we were invited by a Parsee merchant of some consideration to a *nautch*, given in honour of his son's wedding; and, being curious as to the customs of the richer natives, we accepted the invitation and went at about ten p.m. We drove to the entrance of a courtyard, which was roofed in with drapery of white cloth, spangled with stars, and hung with gold thisel fringe. On a raised platform was the band of the 8th Hussars, lent for the occasion. Ascending the staircase, we found ourselves in a long room, beautifully lighted by numerous chandeliers; round the walls were ranged nearly a guests, Mussulmans, Hindoos, Parsees, and a few Englishmen.

The natives were dressed in white, with gorgeous turbans, each guest holding a bouquet and a fan. The effect of these gay colours was light and happy to a great degree, and contrasted well with our heavy uniforms, fastened to the chin, and ponderous with gold lace. As soon as we arrived we were sprinkled with rose-water and presented with betel-nut, a bouquet, and a fan. The Hussar band speedily ceased playing, and the *nautch* dancers took possession of the floor. Two young women, in magnificent dresses, with diamond rings in their noses and silver anklets, commenced a slow and monotonous dance, marking time by a nasal song, most disagreeable to the ear. They were accompanied by two men, one playing a kind of banjo, and the other beating a tom-tom.

There was neither grace in the dance nor harmony in the song. The whole entertainment was hot and tedious; and we left soon after midnight, in spite of the protestations of our host that the dancing would continue until four or five o'clock. Several Parsees present conversed with me in English, and one evinced curiosity to know if the spectacle I was witnessing bore any resemblance to an English ball.

On mentioning this to a friend a day or two after, I was told that at one of the Governor's balls at Hindoo, after watching the dancers for some time, expressed his intention of "sending to England for a ball." He imagined that the guests were exhibitors for money, and that he could purchase some equally good for a specified outlay.

Shortly before our arrival at Bombay, two *sepoys* of the Native Infantry stationed there had been blown away from guns, and a third was transported for life. as far as we can judge, the disaffection does not appear likely to spread—the rebels being overawed by the rapid arrival of European troops. At the time these two executions took place, the English military force in Bombay did not exceed two hundred men, while a regiment of Native Infantry, numbering eleven hundred, was encamped on the esplanade.

The two hundred, however, proved sufficient to maintain order until reinforcements, hastily sent for to the Mauritius and elsewhere, arrived. Of course, various opinions are expressed by the residents. Some imagine that the mutineers are only awaiting the dispersion of the troops to rise *en masse* and murder every English man, woman, and child in Bombay; while others maintain that the disaffection is purely military, and is even now crushed, as far as Bombay is concerned. In the midst of these conflicting hopes and fears, an unexpected demonstration has been made in our favour by the wealthy Parsee residents and merchants, headed by Cursetjee Jejeebhoy, the eldest son of Sir Jamsetjee.

The whole of the newly-arrived English forces, officers and men, together with the Governor, the commander-in-chief, and all the principle officers, civil, military, and naval, have been invited to a vast banquet on the esplanade. A. line of lofty tents, extending for more than a quarter of a mile, and surrounded by temporary walls, has been erected for the banquet, and another of the same extent for the ballroom and supper. The invitation was accepted without much cordiality on the part of the troops, who cannot understand accepting an entertainment from the natives of a country, the soil of which is stained with the blood of English men, women, and children.

Upwards of two thousand men and officers sat down to dinner. All wore either swords or side-arms; and a strong guard was left in camp. The speeches made during the entertainment by the Parsees were most friendly, and I wish I had space to record that of Lord Elphinstone.

No ladies were invited to the dinner; but when the tents appropriated to dancing were thrown open, I was astonished and surprised at their scanty attendance. Amongst the throng of Englishmen, French naval officers, and Americans, there was scarcely a score of ladies, and these I know had hard battles to fight with the prejudices of the rest of the female community. I fancy a fear of losing caste in society, or offending against some ill-denned point of etiquette, deterred many. For on all questions of etiquette the Indian ladies are particular to a curious and amusing degree.

The pertinacity with which claims for precedence are maintained., where there is not a shade of difference in the rank, or rather no rank, of the guests, is very entertaining to a newcomer. I am told that it is often most difficult to give precedence to one without direfully offending all the rest. According to the custom here, the lady who takes precedence must be the first to break up the party; and until she leaves no other guest can quit the room. I witnessed an amusing instance of the consequences of this stringent law.

We were dining at a friend's house, when a lady was taken suddenly ill. The "senior lady" (in regimental phrase) had shown no symptoms of departure. The case was urgent. The mistress of the house represented it; and the difficulty was solved by the lady who took precedence rising and making her *adieux*; but as her carriage was not in waiting, she retired to the empty dining-room, where she sat in state in the dark until it arrived!

Notwithstanding their strict obedience to etiquette, I cannot say that I found the manners of my fellow-countrywomen in India characterized by real politeness. On one occasion we were dining at the house of the highest person in the presidency, himself remarkable for his courtesy.

The guests, about seventy in number, were nearly all strangers to me; and during that *triste* period after dinner devoted by the ladies to the exclusive enjoyment of each other's society, I heard the question asked across the room, "Which is Mrs. Duberly?"

And as loudly replied to by, "There she is, sitting on the sofa, in pink,"

With the comment from a third of, "Oh! is that the Crimean heroine?"—while two young ladies shifted their chairs, in order to take an inventory of me at their leisure.

Intelligence from the interior reaches us very much as the Crimean news did at Balaklava, *viz.*, through the columns of the English newspapers. Neither the local papers nor the people of Bombay appear to give themselves much concern about the turmoil of the northern states. Balls and dinner parties succeed each other rapidly; and I never remember to have seen a more beautiful ballroom, or one better adapted to its purpose, than that at Bombay.

Our stay here will be no longer than is necessary to enable us to procure tents, servants, and a few horses for the officers and men, as we have received final orders to embark for Mandavee, in Cutch, on Saturday, 23rd January. The Calcutta papers, received on the 22nd, contain an account of the reception of the wounded men and widows and orphans from Lucknow. A royal salute was fired, in their honour; and they were met on landing by sympathizing crowds, eager with their offers of shelter and assistance.

Too late! too late! no sympathy can heal such wounds, no friendship can restore the murdered dead. When I think upon this terrible insurrection, and recollect how deeply the rebels have stained themselves with English blood, the blood of English women and of little helpless children, I can only look forward with awe to the day of vengeance, when our hands shall be dipped in the blood of our enemies, and the tongues of our dogs shall be red through the same.

On Thursday the 21st, the heavy baggage, mess-stores, &c.,

were embarked. On Friday, the horses and the rest of the baggage followed; and on Saturday we went on board the steamship *Khersonese*, and at four o'clock in the afternoon, after Lieutenant-Colonel Wilmer, who was found to be suffering from smallpox, had been put on shore, we took the *Persia* in tow, and steamed out of Bombay harbour, bound for Mandavee.

CHAPTER 3

Dangerous Landing

*What mortal in the world, if without inward calling he take up a
trade, an art, or any other mode of life, will not find his situation
miserable? But he who is born with capacities for any undertaking, finds in executing it the fairest portion of his being. Nothing
upon earth without its difficulties! It is the secret impulse within,
it is the love and delight we feel, that help us to conquer obstacles,
to clear out new paths, to overleap the bounds of that narrow circle
in which others poorly toil.*

Wilhelm Meister.

We had watched most anxiously for the mail which. was
due on the 22nd of January, but it did not arrive before we left
Bombay. Unless delayed by an accident the steamboat must have
come in a few hours afterwards, so that the disappointment was
doubly keen. How little can the daily letter-writers of England
imagine the eagerness with, which exiles in a far country look
forward to the arrival of the post, bringing them news from
home. To us letters from England are like voices from another
world.

Bombay Harbour lay serene in the evening twilight as we
sat on deck and watched until we could no longer discern the
houses and the cathedral tower. Fatigue drove me early to my
cabin: but not to sleep. We had been late in going on board, and
found that the only vacant cabin was the one next to that from
which poor Colonel Wilmner had been removed. I went into
it, not without a shiver—and the thought of smallpox, com-

bined with extreme fatigue and the attacks of hordes of fero-
cious insects, deprived me of all sleep. Next morning a head
wind sprang up, retarding our course very seriously. In addition
to the smoke from the funnel sweeping over the after-part of
the vessel, and filling our lungs with gas, we found the crowds of
native servants and. camp followers who encumbered the decks
anything but fragrant.

The *Persia*, a ship of 1,700 tons, was a sad drag on engines not
over strong; and what with bad cooking, undrinkable tea, and
detestable wine, we experienced as many disagreeables as could
well be crammed into so short a voyage.

On the morning of Wednesday the 27th, we were shown
a long line of flat sandy coast, with a small town on the shore,
apparently distant about nine or ten miles. We watched it as-
siduously from nine a. m. until three p. m., but without making
any perceptible approach. The current and the wind were strong
against us; and the water was so shallow that both ships were
compelled to sound incessantly. About half-past four o'clock we
cast anchor two miles from the shore, but at that distance it was
too late to commence disembarking horses.

Next morning business began in earnest, but several men and
officers, and nearly all the horses, remained on board that night
also. At one time it was intended to send us to Gogeh, a seaport
in the Gulf of Cambay, but the landing there proved, to be even
worse than at Mandavee. We found that there would, be no difficulty as to transport as far as Bhooj, thirty-six miles distant, and
to that place the dismounted squadrons were to march on foot.

On Friday, the 29th January, may be said to have commenced
our Indian campaign. We left the *Khersonese* in a large native
boat, with several of the soldiers. It was very rough, and. the old
boat, which must have been built time out of mind, lurched, and
groaned to a surprising extent. It did not reassure us to hear that
a hundred and fifty pilgrims had been drowned two days before
out of a similar boat; however, after a great deal of screaming and
jabber on the part of the native crew, we stuck fast on a sand-
bank, and were carried to the beach. The landing is so bad for

horse-boats at this place that a whole boatload, arriving after the turn of the tide, were knocking about all night; unfortunately our horses were of the number, and as none of them had been fed since the previous morning, we found them on our arrival in camp in a great state of exhaustion, and indeed one was so weak that we feared for his life.

Our tents were pitched upon the sea-shore, in deep sand, which was all very well for the transport camels, but to us. I was particularly struck with the difference between an Indian town and the cities I had previously seen in European and Asiatic Turkey. A traveller who has seen one Turkish town has seen them all. The same narrow and filthy streets, the same figures sitting in the same attitude, in large open shop windows, shaded by a lifted shutter stretching across the street, the same cats and dogs, and the same graceful minarets that are in Constantinople, may be seen more or less in every Turkish town.

The aspect of an Indian town is different; the domed temple of the Hindoo stands out in greater prominence than the airy minaret of the Mussulman. Hideous little carved gods, daubed with red paint, are exposed to public view in wayside temples, like the shrines of the Virgin and the Saints in a Continental town. On certain days these idols are fresh painted and dressed in fine clothes; when devout worshippers appear with mud and rice upon their foreheads, or with bars of white and red mud upon then: cheeks.

This mud, which comes, I believe, from the Ganges, the Sacred River, is worn as a religious emblem, and is hard to reconcile with our European ideas of beautiful adornment. The greater part of the inhabitants of Mandavee are Banyans and Jains, whose creed forbids the destruction of life.

No living creature is destroyed in the town. The fish near it swim unconscious of the hook; cows, being sacred, are of course exempt from injury; whoever shoots a peacock must pay a fine of 500 *rupees*, or 50*l*. Parrots, hawks, crows, and sheep all live as long as nature will permit; but at a village a few miles distant, sheep, fowls, and fish, are purchasable. The hawks, conscious of security, come swooping over the camp kitchens, and carry-pieces of meat, almost from between the fingers of the cooks.

At Bombay there is a hospital close to the sea for maimed, diseased, or aged animals, whither they are brought to await the approach of death. Horses, and other animals, suffering from whatever cause, are there left to linger until nature puts a period to their pain, instead of being mercifully and instantaneously destroyed. The principle is good, which teaches men to refrain from taking God's great gift of life; but I saw enough of animal suffering in the Crimea, to teach me that death is often the greater blessing.

In consequence of this local protection the neighbourhood of Mandavee abounds in game of almost every kind. The Rao of Cutch has a dirty-looking and dilapidated palace here in which his eldest son occasionally resides. Writing of palaces reminds me of something we heard when at Bombay regarding the capture of Delhi. The army which took the place after fearful loss and great hardships, imagined that when the city fell, everything in it would be theirs. Great was their surprise and disappointment when they found that plunder was most strictly forbidden, and that instead of booty each man was to receive a few extra *rupees*. The consequence was that chalk inscriptions were scrawled all over the town:—

"Delhi Taken, and India Saved, for Twenty *Rupees*."

When we heard of the fall of Delhi from the officers of the *Himalaya*, the news kindled the warlike enthusiasm of officers and men. It was imagined that the Avenger would complete his work, and that not a trace would be left of the city to show future generations where it stood.

As they walked the deck, and discussed the news in groups, one of them gave utterance to the following lurid words, which, with all their savage imagery of the days of Tilley and Wallenstein, still seemed to find an echo in most soldiers hearts:——

When the breach was open laid,
Bold we mounted to the attack;

215

Five times the assault was made
Four times we were driven back;
But the fifth time, up we strode
O'er the dying and the dead,
Red the western sunbeams glowed,
Sinking in a blaze of red.
Redder in the gory way
Our deep plashing footsteps sank,
As the cry of 'Slay—slay—slay!'
Echoed fierce from rank to rank.
And we slew, and slew, and slew—
Slew them with unpitying sword.
Negligently could we do
The commanding of the Lord?
Fled the coward, fought the brave,
Wept the widow, wailed the child,
But there did not 'scape the glaive
Man that frowned, or babe that smiled.
There were thrice ten thousand men
When that morning's sun arose;
Lived not thrice three hundred when
Sunk that sun at evening's close.
Then we spread the wasting name,
Fed to fury by the wind;
Of the city but the name,
Nothing else, remained behind.
But it burned not till it gave
All it had to yield of spoil
Should not brave soldadoes have
Some rewarding for their toil?
What the villein sons of trade
Earned by years of toil and care,
Prostrate at our bidding laid,
In one moment won was there.
Hall and palace, dome and tower,
Lowly cot and soaring spire,

Sank in that victorious hour
Which consigned the town to fire.
Then throughout the burning town,
'Mid the steaming heaps of dead,
Cheered by sound of hostile moan,
We the gorgeous banquet spread:
Laughing loud and quaffing long,
At our glorious labour o'er,
To the skies our jocund song
Told that Magdeburg was no more![1]

I shudder as I write these terrible lines. Alas! For the horrors of Cawnpore, and for the retribution which must avenge them!

---

1. Dr, Maginn's *Taking of Magdeburg,*

CHAPTER 4

The First March

In the world's broad field of battle,
In the bivouac of life,
Be not like dumb driven cattle
Be a hero in the strife.

Longfellow

Quale per incertam lunam sub luce malignâ Est iter.

At midnight on Sunday, 31st January, the *reveillée* sounded, and by two o'clock the regiment began its march. The mounted column first, then the treasure-chest on a tumbril, escorted by the dismounted. men, the whole followed by an incredible tram of bullock-wagons and camels laden with baggage. The full moon enabled us to follow the track through a very ugly country; but the wind was extremely cold, and we all hailed the rising sun with satisfaction. Camp was pitched near the village of Bara-Assumbia about nine o'clock, and breakfast followed as speedily as might be. The most energetic of the officers took their guns, and started in quest of game.

During these very early days of marching, before we had become accustomed to it, the mess-dinner was at two o'clock, and the mess-tent, and all others that could be spared, were struck at four, and sent on overnight to the next halting-place, in charge of an officer and an advance party. The object aimed at by this arrangement was to have the tents so sent forward pitched before the regiment came in from the march, that there might be no delay for breakfast; but as the officers selected never marked out the camp until the arrival of the colonel, the plan turned out a failure. Next morning *reveillée* sounded at two a.m., and we started at four.

This was a more adventurous march; for as the tumbril and baggage guards were unable to keep up with the column, at a point where the tracks became intricate, they lost their road, not easily discernible in moonlight, and the whole of the long train of baggage went astray. My husband and I were riding in the rear, and we started in different directions, in the hope of finding either the column or the road. In about an hour and a half, a track was discovered, which to our joy proved to be the right one, and, after much bumping and jolting over deep ruts and uneven ground, and many escapes from falling into holes and *nullahs*, the train of carts and camels eventually reached Naigpoor, about two hours after the column.

Shooting was resumed with unabated vigour, several officers, who had marched on foot, going out immediately after breakfast. Major Chetwode shot a beautiful antelope, and loaded his beaters with game. The next day's march brought us into Bhooj, where we halted for several days. On our arrival, Colonel Trevelyan, Political Resident in Cutch, although a total stranger to me, insisted, with the true spirit of hospitality, that we should be his guests at the Residency, instead of remaining in camp during the halt.

A suite of handsome rooms was given up to us, and our horses were taken in as well. It was the hospitality of a prince; and arriving as we did, all dusty, travel-stained, and fatigued, it seemed as though we could not luxuriate enough in the comforts of a well-appointed house, with its large, cool, lofty rooms, and refreshing baths. Bhooj possesses several objects of interest; amongst which are the tombs of the former Raos. They are of red sandstone, hundreds of years old; some having almost crumbled away, while the one or two that remain perfect are approached by handsome flights of steps, and are rich in ornament as well as beautiful in architectural design.

The domed roofs are supported on clusters, groups, and rows of pillars; while the fantastic and elaborate carvings of every corner remind the spectator of the like ornaments on our fairest English cathedrals. The Rao's Palace, and also several of the tombs, are decorated with figures resembling those seen on English monuments of ancient date. An equestrian statue in chain armour, looking very like a crusader, adorns the palace: and the entrance to the door of the largest tomb is guarded by two figures, male and female, apparently about the date of Henry I.

On inquiry, I learned that many, many years ago, a Dutch sculptor came to Bhooj, and left those traces of his skill. Conjecture wanders in vain over the history of this man. How and why he came so far, a solitary Christian outcast among the heathen, is unknown.

His name has long been lost, but his memory lives long in his works.

Here, in silence and in sorrow, toiling with a busy hand,
Like an emigrant he wandered, seeking for the Better Land.
'Emigravit' is the inscription on the tombstone where lie lies:
Dead he is not, but departed—for the Artist never dies.

The second day of our halt at Bhooj was one of gloom for all of us. The post which arrived in the morning brought us the melancholy news of the death of Lieutenant-Colonel Wilmer, whom we left sick at Bombay. I have since heard that he died neglected, and almost alone. This affected us the more, as although Colonel Wilmer only joined the 8th Hussars on their arrival in India, he had won the esteem and goodwill of all. But a still heavier calamity hung over this fated day; the sportsmen went out to shoot, and with them a young Lieutenant Helme, who had joined scarcely a year ago. He became separated from the rest, and was only attended by his *ghorawallah*, who followed for the purpose of carrying his game.

The young man had his gun over his shoulder at full cock, when his foot tripped, and he stumbled heavily. The gun flew from his hand, and struck the ground with such force that it exploded, and the contents passed through his body. The *ghorawal-lah*, sole witness of the appalling accident, said he had not time to utter a single word, but died as he fell.

The terrified servant ran in haste to some of the unfortunate young man's brother officers, who were shooting near, and meeting Lieutenant the Hon. E. Stourton, brought him to where the body lay. Medical assistance and a *doolie* were quickly on the spot, but he was stone dead. At the inquest, held the following morning a verdict of "accidental death" was returned; and this comfort was left to us, that he is buried in consecrated ground, and amongst his own countrymen, in the English cemetery at Bhooj, where a monument was erected to his memory by his brother officers. He was a quiet and amiable youth, and many were grieved at his untimely end.

Tidings of the evacuation of Awah reached Colonel Trevelyan while we were at the Residency. The rebels had strongly fortified it, and appeared determined to resist. While preparations were being made for the siege, a violent storm of thunder and lightning, with terrific rain, compelled the suspension of all operations; and the rebels taking advantage of the elemental din, and. under cover of heaven's artillery, abandoned the, fort. We heard that a hundred prisoners were made, of whom twenty-four were hanged, and one shot.

I received an intimation from the *Ranees*, appointing an interview with me, and was much gratified at having an opportunity of seeing the interior of an Indian court. Mrs. Jervis, the wife of the resident interpretress. The *Rao* sent his carriage, an English brougham, for us, with an escort both of horse and foot. The courtyard of the palace, an extensive and handsome building, was thronged with people, and music commenced as our carriage drew up at the foot of the stone steps leading to the ladies apartments.

We saw six of the *Ranees*, and the wife of the *Rao's* eldest son. The ladies, who received. us in the *durbar* room, were seated on chairs in a row, surrounded by female attendants and musicians. They rose as we entered, and extended their hands; seats were then placed for us opposite to them.

The eldest lady conversed: the rest sat by in silence. I never saw such a profusion of jewellery in my life. The forehead of each was hidden by a circular ornament, of precious stones, and even their eyelids were fringed with, diamonds; nose jewels, the size and weight of which distorted the nostril, completed the decorations of the face. Several necklaces, some apparently in solid gold, others of strings of pearls, covered the neck and bosom; while massive bracelets, blazing, with rubies and emeralds, encircled their arms from elbow to wrist.

One bracelet I particularly remember; it was a thick and heavy circlet of gold, studded with about thirty emeralds the size of peas. On their ankles they wore three or four chains and. anklets of different patterns, and each toe was covered with an ornament resembling enamelled leaves. The *Ranee* who conversed appeared to be an unusually intelligent woman. She was well informed as to everything relating to the royal families of Europe, and listened with interest for my answers to her various questions.

Mrs. Jervis mentioned that I was the Eglishwoman whom the *Ranee* had heard of as having been with the army during the Crimean war; and her inquiries proved that she was familiar with the leading events of the campaign. Her information was, I believe, acquired from a Persian newspaper, which she receives once a week. She was very desirous to ascertain whether the men of the regiment entertained hostile feelings towards the native population, or only towards such as had revolted. The ladies examined my watch and bracelets very minutely, and then desired their attendants to show me their sleeping apartments.

This was quite exceeding ordinary etiquette, and arose evidently from a wish to make their friendly feeling as manifest as possible. The rooms were dark and close, but the swinging cots were very handsome. That of the eldest *Ranee* was made entirely of silver, and suspended from the ceiling by massive chains, carved into elephants, horses, and palm-trees.

Close to it was a smaller swinging bed in a handsome silver

frame. It was the cot which had been occupied by her son, the heir apparent, when he was a little child; and, mother-like, she still keeps it in her room. The ladies retire about ten or eleven o'clock, and. are rocked and rung to sleep by little silver bells suspended from the chains that swing the cot.

One thing struck me: when in conversation with the *Ranee*, she asked rather eagerly if I had ever been actually present at a battle. And on being answered in the affirmative, she fell back in her chair and sighed. A whole lifetime of suppressed emotion, of crushed ambition, of helplessness, and weariness, seemed to be comprehended in that short sigh.

We quitted Bhooj with great regret on the 9th February. Our first march, of sixteen miles, to Dhunnytee was not commenced till daylight, and during the last three or four miles, the heat was extreme. The next morning we started at half-past three a.m., with the 10th Native Infantry, which had joined us at Bhooj.

This regiment (or rather a wing of it) accompanied us during the whole of our subsequent marches; and no words are too strong to express their fidelity before the enemy, their patient endurance of fatigue, and their cheerful readiness to perform their duties, sometimes under most trying circumstances. As we had no longer the benefit of the moon, and the leading squadron was marching nearly five miles an hour, the rear squadron, owing to some slight delay, lost sound of the rest of the column, and we had about two miles of hard trotting across country in total darkness, over ground fall of large holes.

The next morning our ride was more exciting still; for our guide lost his way, and brought us to a river, which we had to ford. It was so dark that we could, not distinguish the ground at all, and we had to ride on, although our horses floundered shoulder-deep into holes, or stepped and scrambled over rocks, every moment. The fourth march brought us to Chowbarree, where we dismissed the beautiful bullocks and handsome carts which had carried our baggage from Bhooj. As we hear that the bullocks in the northern and central part of India are mostly a miserable and half-starved race, we have purchased a pair of the magnificent white ones, for which Cutch is famous, to draw our *gharry*.

The country now slightly improves in beauty. At intervals there are trees and patches of cultivation, and we have passed several large tanks, covered with water-fowl. Game continues very abundant; and the wild dogs and jackals prowl at night close to the tents, making the air reverberate with their screaming laugh. Jeesra and Geree, where we encamped in a dry salt marsh, full of tall reeds, which kept us constantly on the watch for fear of fire, Moorania, and Fowar, were passed before our next halt. Between the two last we crossed the Runn of Cutch, the eastern boundary of the Rao's dominions, and entered the Palampoor States.

The Runn is alternately a sandy and muddy stretch of land, which, during the monsoon, is covered with salt-water. .Alter crossing four miles of dry mud, we came to a small sandy island, called "Gadka Gate," covered with grass and small bushes. Entering again upon the Runn, we reached another island, called "Blurdia," of the same kind as the first. The Runn, which becomes hard and consistent by December, presents no obstacles, except in cases of unseasonable rain; and at this point is about twelve miles across.

After marching through Babra and Warye we halted again for a day at Radhinpoor, which is a large and prettily situated native town, surrounded by a wall. The political agent for the Palampoor States resides here, as does also the *Nawab*, whose gardens are extensive, and afforded us a shady and agreeable promenade. We despatched letters to England from this place *via* Deesa, whence ours were forwarded to us at Warye, dated 4th and 15th January.

On the 25th February we quitted our pleasant camp at Radhinpoor, and betook ourselves along one of the dustiest tracks I ever rode, about thirteen miles to Ooun. The moon lighted us for the first hour of our march, which began at three a.m.; but several times, although the night was clear and bright, I was unable to discern the man riding immediately in front of my horse's nose, owing to the intense dust in which he was enveloped. It was no wonder that the eyes felt as if their lids were lined with sandpaper, or the skin as though rivers of water would scarcely slake its thirst.

The *Nawab*, by whose orders carts were supplied to the regiments, is said to make a good thing of the troops who pass through his States, The carts which he provided for the baggage transport were charged to us at the rate of two *annas* a mile for the thirteen miles, and as each officer employed two, and some six, a goodly amount was paid over to the *Nawab*, who, according to report, gives the unlucky *gariwallah*s what he pleases, and keeps the rest himself.

We marched into Deesa on Sunday morning, the 28th February, at about eight o'clock. With the exception of the few days' halt at Bhooj, we had lost no time upon the road, never marching less than nine miles, and generally doing from twelve to sixteen miles a day. Deesa being the first English station on our march, we naturally approached it with feelings of curiosity and excitement; it was, moreover, the extreme frontier of the quiet districts, and its cantonments once passed, tents can no longer be sent on overnight, and no messman will be ready to greet us with tea or coffee on our arrival in camp.

We were prepared after leaving Deesa to renounce all the luxuries of the campaign; but we hardly anticipated the fatigue and discomfort that lay before us. The stern schooling of the Crimea had taught us to make light of difficulties, and although even at this early stage of the march, we were glad to halt for two or three days, we nevertheless looked, forward to the future without fear or anxiety. Deesa is a large, straggling cantonment, with comfortable-looking bungalows scattered here and there; but the soil is so sandy that with the slightest wind the dust becomes intolerable. In the native town there are two Parsee shops, which appear to carry on a thriving trade.

One of these shopkeepers is the agent of our regimental agent in Bombay, and the Mess President endeavoured in vain to induce him to take charge of some superfluous stores, so that our baggage was ultimately given over to Government and stowed away in the barracks. Our encampment was pitched on a large plain just outside the cantonment. We found here the Queen's 89th, the 17th Native Infantry, a native cavalry regiment, and Captain Bolton's company of Royal Artillery.

Although we knew that our destination was Kotah, we were at first in ignorance of the route which we were to follow. It was evident that we were to lose no time upon the road; and in order that we might save about sixty miles, it was proposed that instead of going by Nusseerabad, we should take a more direct track, leading over the Chutterbooj Pass, which no regular troops had ever crossed before.

This route at first sight appeared totally impracticable for cavalry, as no stores could be carried on carts, and as the Commissariat declined to enter into any contract with the natives for the supply of grain and grass, having no hope of its punctual fulfilment. Another serious obstacle on this new route was the apprehended deficiency of water. However, after a great deal of consultation and consideration. Colonel De Salis, who commanded the column, resolved on proceeding by the main road as far as Erinpoora, and there awaiting final instructions as to whether he should or should not proceed by the Chutterbooj Pass.

Three hundred pack bullocks were furnished to the regiment to carry grain from Erinpoora, to be used in case of the failure of local supplies, and fifty fresh troop *ghorawallahs* were also procured to supply the places of the Sindians who left us at Deesa, the enormous pay of fifteen *rupees* a month not being a sufficient bribe to induce them to remain. Of course we had to reduce our baggage to the smallest possible amount, and we suffered great inconvenience in consequence during the rainy season, having neither warm clothes nor waterproofs with us.

Indeed, I should probably have lost my life had not an acquaintance, made at a later period, given me the thick cloth cape of a regimental cloak as some protection when in my saddle.

At one a.m. on Thursday morning, March the 4th, we left Deesa, and marched sixteen miles and a half to Koachawarra.

We had crossed two shallow streams, and passed two villages, when one of our vicious little troopers struck out at Sergeant Major Warde, who was riding up the column, and broke both the bones of his leg below the knee. He continued to ride for three or four minutes without being aware of the extent of the injury, and was then placed in a *doolie* and sent back to Deesa, where there is a good hospital. We subsequently learned that when he had recovered from the accident he was sent to regain his strength at the sanatorium on Mount Aboo, where he was attacked with pneumonia and died.

Being entirely dependent upon camels for the transport of our baggage, the labour of shifting camp is immense. For the mess alone, seventy camels have to be laden. As in many instances they will not allow a European to approach them, and as the native servants occupy an interminable time in arranging the load of each, the packing occupies the greater part of the night. My husband indented at Deesa for twelve camels, but after a few marches sickness overtook them, and we found fifteen requisite to carry our tents, with the servants baggage and our own. We expected to be tolerably tired of marching before reaching Kotah, which at that time we looked upon as our final destination, and were already somewhat inclined to agree with the butler of one of the officers of the 8th Hussars, who begged to give him warning, for he found it too much

On Friday, the 5th, we made a thirteen-mile march to Muddar, of which the latter part was as varied and beautiful as the first was monotonous and wearisome. We were now surrounded by rocky eminences, and in sight of the Mount Aboo range of hills. Our camp was pitched, for the first time on tolerably hard ground, instead of on the everlasting sand, and we placed our own tent beneath a wide-spreading tamarind tree, the green branches of which afforded a delicious shade.

The next day we pushed on to Reodur, ten miles nearer the beautiful hills. Where we also enjoyed the advantage of a cool and shady camp. H.M.'s 95th Regiment, which preceded us on this march, attacked and tools the village of Rowa, about six miles from Reodur, It was occupied by the rebels, a gang of whom, to the number of two hundred, infest these heights, and are the annoyance and terror of all the countryside. Secure among the fastnesses of the mountains, they descend like vultures upon the plain. One day they appear on the northern, the next day on the southern side of the hills, and swoop down upon some devoted village, which they sack without

Major Chetwode went out from this place in quest of a tiger, from the ravages of which the inhabitants had suffered severely; but as the regiment made no halt, he was unable to devote sufficient time to the pursuit. Lieutenant the Hon. E. Stourton, who had been for some days suffering very severely from fever, has experienced so grave a relapse that the medical officers determined on leaving him at the sanatorium, whither he was conveyed from Maira, our next encampment, directly at the foot of Mount Aboo.

My recollections of this camp are most pleasant. The mountain, in all its solitary grandeur, rose before us, unmarked by any dwelling or footprint of man. Now and then the wild cry of a hawk might he heard, as he wheeled high over our heads; and beneath our feet were little star-like flowers and blossoming shrubs. As the shades of evening gathered around us, we walked towards the mountain—tearing our feet with thorns and filling our hands with flowers; nor did we turn back until it was dark, and when we reached the camp it was so late that we had little more than two hours to sleep, before the *reveillée* (that remorseless call) summoned us again to our saddles.

It appears to be General Roberts' intention to wait at Nusseerabad until we can join him. We are certainly hastening towards him with all speed, having marched six days without a halt. The fatigue, however, begins to tell heavily on the three-year-old horses, and also upon the 10th Native Infantry and Captain Bolton's company of Royal Artillery, who accompany us as far as Erimpoora.

At length, after six days' marching, came a blessed day of rest at Serohee. I do not know one of my English acquaintance who can thoroughly appreciate a day of rest. A halt-day is to us what the Sabbath is to a man employed in monotonous and toilsome labour all the week. It seems to me as though when the halt-day comes I cannot rest enough. Oh! The inappreciable luxury of a whole clear day, with no *reveillée* to disturb one at midnight, no camels to pack, no sleepy horses to rouse up and saddle, no tents to strike, no dusty march and long-delayed breakfast, no dinner hurried over that the large tent may be struck before dusk!

Serohee is a large town, well situated on the side of a hill. It is famous for its manufacture of swords, which are of considerable value and beauty.

Letters of the 2nd February were received this morning. The *Home News*, of the same date, which had arrived three days before, contained a detailed account of the marriage of the Princess Royal, and also of the attempt to assassinate the Emperor of the French. It is quite refreshing to see that the French army has abandoned all pretence as to *La Belle Alliance*. As far as individuals were concerned, it was a humbug throughout. The national antipathy has not diminished, and the inconceivable bombast of the French soldier oozes out in the pompous addresses to the Emperor.

We have gained one great advantage by entering the disturbed country, and that is, that the servants and baggage-men, duly impressed with, the fear of being cut off, keep up much more closely with the column than heretofore; so that our tents are pitched and breakfast ready almost in time to save me from fainting either from exhaustion or the sun. One of our *ghorawallahs* has provided himself with a sword; and Lieutenant-Colonel Naylor's servant has procured a bow and arrows, just like the fatal instruments in the tragedy of "Cock Robin."

One or two more have armed themselves with boar-spears; and this reminds me that, a day or two before we arrived at Serohee, a wild boar charged through our column when on the line of march. It is well known that a boar will never swerve from his straight course for the purpose of attacking any object: so, as a passage was quickly made for him, he shot through without injuring man or horse.

The Rajah of Serohee visited our camp, and rode through it in state, during the day we halted there. He was escorted by a large armed party, who were at first refused admission into our lines, through a misapprehension, which was rectified almost as soon as it was made.

It was interesting, as our march wore on, to see the various wild animals with which India abounds; for instance, between Serohee and Palree, two bears (these were more strange than pleasant) passed through our column, on their way from their nocturnal wanderings to their den in the mountains. One or two officers fired revolvers at them, but I fancy without much effect; had my husband been riding near, he might have given another proof of his great accuracy as a pistol-shot. On the day we reached Erimpoora, graceful little antelopes came to wonder at us. It was here that we for the first time came upon traces of this terrible mutiny. Ruined bungalows and gardens laid waste, showed how ruthless had been the destroyers.

The Bengalees of the Joudpoor Legion, some of whom were stationed at Erimpoora when we passed through, were the instigators and executors of the revolt. Captain Conolly, who commanded them, and who was at the time the only European officer residing at the station, was saved through the connivance of some of the native officers who remained faithful. Reports differ as to the manner in which he effected his escape.

I was told that he overheard some of his men planning his death, and while at his wit's end to know how to escape, a friendly *subadar* came to him and said, "You will find a horse waiting for you outside the cantonment. Get to him unperceived, as best you can, then mount, and I need not tell you not to spare your spurs."

The last injunction, my informant added, he fulfilled so well, that he did not check his gallop till twenty miles lay between him and his would-be assassins. Now, for the correctness of this I cannot vouch —

I know not what the truth may be,

230

I tell the tale as 'twas told to me.

Two of this same legion acted as our guides for several days, and a few were not a little suspicious of them. However, they proved faithful and harmless. The detachment of Royal Artillery under Captain Bolton left us today, and proceeded to Nusseerabad. It was believed that General Roberts would take with him to Kotah the artillery then at Nusseerabad, and that Captain Bolton's men would supply their places there; but after we had been some days before Kotah, we had the pleasure of falling in with them again.

The authorities appear resolved to try the mettle of the horses and the constitutions of the men and officers of H. M's 8th Hussars; for, besides giving us a route never passed before by any troops, except when on one occasion five hundred of the Joudpoor Legion scrambled along it, we find that the marches are, in reality, much longer than they are reported to be in the book of the quartermaster-general.

Our first march from Erimpoora to Ballee was entered as fourteen miles, but it proved to be seventeen. The next day, to Gomerao was mentioned as fifteen miles; but the infantry were seven hours and five-and-twenty minutes on the line of march, and the cavalry, who started at three a.m., did not reach their camping-ground until fifteen minutes past nine, although they never halted for more than a quarter of an hour at a time. The regiment is supposed to march from three miles and a half to four miles an hour, after the first mile or two, during which they move faster.

The luckless *ghorawallahs* and camp-followers, who were on foot, came in quite useless from fatigue; and our sick men began to increase in number. There were two officers on the sick, report, Lieutenant-Colonel Naylor, and Hon. E. Stourton, who was left at Mount Aboo, and of whom no tidings were heard for a long while. The increasing heat of the weather deprives us of nearly all the refreshment of the day's rest. We keep our hearts up, nevertheless, with the hope that when we arrive at Kotah we shall be repaid for the hurry of this march, said, by officers who have previously served in India, to be the most harassing they ever undertook.

I do not know whose coughs are the worst, those of the native servants or those of the horses. During the few hours allotted to rest, the noise of coughing horses, choking natives, and remonstrative camels, is enough to banish sleep from everyone in camp.

As many of the camels are weak and ill-fed, they not unfrequently fall with their loads; and it is no unusual thing to see a bedstead arrive in two or three pieces, a chair minus the seat, or a table wanting a leg. Lucky, indeed, do we consider ourselves if both chairs and table survive the breakfast, without giving way. Here let me remark, for the benefit of others, that the only chairs suited to such. an expedition as ours are the portable iron ones manufactured by Messrs. Brown and Sons, of Piccadilly. They fold quite flat, and are easily carried, besides being strong and comfortable.

Our bullock *gharry*, while following the baggage on the line of march from Gromerao to Sommair, was upset into a dry well, It fell completely over, and, strange to say, neither of the bullocks were injured. On its arrival at Sommair, it was taken to pieces, previous to being carried over the Chutterbooj Pass by *coolies*.

CHAPTER 5

Panic at Poonah

All in a hot and copper sky,
The bloody sun at noon,
Right up above the mast doth stand
No bigger than the moon.

Coleridge.

And sometimes thro' the mirror blue
The Knights came marching two and two.

Tennyson.

On the morning of the 16th March, the *reveillée* sounded at three a.m., and shortly before five o'clock the regiment started, as the day broke, to march to Jeelwarra. Lieutenant-Colonel Naylor, whose *gharry*, like our own, had been taken to pieces, started his *coolies* at midnight with their load, and mine followed an hour or two later. The troops soon found themselves on a rough and rocky path, leading towards the heart of the mountains.

We crossed two little hill torrents, and passed at first under thickly-spreading trees, which diminished in beauty as we ascended. I have no doubt that in the clefts and caves of the rugged hillsides many a fierce she-bear lies amidst bones and blood; and, in fact, a bear was seen near the centre of the column. On and upward we scrambled in single file, over masses of rock and large loose stones; passing with difficulty in one narrow place an unfortunate camel of our advance party, which had laid down to die. Once the road was cut out of the side of the mountain, and we looked down, a most uncomfortable depth. It was singular that the Arab horses, so careless when the road is level and smooth, should on this day pass without hesitation or mistake over ground where a false step would have been irrecoverable.

A sufficiently hazardous undertaking it was to move troops up so narrow and steep a pass, commanded by a fort, and by eminences from which. twenty men might have most seriously annoyed the two regiments. A part of the 10th Native Infantry marched in front, and the remainder of the 10th, with forty of our own men, who were dismounted for the purpose, acted as rear and baggage guards,

We marched as quickly as possible through the gorge, occasionally dismounting and leading our horses up the most difficult places. The Pass extended, I believe, from seven to eight miles; and about two miles and a half after we had reached the more open ground at the top, we came to Jeelwarra, most inhospitably situated on a bare and rocky soil; producing, however, one fine banyan-tree, under which we were so fortunate as to be able to pitch our tent.

I felt at this time the first symptoms of over-fatigue and want of sleep, and found that the three, or at most four hours allowed for repose were no longer sufficient to compensate for the fatigues of the day. Satisfied, however, with the report of an easy march for the morrow, I endeavoured to compose myself to sleep. As we were to descend the *ghaut*, and pass over more rough ground, the *reveillée* did not sound until half-past three; and when parade sounded at about twenty minutes after four, we mounted and groped our perilous way to the front of the column, where we remained until the first streak of dawn, when we commenced the descent.

The "good road" proved very like the one of yesterday, except that it was downhill, instead of up. After slipping and scrambling down the rocky paths, we reached the town of Chutterbooj, and came to a rather more sandy and comfortable country. Here we were met by a riding-camel, with a native bearing a note from the officer of our advance party, who had gone on the previous day at noon. The note contained the cheerful intelligence that the road was a very bad one; and that instead of the distance being eleven miles, as stated, it was a good five-and-twenty. By this time the sun was up, and he caught the sides of our faces, which scorched as though blackening beneath his touch.

The anxiety that we felt was not so much for ourselves, mounted as we were, but for our unfortunate servants, *ghorawallahs*, and camels. Many of the young troop-horses were also greatly fagged. It appeared to us that great carelessness had been manifested in the route chosen, and that the political agent of the Polampoor States must have been satisfied with very inaccurate measurements. It is always difficult to judge of distances in India, as the *kos*, or native mile, differs in different parts of the country. Sometimes we found a *kos* to signify two English miles, and sometimes three.

On the day of which I am now writing the men fell into parade at Jeelwarra at a quarter-past four a.m., and they dismounted at the camping-ground at Aimatti at about twenty minutes past one p.m., while the baggage-camels did not come up until between five and six o'clock in the evening. I would not have changed places with the officer of the rear-guard that day upon any consideration; as it was, when the halting-ground was reached, I was obliged to be assisted from my saddle, being too cramped to dismount without help.

There was no dinner at mess that night, and our own servants did not arrive until so late, and were so knocked up when they did, that it was useless to expect any dinner from them. Had it not been for the hospitality of the officer who commanded the advance party, we should have gone fasting to sleep. The Rajah of Aimatti is related to the Rajah of Kotah; and his town, when we were there, was garrisoned by 2,000 men. The walls look as though they were built of gingerbread-nuts.

No European soldiers were admitted within them; but our native servants were supplied, willingly enough. The inhabitants have some expert thieves among them; for they stole two swords and a carbine from a tent, with securely-fastened doors, in which. eight men were sleeping at the time.

We halted for a day at Aimati, as well we might; and on the following morning a march of six miles over a smooth and level country to Lowa enabled, us to place our camp between a grove of fine tamarind-trees and a very picturesque, although ruined, fort. Here we had an opportunity of watching the natives extracting opium from the fresh and green poppy-heads, the flowers of which had just fallen.

Large tracts of country are devoted, to the cultivation of this gaudy, but misused plant; and we most imprudently stayed in the sun, watching the labourers, who, with an instrument resembling a three-pronged fork, were making incisions on each side of the poppy-head. The morning after this operation, they return provided with a knife, the blade of which resembles a small sickle, and on this they scrape off the dark juice which has oozed through the incisions. The quantity taken from each head is so small, that the labour of collecting it is very tedious. The syrup, when collected on the knife, resembles a juicy pulp of a dark brown colour.

I should not omit to mention that this day's march, which we found in the route furnished to Colonel De Salis to be twelve miles, was barely half the distance. May the mistakes in future be always on this side! The commissariat arrangements are now so bad, that sometimes after a severe march a very insufficient quantity of hay, and only 3½ lbs. of grain, instead of their allowance of 10 *sirrs*, or nearly 12 lbs., are issued for the horses. Our private letters from Poonah and Kirkee speak strongly of the mutinous feeling which smoulders at those places.

Secret meetings are being held, and great hopes are excited that the Nana, who is reported to have slipped his northern moorings, will hasten down to the vicinity of Poonah, and rally the Mahrattas to his standard. Strange scenes, the effect of panic fears, are said to have been enacted by the residents at that place, where an elderly officer, who happened at the time to be quite disabled, in consequence of a fall from his horse, was in great request to sleep in the houses of the ladies whose husbands were absent, by way of guard.

A march of twenty miles (stated to be ten) brought us the next day to Gangapoor, a town of some importance as to size. We encamped near it in what was evidently the bed of a tank in. the rainy season. Water was abundant in the neighbourhood, two large and picturesque lakes, covered with waterfowl, were on our right hand, and a tank near the town on our left.

The birds of India are an interesting study. If their voices are unmusical,—and there is a proverb in India, that "the birds have no song, the women no beauty, and the flowers no perfume,"— the beauty and brilliancy of their plumage far exceeds that of our northern songsters. It is no unusual thing to see fifteen or twenty peacocks at a time. We frequently pass them in the grey morning, roosting on the trees, or coming down in clusters to feed. Then there is the Sáras,[1] of a French grey and white colour, with red near the bill: this bird is nearly as tall as a man, and often in the morning light appears of gigantic proportions.

The white egrets, and paddy-birds, Brahmin kites and hawks, are amongst the larger birds, as well as several others, apparently of the flamingo and bittern tribes, which my ignorance does not enable me to name. Parrots, orioles, jays, mainas,[2] mango-birds, and others, small but brilliant, dart through the sunshine like flashes of light Every sort of duck can be shot upon the tanks; and a day or two before we reached this place Major Chetwode killed an alligator which he saw basking on the bank. It moved towards the water directly it perceived him but having a rifle, he fired instantly: the ball entered behind the shoulder, a second shot was quickly given, but the creature, although mortally wounded, took to the water. None of the beaters cared to go in and bring him out

There was no time to lose: so Major Chetwode, whose promptness and decision are well known amongst sportsmen, sprang after him, and dragged him on shore. Although the crea-

---

1. A crane, *Grus antigone.*
2. The maina is a name applied to several birds of the starling' family.

ture measured only about eight feet in length, I looked with wonder into its enormous mouth, the jaws of which, if roughly closed, sounded as though made of hard wood.

Gorlam, distant from Gangapoor about fifteen miles, was the next place where we pitched our tents. A proof of the dryness of the Indian atmosphere was afforded this morning by the showers of electric sparks which flew from the tail of the horse immediately before me. At times the flashes of light were as strong as those which his iron shoe would have caused had it come in contact with a flint.

The next day's march brought us to Bheelwarra, which is surrounded by fine trees and cultivated ground. To arrive at our encampment we had to pass through the town, which is handsome and well built, with broad streets and open squares. Never before had the inhabitants experienced so great an excitement. The streets were thronged with spectators, and the roof of the principal temple was literally covered with human heads. We observed a long and low house near the gate by which we made our exit from the town, the frontage of which was richly carved and painted; while the massive doors were fastened by bright steel chains.

This proved to be the bank wherein, during the stay of the gallant 8th Hussars before their walls, the careful inhabitants locked up their women. I was shown a handful of small change from this repository of treasure, of which a *cowry*, or small shell, formed the most valuable ingredient. I afterwards saw a quantity of these *cowries* stored up in the strong closet of a merchant's house at Kotah. There are here two large wells or tanks of great depth, one in the centre of the town and. the other outside the gate. They are surrounded with ornamental walls and are approached by flights of steps descending beneath archways of stone, supported on light and well-proportioned pillars.

During our halt of one day at Bheelwarra we heard of General Roberts being actually before Kotah. We were most unwilling to believe that he had advanced without waiting for us, who have been making such efforts to join him. We still hope that the information is premature; but our uncertainty will cease on our arrival at Jehazpoor, four marches from hence, where Colonel De Salis will receive a communication from the general commanding the division.

Three days before our arrival at Bheelwarra we buried the first man who died during our march. He had long suffered from depression of spirits—a sure forerunner of disease in this climate—and died of dysentery while being carried on the line of march. Our hospitals are now filling, nor can we wonder at it, as so many of our men have to undergo the unusual exertion and exposure to the sun consequent upon attending to their own horses, a thing forbidden in this country, where it is customary for all European regiments to have native grooms. In one troop of the 8th Hussars at this time there are but five *ghorawallahs*, the rest having absconded soon after leaving Deesa; at which place they were hired, and where they mostly received wages in, advance. Our soldiers are thus much exposed, especially in having to transport large sacks of grain from the commissariat to the troop lines.

On the second day's march from Bheelwarra, we readied at sunrise a wide plain with a cluster of trees which sheltered a large tank. Behind them rose the walls of a palace which, at a distance, appeared beautiful and fairy-like enough, to gratify the ideas usually entertained by those who have never seen them of the architectural beauties of eastern buildings. This turned out to be the residence of the Rajah of Shahpoora, who, soon after our arrival, came with several elephants, and an escort of mounted men, to inspect our camp.

Later in the day, when we proposed visiting the building which had caused us so much admiration in the morning, we were told by an officer returning from it, that it was a mere ruin of paint, and plaster, and dirt. And yet India can boast of one building, the purity and beauty of which is as transcendent as it is wonderful and glorious. I allude to the gorgeous tomb at Agra, erected by the Emperor Shah Jehan to his wife,

Although fallen from its original splendour, it is still a marvel;

and Government allots a certain sum to save it from decay. But its gates, which like those of the shrine in the church of St John at Malta, were of pure silver, have long ago been coined into *rupees*. Tradition also tells of a door formed of agate, which exists no longer. The tomb itself is of white marble, and. the Emperor is said to have planned the erection of a similar resting-place for himself close by, connected with it by a span of white marble.

It was reported in our camp, as we marched next morning, that the Rajah of Shahpoora had sent a thousand armed men to join the force before Kotah. The warriors whom we saw on the previous evening carried matchlocks and round shields made of thick leather. A party of them, accompanied by three elephants and a concourse of followers, came into camp before sunset, and amused us by a display of horsemanship. They described circles and figures when at a gallop; they rushed forward at full speed, and then checked their horses suddenly and stood still. The process as practised in India is a cruel one. The bit is so exceedingly severe that it is not unusual to see the horses' mouths streaming with blood. After all said and done, there is no horseman in the world to be compared to an Englishman who knows how to ride, plainly and neatly turned out on a hunting morning, and mounted upon a handsome thoroughbred English or Irish horse.

The native Indian, the Turk, and the Arab carry all their bed and household appendages upon their horse's back, so that the animal, to our notion, is loaded, before he is mounted by his rider, whose seat, owing to the width of the accumulated loadings, is very ungainly. The fashion, too, of confining the horse's head close to his chest, by a tight band or martingale, deprives him of all freedom or grace of motion, and causes him to be covered with sweat and foam.

This neighbourhood, and also that of Jehazpoor, is rich in garnets, and at the latter place they can be procured, ready polished, for a mere trifle. Camp gossip becomes rife as we near Kotah, and it is now asserted that the town is defended by 22,000 rebels. The guides on our next march performed their task very unwillingly, and ours twice asserted that he had lost his way. That of the 10th Native Infantry lost his so completely that the regiment did not arrive in camp until two hours after we had pitched our tents. The consequence was, that many baggage camels went astray. As soon as the 10th reached the ground, they gave their guide a couple of dozen lashes. A dozen was also administered to one of our troop cooks, whose habit of loitering on the march delayed the men's breakfasts an unwarrantable time. I hear that he took it with perfect philosophy, and when released, laid down, and slept the remainder of the day; but the next morning the breakfasts of the E Troop were ready before the rest.

On the 26th March, for the first time, we felt the hot winds. They blew like blasts from a furnace, inducing a thirst that nothing could allay. One officer, complaining of this, said "I drink twenty-five hours out of the twenty-four, and yet cannot quench my thirst."

Mr. Russell, *The Times* correspondent, writing a short time later, thus describes his sensations, which I quote, as entirely resembling my own;—"The hot winds, which set in about ten o'clock, are all but intolerable, charged as they are with dust, which fills every pore and fires the blood—which seems to penetrate the internal mechanism of the body, as it does, in reality, force its way into the works of a watch—which renders an out-of-door exercise a sort of severe penitential infliction, and makes dwelling in tents utterly miserable and hopeless."

To the increasing heat, he goes on to say, "will be added length of days, greater power of the wind, and, if possible, more dust. Of the latter it is quite beyond the power of description to give an idea. It is so fine and subtle, that long after the causes which have raised it have ceased to exert their influence, you may see it, like a veil of gauze between you and every object. When this dust is set in motion by the hot wind, and when the grosser sand, composed of minute fragments of talc, scales of mica, and earth, is impelled in quick successive waves, through the heated atmosphere, the effect is quite sufficient to make one detest India forever.

The regimental orders of this day contain a notification that on our arrival at Jehazpoor a communication will be received from General Roberts, which will probably hurry us as much as possible to the front. We are therefore ordered, to hold ourselves in readiness for forced marches. A ride of five-and-twenty or thirty miles at night does not appear formidable, after our march till after "the deep midnoon" from Jeelwarra to Amatti. The next day, according to expectation, the communication came. It enclosed a route containing six marches to Kotah, and gave no directions as to the time in which they were to be performed.

CHAPTER 6

Escape of the Enemy

Bardolph.—On, on, on, on! to the breach, to the breach!
Nyh—I pray thee, Corporal, stay; the knocks are too hard: and,
for my own part, I have not a case of lives; the humours of it is
too hot, that is the very plain song of it.
Pist.—The plain song is most just: for humours do abound;
Knocks go and. come God's vassals drop and die;
And sword and shield
In bloody field
Doth win immortal fame.
Boy—Would I were in an ale-house in London! I would give all
my fame for a pot of ale, and safety!

Shakespeare.

After a march of fourteen miles, we had set up our camp for the day at Thanna, when, looking out of our tent, we descried a riding camel with a very gay saddle, and we knew that despatches had come in. Overcome with heat and fatigue, I soon after fell, asleep in my chair, when an orderly awoke me, and said that the colonel had received a despatch, to hasten the regiment to the front, and that we were to march, at eight p.m., twenty-two miles, to Boondee. Officers were so far fortunate that they could have a change of horses, and the troopers, when they started, were wonderfully fresh.

The country through which we passed must have been lovely, although we could not see it. Our road defiled through mountain passes, with a gate and fortification erected on the summit.

Thence we descended until we reached a fertile valley, and a river, wherein the horses were watered; soon after we passed the lake, above which frown the walls and towers of Boondee, and by half-past three a.m. had reached our halting-place on the far side of the town. Several hundred .Bengalee *sepoys* were reported to be in this place, the fortifications of which, natural and otherwise, appeared of immense strength. The inhabitants manifested an unwillingness to supply our advance party, which preceded us by a few hours, but brought provisions readily enough to us.

On our arrival, at half-past three a.m., very few tents were pitched, as we only rested until the horses and camels were refreshed. I was indebted to the great kindness of the officer in command of the advance party, who, directly I arrived, insisted on giving up his tent for my use. Thick groves of mango, pomegranate, tamarind, and palm trees, formed a screen from the sun winch rendered a tentless necessary. "Boots and saddles" sounded at two o'clock, and by three p.m. we were again on the line of march.

The sun blazed down upon the white and dusty road, but every hour decreased his fierceness, a fortunate thing for us, as one-and-twenty miles still lay between us and Kotah. It was about half-past eleven p.m. when we first discerned in the distance the lights of the camp. About a mile from our encamping ground two men of the 1st Bombay Lancers, whose admirable conduct at Nusseerabaci, when they escorted all the Europeans to places of safety, is worthy of the greatest praise, met us and showed us the position we were to take up. Looking at my watch by the moonlight on arriving in camp, I found it was five-and-twenty minutes to two a.m.

During the four last miles we had heard the guns firing on the town; but our astonishment was great, on our arrival, to see Colonel De Salis reading brigade orders before the men had dismounted, to the effect that an assault was to be made at noon, and that the cavalry, 8th Hussars included, would turn out at seven a.m., prepared to take their share in the action!

This was sharp work "and no mistake." And I must say that

I observed with pleasure and with pride, that after two months' wearisome marching, after fifty-six hours of great exertion, with tired horses for which not a draught of water could be procured, without rest, or refreshment for themselves, save what the bare earth afforded, there were none who did not show that eager excitement and cheerful readiness which never seem to desert the English soldier in the field. By half-past seven the cavalry brigade marched off the ground, 1,500 strong, and apparently as fine a body of men as one would wish to see. There were 8th Hussars, and Bombay Lancers, Jacob's Sind Horse, some Belooches on their little ragged tattoos, and Lieutenant-Colonel Blake's troop of Bombay Horse Artillery.

We, who were thankful enough for some few hours rest from our saddles, whence—

We had oft outwatched the bear,

—and the 150 men left to guard the standing camp, waited with a thirsty anxiety for news. The firing on the town struck us, who were accustomed, to the ram of shot at Sebastopol, as remarkably slack—far too much so to justify the information we received last night, which was, that the town was to be bombarded from daybreak until about ten o'clock, when the infantry were to force their way into the place by the *Rajah's* gate, and the cavalry having crossed the river by a ford about seven miles up, in order to reach the only open side of the town, were to intercept and destroy the rebels should they attempt to escape. As we were not then aware that the greater part of the garrison had already fled, the plan appeared an admirable one. In theory it was perfect—in practice, however, it turned out the reverse.

At two o'clock a rattle of musketry, which continued for about five minutes, made us order the least weary of our horses, and start in the direction of Kotah, distant about a mile, and a half. Nothing occurred to interrupt us, and we rode on without any incident beyond the astonishment caused by the apparition of a lady in camp to a native infantry officer, who involuntarily checked his horse and continued staring until we were nearly out of sight.

We soon gained an eminence overlooking the river and the *Rajah's* palace, together with the gate by which our troops had already entered the town. Just as we reached this spot a great explosion took place, fatal, as we afterwards learnt, to several men of the 95th Regiment. Some foot soldiers and several of the Sind Horse were visible near the gate, and the noise made by human voices inside the walls was perfectly incredible; it was like an enormous beehive.

The heat of the sun was intense; and as we could see nothing besides the fortifications, and could gain no information, we returned to our tent. We heard the next day that while we were watching the town, between two and three p.m., the remainder of the mutineers were escaping from the opposite gate. They evacuated the town in haste, but without disorder, passing quickly over the plain until they reached a few houses known as "The Rebels Village," where they formed for their march.

It will naturally be asked—"Where were the 1,500 cavalry and artillery at this time, and what were they doing towards the destruction of the flying enemy?"

The cavalry and artillery reached the ford at the appointed time, and had traversed half its width, in spite of the difficulties which it presented, when someone with keener eyes than the rest discovered what he declared to be a gun pointed on the wading force. On nearer and careful examination, it proved to be a black buffalo grazing. At last, after a good deal of delay, and some little disorder, the ford was crossed. I hesitate to describe what followed.

The cavalry and artillery were immediately halted on the river bank, and the men remained standing to their horses or lying under the trees until two o'clock, when the enemy, unable to endure the fierce assault of the infantry, fled across the plain, carrying with them their arms, ammunition, and treasure! Surely on receipt of this intelligence, the cavalry must have started in hot pursuit. No. Far from it. They remained where they halted all that day and all that night; and the next morning they marched into Kotah, and then returned to their original halting-place by the ford!

Greatly disheartened and humiliated did both officers and men feel at this ignominious termination of their gallant efforts to get up in time to take part in the siege. They were forced into this false position without any obvious reason, and at a time when a fair opportunity offered of adding fresh honour to their Crimean name. On the evening of the next day an order was sent to our camp desiring us to join the regiment at the ford. do we struck our tents and mounted our horses, starting a little before ten.

It was fortunate for us that the moon was up and near the full, for after marching about seven miles we came to the broad, broad river; it did not reach our horses girths, but its bed was filled with masses of rock and large boulders. Slowly the horses crept across, now plunging up to their shoulders as they slid off a boulder, now poising themselves on a rock which rose above the surface.

The white Arab which my husband, rode shivered and snorted at every step, but "Prince," who carried me, was calm and brave, and only lost his footing once or twice. We crossed far more easily than did the main body of the regiment the day before, when, as I am told, many horses were down. It was one o'clock when we reached the camp, and. we found all the officers astir, for the flying column which was to go in pursuit of the escaped rebels was being organized, and the orders then just issued were for two squadrons to join detachments of other cavalry regiments and artillery, and to start at daybreak.

A harassing night to men and officers resulted. Orders and counter-orders, a delayed commissariat, and other reasons, prevented the one squadron, which eventually went under the command of Major Chetwode, from marching until four p.m. It was hard upon the men to arouse them at midnight for a service upon which they were not required to start until sixteen hours afterwards! And had the brigade been otherwise commanded there would have been no necessity for a pursuit at all, for few

247

Acting Brigadiers would have halted their men for twenty-four hours with a flying enemy almost in sight. The fugitives, who had gained fifty-two hours' start, were now to be pursued by our troopers in full marching order and on jaded horses!

The 95th, 10th Native Infantry, and the artillery, with their *doolies*, camels, *gharrys*, grass-cutters and camp-followers, marched by our tent-door before eight o'clock. Amongst the camp-followers was a handsome clumber spaniel which had lost sight of his master. He came for a moment to the shade of my tent, and then left it in search of his owner. I fetched a *gindy* full of fresh water, and had it waiting for him, for I felt sure I should see his foolish, honest face again, and after about half an hour back he came. Poor thirsty dog! How he panted and lapped, and then laid down close to the water, and made himself quite at home till evening, when he wagged his tail to me, and wandered forth again.

It is a mistaken feeling of affection which brings English dogs into this fierce climate. They suffer cruelly, and are rarely long-lived. Even "Jim," the dog of many fights, who has been with the 8th Hussars ever since they landed in .Bulgaria in 1854, who went through the Danubian expedition, and was present at Alma and Balaklava, and was wounded at Inkermann—who wore a Crimean medal for twelve months at Dundalk, and accompanied the regiment on its voyage to Bombay, and on its march to Kotah—even he, although "held up bravely by the brave heart within, begins to show the effects of heat and thirst.

When leg-weary on the march, he will fall back until he recognises one of his particular friends amongst the men, when he puts his fore-paws on the stirrup-iron, and gets a ride on the front of the saddle. Great will be the grief, universal the mourning, whenever death claims "Jim:" and sturdy and quick Is the vengeance wreaked upon man or dog who presumes to molest this regimental favourite.

On the afternoon of the 1st April, an explosion took place in the town of Kotah, winch was distinctly visible in our camp. A quantity of the enemy's powder which had been parked, previously to being transported to our lines, had been left under a native guard. Some disaffected persons in the town ignited, it, and several men and two officers of the 95th were killed and others wounded by the explosion.

A *havildar* and two men, forming part of the guard, who happened to be in a shed inside the yard where the powder was, were blown to atoms. Two native sentries outside the wall never moved from their posts. They stood firm, although to have done so must have appeared to them certain and instant death. Strange to say, neither of them was hurt. They were especially recommended to General Roberts commanding the division.

An arbitrary abuse of power has for some time caused great annoyance and discontent throughout our regimental camp. No officer is permitted to purchase forage for his horses, nor even to leave the camp, until the commissariat offiicer has supplied the proper amount of forage to the troop-horses. In India every officer buys forage for his own horses at his own cost, independently of the commissariat; and now, if he purchases hay, even at a distant village, it is taken from him in case the troopers, through the neglect of the commissariat, have not received a fall supply.

To visit the failures of the commissariat upon every officer in the regiment, seems to me both unjust and unwarrantable; and I write feelingly, as in consequence of not being permitted to purchase what is freely offered for sale, our beautiful white bullocks have had no grass for two days. Of course our horses, and I believe those of every officer in the regiment were equally deprived of their grass.

At the end of this our most unsatisfactory first act, we are told that our destination is either Neemuch or Nusseerabad. We have heard today, April 8th, that the rebels, having got away from Lucknow, are making for Central India. It is thought that the delay of Sir Hugh Rose's column at Saugor has afforded them the opportunity of going southwards. It is easy to foresee that this will give us employment; so we no longer reckon with delight and certainty upon the bungalows of Neemuch. Indeed, it appears that so long as we remain in what our Bandmaster

Herr Adolphe König energetically calls "this detestable country," we must always be engaged either in flight from, or in pursuit of an enemy.

The foe that especially annoys us now is numerous, and always acting on the offensive—harassing us night and day; destroying, not only our comfort, but our clothes. It is none other than that scourge of India, the white ant. It is impossible for anyone who has not resided in the country to form an idea of the depredations committed by these destructive little insects. Wooden boxes, carpets, leathern bags, straps, saddles, linen, bridles, boots, tent and tent-poles are all equally the objects of their rapacity. Nothing excludes them but glass or tin, and camphor wood, which they cannot endure. So secret and so speedy are they, that it is no unusual thing to see the soles of boots, which have lain by for only one day, half-eaten through.

Fortunately nearly all our boxes are lined with tin; and we have taken the additional precaution of raising them from the ground on bottles. Carpets, &c., require looking to, at least twice a day; and it is a good plan to put all small leathern articles on tables, the legs of which stand in iron saucers filled with water.

An instance of antique heroism, uncommon in these civilized days, occurred during the assault on Kotah. The rebel chiefs were endeavouring to make the most favourable disposition of their forces, and one of them rode with considerable difficulty to the top of a fortification, from whence he could command a view of all that was going on. As the mutineers began to fly, and the English pressed into the town, it became evident to him, that, before he could descend, the enemy would be upon him, and escape would be impossible.

Choosing death, rather than the disgrace of falling alive into our hands, he gathered up his reins, and plunging his armed heels into his horse's sides, rode him at the parapet wall. The horse rose bravely at his last leap, and falling headlong with his rider a depth of 120 feet, both were crushed in one mangled mass together. In the days of Saladin and *Coeur de Lion*, that corpse would have been carefully gathered up, and reverently buried, instead of being left to be devoured by the pariah dogs and pigs.

We have at last received news of our flying column, which has been out for eleven days. A. despatch has come in, saying that although they have been unable to come up with the main body of the rebels, yet they have taken seven guns, and are now waiting for orders. The squadron of the 8th Hussars reports only one man sick, and only four horses with sore backs—wonderfully less than we anticipated.

On the first afternoon that there was a slight breeze, we started on horseback, a party of four, to ride into Kotah, and see as much as we could of the town. We passed the camps of the 10th Native Infantry and Her Majesty's 95th, and shortly after came upon the ruins of the bungalows that had been destroyed. The principal of these was the Residency, where Major Burton had lived, whose murder the rebels have now such deep cause to regret; and near it is the burial-ground, where his daughter lies buried underneath a handsome tomb.

The houses, pleasantly situated amidst large trees and flowering shrubs, presented mere shells, and all things around told the same tale of desolation. A large ornamental well, with broken trough, stood in one of the enclosures; but the only beings at home amongst the general ruin were the monkeys, which played among the trees, and sprang from branch to branch, as gaily as though no human blood had ever stained the soil beneath them. The fortifications which surround the town of Kotah are wonderfully massive.

We read in the Bible of persons inhabiting houses built in the thickness of the wall at Jericho, but these walls are so thick that there is a deep moat between the outer gate and that which opens into the town. The streets were so strewn with plunder, that our horses positively walked over cushions, garments, bedsteads, sofas, and Persian MSS. We had difficulty to induce them to follow such a gaudy path, and they proceeded with many snorts and shies until they gained a clearer thoroughfare. A few wailing old men and women were alone left to mourn for the city; and starving dogs and bullocks roamed about—gaunt, hungry, and grim. We went into some of the temples, but found nothing of interest. The streets are narrow and ill-paved, and the town was pervaded by that strong and pungent smell peculiar to the whole of the East.

As we were riding out of the town, we met with an enormous boar which had come in, scenting future feasts on "all uncleanness." His tusk gleamed by his dusky upper lip, and when he saw us he gave a grunt and began to increase his speed. Fortunately we were riding in single file, and he passed me and Lieutenant Hayes, who rode next, without notice; but seeing more horses than he liked, he made a dart at "The *Rajah*," who avoided him by springing up a side street. He then charged the last horse of our party. The ill-paved street was so slippery that I feared the horse must lose his footing; he did not slip, however, but wheeled sharp round, and darted off at a rate which showed that he appreciated the tushes of his foe.

The native servants are possessed by the love of plunder in an unconquerable degree. A provost-sergeant was stationed at the gate nearest camp to search all out-comers, whom, in case of resistance, he had power to flog. Several camel-drivers eluded him by concealing plundered articles in the hay with which the camels were laden; but a *ghorawallah*, who accompanied his master into the town, endeavoured to cheat "Cerberus" by tying various articles round his waist, underneath his clothes.

"Hullo!" barked Cerberus, "You looks fatter than you. did when you followed your master into the town. *Iderow* (come here), you *ghorawallah*!"

And the poor fellow, as he was unwound, bid—

Farewell, a long farewell to all his greatness,

—with, a sorrowful and disgusted face.

Having made ourselves acquainted with the interior of the town, we organized another party to inspect the outside of the fortifications. To gain those on the eastern side (the one from which the rebels had escaped), we passed through spacious

252

and shady gardens, and came upon a group of twenty or thirty tombs, some of them elaborately carved and adorned with, rich, fretwork.

Each of these temple-tombs was approached by handsome flights of steps, ornamented with. carved horses and elephants in bold relief, while colossal elephants guarded the sacred portals. Large trees added to the beautiful effect of this secluded spot, after passing which we came to the deep, wide lake, in itself a fortification.

As we neared the massive walls, flanked by towers and bastions, with buttress and moat, we saw revolting evidence of the work of death. The dogs and pigs were busy at their work, and it was frightful to see them tearing at the limbs of the dead. Near one of the towers lay two men and three horses; the latter had their legs hobbled and tied together, as though the slings had broken in an attempt to lower them from the top of the tower. At the foot of another tower lay the man who had been seen to leap over.

We scared away the unwilling dogs; and I could not help noticing, that where men and horses lay together, the men were devoured, before the horses were touched. We returned home through the gardens (needing the fragrance of the flowers), and watered our horses at an irrigated rose-bed.

About this time the inhabitants were permitted to return to the town, which, after many conferences, had been given back to the *Rajah*—an arrangement which disappointed the hopes of those who were calculating on a large amount of prize-money. At first it was reported that ten pounds weight of jewels had been seized, and that captains would receive at least 400*l.* and *subalterns* 200*l.*, but these golden visions soon faded away. However, as by general orders of April 7th a return of fighting men and enlisted camp followers was to be sent into head-quarters, it is probable that the rebels left behind them a sufficient sum for every man to receive a share.

I have been over the Residency today, and have seen the floor of the supper-room all smeared with blood. It appears that Major Burton's head clerk, had conceived a spite against him, and seeing the rebellion ripening he suddenly attacked the Residency with 1,500 men and two guns. Major Burton and his two sons retreated to an upper room, and prepared to defend themselves in spite of the odds of 1,500 against three, and of the round shot from the guns in the garden, which burst every moment through the walls.

The river runs by the back of the Residency; and the old man vainly entreated his sons, who were expert swimmers, to leave him and to save their lives. Firing from the veranda on each side of their father, for three hours, they kept the 1,500 men at bay, expecting that the Rajah of Kotah would send boats down the river to their father's relief. The traitorous Rajah sent no boats; and at last they were wearied out and overpowered by numbers. The blood-stains are still visible on the floor where they fell, and across which they were dragged, that their bodies might be flung over to the populace below.

On the 9th. April the force before Kotah began to disperse. The left wing of the 8th, under Lieutenant-Colonel Naylor, marched for Nusseerabad, expecting to go into cantonments there; and on the 16th the detachment of Sind Horse also left us, having before them a playful little march of 1,200 miles to Jacobadad.

CHAPTER 7

A New Brigadier

Trait'rous knaves, with plots designing,
Trembled at our sheathless sword,
Knowing that; its splendrous shining
Was the glory of the Lord.
The sunbeams are my shafts, with which I kill.

Shelley.

I have lived my life, and, that which I have done
May He himself make pure! But thou,
If thou shouldst never see my face again,
Pray for my soul.

Morte d'Artur.

The flying column returned on the morning of the eleventh of April, bringing with them the captured guns and a considerable quantity of ammunition. They had pursued the flying foe as rapidly as possible, obtaining as they went very little information, and that little, vague and unsatisfactory. Once they heard that the main body of the rebels was sixty miles ahead, and it was debated whether the cavalry should push on the whole distance at once., but this plan was wisely rejected; for, independent of the fatigue, the exposure of Europeans to the sun must have been attended with fatal consequences.

When they had penetrated as far as the borders of Gwalior, they learnt that the fugitives, whose track was marked by the bodies of slaughtered men and women, had buried their treasure and dispersed. During their flight a number of *sowars* always preceded the rebel force, and pressed all the carts and bullocks of the village., and any attempt at opposition was answered by death. By these means their march was never hindered for want of transport. The exhausted horses, or bullocks, were unharnessed and turned adrift, while pressed ones took their places. So great was their haste, that if a cart broke down it was pushed aside out of the road and left.

At one village the atrocities they committed were so outrageous, that the inhabitants, in desperation, rushed out to attack them under cover of the night, crying, "The English are coming! the English are coming!"

The effect of this war-cry was magical. Like the Syrians of old "they arose and fled," leaving their camp as it was. The seven guns thus abandoned fell into the hands of the pursuers, who were in reality nearer at hand than the brave villagers had supposed. Some distance further on an eighth gun was discovered among some bushes. We rode up the next day to inspect the guns, which are of brass. One is a small camel gun; and the rest, although possessing great weight of metal, will only carry a shot of about five and a half or six pounds.

I mentioned before, that amongst the cavalry at Kotah, there were detachments of Jacob's Sind Horse, and also of Belooches. The former, judging by those we saw, must be a very fine body of men. No married man is enlisted into the corps, or permitted to remain in it; and the anxiety of the Sindians to be admitted into it is said to be very great.

The candidates, if satisfactory in other respects, are mounted on horseback, without a saddle, and with a plain watering-bridle. They are then taken to a steeple-chase ground, extending over two miles, and supplied, artificially and naturally, with every kind of obstacle, and told that the first men in will be chosen. Even before I had heard of this initiatory process, I used to admire these dashing riders, who sat so easily on their horses, and looked so well.

During the expedition of our flying column there was a ford

to be crossed—deep, wide, and difficult; but they made no check. Plunging into it, they splashed and scrambled through it in ten minutes; while it took our people, with their steadier notions, twice that time to cross. They are allowed a certain sum, out of which they provide their own horses, or Government perhaps would hardly approve of such expeditious movements.

The Belooches are a kind of Indian Bashi-Basouks. They wear their own dress, ride their own *tattoos* (little native ponies), and are the most inveterate plunderers. On entering a village they disperse and scramble over the roofs, or in at the windows; anyhow, or anywhere, so long as anything in the shape of booty is to be obtained. On one occasion, a native of one of the large villages came, with clasped hands, to prefer a complaint "They have robbed me and my wife of everything that we possess; we are stripped, and utterly ruined."

The accused were searched, in spite of profuse protestations of innocence, but nothing was found At last suspicion was directed to a saddle; it was taken from the horse's back, and when the lining was ripped open, the stuffing was found to be composed of shawls, scarfs, turbans, and money.

"Yes," said the plundered victim, "these are mine; but these are not all, there are yet more shawls."

The ingenuity of the searchers was at fault, until somebody bethought them of the nose-bags of the horses. There was grain in each; but when the bags were turned upside down, with the grain fell out the missing property. The officer commanding the Belooches having been requested to punish the guilty men severely, as a warning to the rest, soon after sent to say that their horses would be sold and the price put into the prize fund, that they were to receive fifty lashes, to march on foot, and to be imprisoned for six months; at the same time he requested to .know whether these punishments were considered sufficient, or whether he should add anything else.

The irregular cavalry rarely unsaddle their horses, lest by doing so they should disclose the fearful sores upon their backs. So long as their horses will feed, they do not trouble themselves about anything else; but they are careful to provide them with sufficient forage, knowing that without it the little creatures could never perform the work expected of them.

The news of the fall of Jhansi, which readied us yesterday, is continued by Colonel Price, commanding the Royal Artillery here.

The head-quarter wing of the 8th Hussars, on leaving Kotah, was to march into cantonments for the hot and rainy seasons at .Nusseerabad; but as Colonel De Salis had taken a house at Nee-much, he exerted all his influence, and eventually with success, to have the head-quarters ordered to Neemoch. Courts-martial on our prisoners have been busy for some time; and on the 10th April sentence was passed upon Kedra Bux, and Alem Gha. The former was acquitted, and the latter sentenced to transportation for life, for aiding and abetting in rebellion against the Government of the East India Company. Several men have been hanged; but as these executions took place, happily for us, on the other side of the river, they did not create interest or disturbance in our camp.

The sun in this perfectly unsheltered plain grows more and more intolerable every day; and living as we do, surrounded by camels, horses, bullocks, and dogs, within a dozen yards of our tent, a standing camp soon becomes unhealthy. The thermometer in our large tent, at noon, is either 108^0 or 109^0, and in the *baychuba* (a single-roofed tent) one degree higher.

The sun blazes and blisters, and "being a God, kissing carrion," corrupts everything exposed to his fierce heat. I now feel the effects of our severe march. My strength is gone. I am unequal to any effort or fatigue, and look with absolute dread upon the horses, knowing that I shall soon be compelled to ride them, however unfit I may be. My mind—overwrought and exhausted—fell back during my illness to places long ago left, and to friends many years dead.

I fancied myself a child, once more at home. I could not account for my prolonged absence, nor why mamma had not sent the carriage to fetch me—that mother whom I last saw in my golden childhood laid out in her coffin just twenty years ago. It is satisfactory to know that our bandmaster, Herr Adolphe König, has reached Bombay, as the want of his delicious harmony has been felt and acknowledged by most of us. The band instruments, however, are all in store at Deesa, as they were found to have been injured by frequent falls from the backs of unsteady camels.

We left Kotah on the 19th of April, and recommenced our wanderings. General Roberts, with a party of his division, preceded us by one night on the road to Neemuch; whither, as we believed, we were all bound. Brigadier Smith, who had been detained on his march from Bombay, had lately joined General Roberts, and taken the command of his brigade.

We started in the expectation of making an eighteen days' march to Neemuch, with the prospect of settling in cantonments either there or at Jusseerabad. It was well we left Kotah when we did, for it is supposed to be one of the hottest and most unhealthy places in this part of India. It becomes of great importance to us to know our destination before the rains, as in consequence of having left our mess-stores at Deesa, we are quite out of supplies. No sherry, no beer—although, indeed, both are procurable in small quantities from Parsee rapacity at four guineas and two guineas a dozen respectively.

Our first march of eleven miles, to Jugpoora, was accomplished without incident or adventure. We passed the fragrant trees that shadow the gardens on the eastern side of Kotah, and then emerged upon a rocky plain, which must have given the staunch little horses of the artillery rough and slippery work. Our halting-place was near a grove of palm and mango-trees, which shelters a spring and stream of clearest water.

The next day's march, of eight miles, brought us to Hunoubra, and here we were nearly having an adventure. The camel-drivers, after each days march, take their camels to graze in the vicinity of the camp; and it appeared that some camel-drivers of General Roberts' force, which had passed through Hunoubra on the previous day, had torn down branches from the mango-trees to feed their beasts. The villagers sought to indemnify themselves by seizing two of our own private camel-men, whom they beat severely, robbed, and finally sent back to camp without their camels.

They came to us immediately to complain, and the matter was reported to the brigadier; upon which, some European soldiers, with an interpreter, were despatched with orders to bring in the culprits and the head man of the village. They came, escorted by the Hussars, and looking in a terrible fright. The punishment, however, was merely an order to refund the stolen money (ten *rupees*), and the administration of a few blows to the head man, to remind him that it was his duty to keep order. It was thought that more notice should have been taken of the matter; for the bungalow, formerly occupied by the sergeant employed to survey the roads, had been reduced by the inhabitants to a heap of ruins; and they were reported to have cut the throats of two camel-men, who passed through on a previous occasion with a European force.

Last night, during our long and rough march to Anmedpoora, my husband's horse became alarmed; and, springing aside, lost his footing, and rolled over a steep embankment. Fortunately, neither were beyond a few cuts and bruises; but when the white horse galloped wildly away across the boundless plain in the dim twilight, I never expected to see him anymore.

The villagers scowl at us as we pass. We are now in the territory through which Holkar chased General Munsen after having defeated him near the Mukundra Pass. The roads are infamous. Surely the Government of India might oblige the various *rajahs* to make passable roads through their several districts. It would very much facilitate the passage of troops, if it were productive of no other good; and would entail but a small tax upon each state.

The Rao of Cutch has made a really fine road, elevated and drained, with bridges, and in places a footpath, extending from Mandavee to Bhooj, merely on the suggestion of the Political Agent; whereas we often marched over very bad and rough tracks, which, with a little trouble and labour, might have been level and sound.

In going up the Mukundra Pass, we rode over rocky ways that for a couple of miles were all but impracticable for guns. Large masses of rock impeded us at every step, while at one time we descended a path resembling steep and uncomfortable narrow stairs, which thirty or forty men, with hammers and blasting-powder, might in a few weeks have converted into a good road. Bridges might be constructed by the same means over the many rivers, which are impassable during the rains; and which, even in the dry season, present deep, rocky, and dangerous fords. On the trunk-road, near Mahona, it was a real pleasure to see a beautiful and well-built bridge.

CHAPTER 8

Woman's Fortitude

Helas! helas! que la mort est amère!
Hier encore nous étions si joyeux—
Adieu, Marie! Adieu, ma pauvre mère!
Deja je sens appesantir mes yeux
Le Soldat Mourant

Marching, marching, ever marching
'Neath the Sun-God's madd'ning glow—
Soul-sick, weary, staggering, parching,
Following still a phantom foe.
Anon.

After crossing the Mukundra Pass, we came to Beheeborra, where the faithless *vox populi* said we were to halt for a day, as General Roberts and the rest of the division were waiting there. Besides our own brigade, which consisted of 1st Bombay Lancers, 8th Hussars, 3rd Troop Horse Artillery, Her Majesty's 95th, and the 10th Native Infantry, we brought in the heavy guns, which had been obliged to halt for a day at Mukundra, in order that the bullocks might recover the shaking and exertion of drawing the siege-train up the Pass. Before finally arranging our tent, I thought it would be advisable to ascertain whether the report respecting the halt was true or not. The Colonel's answer took me aback.

"Halt! Oh, no. On the contrary, the brigadier has just informed me that we start tomorrow morning in pursuit of the escaped rebels; that is to say, we are to march down to the Grand Trunk Road, as Sir Hugh Rose is advancing, and requires our brigade to protect his rear. We are ordered to send our sick to Neemuch, and to take provisions for a month."

So we found that there was more work to be done before going into cantonments, but we little thought at that time how long it would last. We were comforted by the assurances of all the officers who had previously served in India, that it was impossible that we could remain out another month, as the heat would render campaigning impossible.

"I remember," said one officer, "being out in the Punjaub until the 28th April, but that was quite unprecedented."

At two o'clock on the following morning (April 25th,),the brigade marched for Jubra-Patten. We were told the distance was eight miles; we found it considerably nearer eighteen. Just before reaching camp, we crossed a branch of the Chumbul River by two fords, and most delicious and refreshing was the cool water, in which our horses pawed and splashed, and buried their dusty heads. Turkey possesses a great advantage over this country in its clear fountains, with their large troughs of pure water, which are immeasurably superior to the tanks and wells of India.

The water of the latter, nearly always more or less stagnant, is often the colour of mud; and I have sometimes fancied that it has anything but a cleansing effect upon the skin. Our *bheestie* frequently goes to four or five wells, before he can procure water fit to drink; and it usually has an earthy taste, which, if not unwholesome, is at any rate excessively disagreeable. When poured into the common earthenware "*chatty*" of the country, which is very porous, and placed, in the hot wind, it becomes almost as cold as through the agency of ice. The thermometer has now risen to 114° to 115°. I hastily took up a bunch of keys winch had been lying for some time on the table in the tent, exposed to the hot wind, and had to drop them very quickly, for they burnt my fingers.

This is the anniversary of the day on which we had left England for Constantinople and Bulgaria in 1854, and of that on which we had embarked at Ismid to return home in 1856.

Jubra-Patten is a large fortified town, well supplied with water, and possessing really fine gardens, in which, notwithstanding the heat, we were tempted to stroll at evening-tide. We are unable to halt here on account of the *Rajah's* troops. They must be a lawless set, for their own *suzerain* is afraid of them, and earnestly requested that none of our soldiers might be allowed to communicate with them, or to visit their camp. He will not admit them into his town at any time, and at night he shuts his gates, and points his guns on their lines.

It was half hoped that an excuse might he found for attacking them; but nothing of the kind occurred, so we continued our wanderings, crossing a dry, but very wide river bed, believed to be a tributary of the Chumbul. At Usawarra, where we halted, after eight days' consecutive marching, we thought ourselves fortunate in securing a group of trees,(beneath which the brigadier and staff and several officers pitched their tents. The shade was an inestimable blessing in the daytime, but we soon learned the disadvantages of sleeping where a free current of air cannot be obtained.

I spent the whole night myself with an English fan, for we had not at that time even a hand-*punkah*. We are now in the Bengal Presidency, and many of our servants, who look upon the frontier of Bombay as upon the boundary of another world, give indications of a desire to run, which obliges us to watch them closely. An officer having incautiously mentioned, in the hearing of one of them, who understood English, that we should not return to Neemuch, first caused the alarm,

Our next halt, after three days, marked by no particular incident, was at Chuppra, a large town on the borders of Tonk and Gwalior. We forded two rivers during the last march from Berodi. After passing the second, which was deeper than usual, and in the middle of which a cart, drawn by two bullocks, was upset, we met the chief man resident in Chuppra. He is secretary to the *Nawab* of Tonk, and had come out with, an escort of fifty men to conduct us to our encamping ground.

The foot soldiers of his party were armed with swords and matchlocks, and the cavalry carried blunderbusses. They rode the horses of the country, and the costumes of some of them were wondrously grotesque. The Secretary himself was handsomely dressed in a green velvet head-dress, very like the cowl of a chimneypot, and a black robe extensively embroidered. One of his officers rode a trained, charger, taught to adopt a showy and graceful prance, which had, however, entirely superseded his natural action. I inquired if he were for sale, and was told that "no price could be put upon him, but, if he pleased me, he was mine as a gift."

The inhabitants, who manifested a very friendly spirit, informed us that Lalla, with a body-guard of rebels, had lately passed within six miles of them, and that he was supposed to be still in the neighbourhood; but as he is not permitted to enter the villages, either here or in Gwalior, it is presumed that his followers must be starving in the jungle.

On the evening of our arrival at Chuppra the Secretary courteously sent an elephant, that I might ride on it to see the town. The sonorous voice of a large bell attached to his trappings, announced his approach. He was an enormous fellow, although expression almost ludicrous, of cunning and wisdom; in his little bright, twinkling eyes. His approach to our tent frightened the horses nearly out of their senses. To our disappointment there was no ladder or means of climbing into the *howdah*, unless by scrambling up his trunk or his tail, so he had to return the way he came, trumpeting to show his satisfaction, and bundling himself off with more expedition than grace. There is something very laughable in the hurried gait of an elephant. His hocks bending inward, like the human knee, suggest the idea of an old man shuffling along in a hurry.

There are here very handsome stone tanks and wells, containing deliciously clear water. On the last day of our halt, by special and urgent invitation, we accompanied the brigadier and a large party of the natives to the gardens of the *Ressildar*, "to see the fountains play." We rode through the ill-constructed and unsavoury town, and, after many ups and downs, came to the gardens, which were thronged with an expectant crowd. On our arrival, five or six jets began dribbling into a small basin in the most melancholy way, to the admiration and. delight of the inhabitants, whoso imaginations were not haunted by the memories of Sydenham or Versailles. The next day we—

Folded our tents like the Arabs;

—and as the heat of the sun renders a standing camp intolerable after a few days, we were not sorry to change the ground, and march towards Shikarpoor. The first ten miles were smooth enough; but we then descended abruptly, and came to three streams, forming in the rainy season the one enormous body of the Parbuttee River, the bed of which is composed of rock and large loose stones, affording very uncertain footing. We passed these "uncanny" fords with only one horse down, and camped in some very pretty and green jungle on the other side.

The next morning Brigadier Smith started with the Bombay Lancers, four guns of the Horse Artillery, one troop (or rather two half troops) of the 8th Hussars, the greater part of the 95th and 10th Native Infantry to Pardoun, in the hope of coming across the rebel force and capturing Lalla, who was reported to be hidden in a cave in that neighbourhood. The expedition resulted in the capture of an elephant, and, I believe, two guns. The rebels, aware that they were pursued, fled just in time to save themselves, leaving their spoil in the hands of the pursuers.

Whilst the brigadier and the greater part of the force were gone to Pardoun, the remainder recrossed the rocky fords, and moved out of the thick jungle, which was reported to contain tigers, encamping on open ground close to the village of Shikarpoor, which owes its name to the quantity of large game in its vicinity, *Shikar* in Hindostanee meaning, I believe, sport, and Shikaree sportsmen.

On the third day of our halt, while my husband and I were angling for little fishes in the Parbuttee, Lieutenant Webster came in from the brigadier, bearing an order for the force to march at

3 a.m, on Futtyghur. I was too tired with my excursion in the sun to be able to start before daybreak, and then my mind was full of uneasiness about certain bottles of lemonade and ginger beer, which I feared would be broken if trusted upon the back of a camel.

Those who have campaigned in an Indian summer will enter into my anxieties, and can judge how tenderly the bottles were laid in a circular basket filled with hay, and how carefully they were deposited in a corner of the *gharry*, Beer we had none: nor sherry, nor vegetables of any description save our old Bulgarian friend, the onion—blest vegetable, that diffuses its odour over most of the desert places of the earth. We expected to suffer a good deal from the want of necessary supplies, nor were we deceived.

After traversing a rocky, precipitous and slippery road, we encamped beneath some trees close to the fort of Futtyghur, from which the Rajah fired a *feu-de-joie* at our approach.

The brigadier, whom we found here, informed us that our destination was again changed, and that Sepree, a small station in the Gwalior territory, sixty miles from Jhansi, and situated north-east of Mhow, was to be our quarters during the rains. All hope of shelter from the hot weather we have abandoned. The heat is now at its highest, the thermometer ranging up to 118° to 119°. Bungalows, at least the ruins of them, are reported to exist at Sepree; and as it is upon the Trunk Road, we begin to hope that it may be possible even during the rains to get up supplies from Bombay. We despair of obtaining all our own special comforts left at Deesa; linen, dresses, gloves, writing paper, books, boots, lamps, &c.; indeed we shall be lucky if we see them next year.

We left Futtyghur by a stony *nullah*, through which it was scarcely possible to drag the guns; and., after about five miles, reached Jaighur, where we awaited our baggage in the friendly shelter of a temple overlooking a shaded stream, in which the men were soon busily engaged fishing; and with a very rude kind, of rod, one of them, landed a large water tortoise and some spotted fish resembling trout.

The next morning, at 3 a.m., we resumed our march and. halted at Goonah, a station on the Grand. Trunk Road, with several bungalows, the ruinous condition of which gave evidence of the ravages of the mutineers. As we approached, we wore met by Captain Mayne and an escort of the Irregular Horse he commands. We were struck with the soldier-like appearance of the party, and with the superior class of horses they rode.

One of the native officers, a large stout man with a decoration on his breast, comes from Delhi, where he possesses considerable property. Every effort had been made to induce him to abandon his allegiance to the English, but in vain. He was tempted and threatened by turns, and at last his property was destroyed. His loyalty and courage have gained for him the confidence of his commanding officers, and the sympathy and admiration of all to whom his history is known. Captain Mayne—whose family and mine are acquainted, as I afterwards discovered——showed us every attention and kindness, and endeavoured as far as possible to make us forget our harassing march.

While sitting in the cool shade of his spacious Bengal tents he recounted to us the story of his own and his wife's escape from the mutineers—a story full of anxiety and dread on his part, and of deep suffering and almost loss of life on hers; for, forty-eight hours after she was aroused in the middle of the night, and compelled to conceal herself in the garden until her husband could convey her to a carriage, her child was born. How little we know of the cases of individual suffering these mutinies have caused!

Not content with burning the bungalows, the rebels defaced the tomb of a child, the daughter of Mr. Belton, formerly in the Contingent here. In times of peace a bullock train runs from Bombay to Agra along the Trunk Road, and even now we found the advantage of being upon it; as at Mhow, only two days post from Goonah, there are several Parsee shops where all kinds of stores can do procured.

We expected to remain here for three days, and then to proceed up the Trunk Road to Sepree, only about sixty-five miles further in a northerly direction. But the 15th of May brought the frustration of these hopes.

About five o'clock in the afternoon of that day a party of natives rode into camp, bringing the information that the rebels, to the number of 6,000, had assembled and retaken Chandaree, a fortified town from whence Sir Hugh Rose had ejected them in the previous month of March. The fort was then garrisoned by the soldiers of Scindia, Maharajah of Gwalior, and the guns left in position. When the rebels attacked it, these men, after losing about a hundred of their number, ran away, leaving the enemy in possession of fort and guns. Brigadier Smith, upon receipt of this intelligence, lost no time in putting himself in communication both with Sir Hugh Rose and with General Roberts, as its occupation by a rebel force not only affected the town of Chandaree, but rendered the road between Goonah and Jhansi unsafe.

We have just had an instance of the wonderful things women can do. Mrs. Cotgrave, the wife of an officer in the 3rd Europeans, who was stationed at Jhansi, and had obtained permanent employment there, determined to join her husband. With a little graceful and delicate child of four years old, and her *ayah*, she left Poona, and travelled by bullock tram to Mhow. Here great difficulties were made, and reasonably, on the part of the authorities, as there was danger in allowing her to proceed. Fearing she would be detained, she left Mhow one night unexpectedly, and travelled in a *gharry* without an escort of any kind. As they were passing through thick jungle, the *gharry*, with its helpless freight of two women and a little girl, broke down.

The native cart, containing the baggage, had gone on, and was some distance in front. Mrs. Cotgrave's fear of tigers and wild beasts was very great; but she told me that she sat by the wayside during more than an hour, with her little child held tightly in her arms, and trembling with fear, for the jackals were screaming round her with their frightful and unearthly laugh, while the *gharrywallah* mended the cart.

After many delays and adventures, she reached Goonah; and I had the satisfaction of hearing, some time afterwards, that she had rejoined her husband at Jhansi in safety. On the 18th May, we shifted our camp, which the sun was rendering unsavoury; and on the 20th May, we again started on our pilgrimage; this time bound to Chandaree, to dislodge the rebel occupants of the fort The brigade was divided; a part of the force consisting of Bombay Lancers, and some of the 10th Native Infantry going to Kollariss. near Sepree, to keep the Trunk Road open, while the rest marched first on Pinnigutti. Here we were encamped on an open plain to the east of the Sind River, which we forded just before we set up our tents.

Many of the rebels who fled from Kotah are now forming part of the garrison at Chandaree, and the newspapers are demanding an explanation of their escape. No place in this part of the country appears to be secure. Colonel Whitclock, coming down from Agra, was shot on the Trunk Road about four days since, having fallen in with a body of rebels. We have been gratified by reading in one of the Indian papers a just tribute to Brigadier Smith's column, and to the courage with which it has supported the trials of a most harassing march.

The 95th are, many of them, now obliged to wear native shoes, their own being entirely worn out. Some of the 10th Native Infantry have been despatched from Goonah to Jubra-Patten, to bring up supplies of shoes and boots. But when will they rejoin us, or where? In the meantime the. 95th must march on, footsore and weary, as best they can. The doctors fear that scurvy will show itself on account of the absence of nourishing food, beer, and, more particularly lack of sleep.

We might almost have been said to have groped our way to Chandaree, so uncertain, unsatisfactory, and contradictory was the information afforded to the brigadier. On one point, however, all seem agreed, namely, that the rebels are in force.

On the 21st, we marched to Shahdowra, reaching our camp at about half-past five a.m., and so being housed before the sun acquired much power.

On the 24th May, the Queen's birthday, we advanced to Jharee, and, whilst on the march, came to villages which had been plundered but a few hours previously by five hundred of the rebels, who were reported to be encamped on the other side of the river, on the banks of which we were to set up our tents.

Our fighting instincts were once more aroused. We fully hoped to come up with, and account for, an enemy who appeared so close at hand. It is, however, scarcely necessary to say that no opposing force appeared to interrupt the even tenor of our, way. An extra ration of grog was served out to the men in honour of the day. The natives, who rode into camp towards evening, still persisted in the proximity of our invisible foe. They told the brigadier of a *ghaut*, with a fortified gateway, in our next march, which would probably be defended.

One of the men of the 8th Hussars remarked today: "I should like to see a live rebel; we've been going after them so long, I begin to doubt if there are any at all."

Although thick jungle, *ghaut*, and gateway would all be in favour of our enemies, very few were sanguine as to meeting them, though all concurred in hoping that fortune would befriend us. Our brigadier is so beloved for his unselfishness, kindness of heart, and urbanity of manner, that even one desires a victory on his account, as well as on their own.

The strong winds preceding the monsoon had now been blowing for two or three days, and we were in hourly dread of the commencement of the rain. In that case, goodbye to all comfort or even locomotion. Had the heavens unlocked their flood-gates at this time, we must just have remained where we were; for the poor attenuate camels that pervaded our camps, wandering with silent footsteps, like ghosts, could never have transported our baggage for another march. Twenty-four hours' rain would, moreover, have made it impossible to cross the Betwa River.

On the 25th May we left Khorwassan at daylight and marched in search of the *ghaut* and gateway. The gateway proved a fiction, but we crossed a wide river with banks so steep and difficult that it would have been an admirable place for acting on the defensive. The jungle all through the march was thick as to necessitate strong flanking parties on each side of the track; and six prisoners, whom we captured the day before, persisted in asserting that it was haunted by the mutinous forces. A single cluster of tombs, with plain Grecian porticos supported on rows of pillars, and tall bulbous roof crowned the river bank.

The brigadier and brigade-major each took possession of a house in the village. We preferred our own tent to the by no means tempting-looking rooms, notwithstanding that the brigadier courteously offered us his house. We halted nine miles from Chandaree, without having seen an enemy; but soon afterwards an exciting scene of a different kind occurred. The greatest animosity exists between Arab horses and the little ponies of the country, commonly called *tattoos*. Some of these wretched animals belonging to the grass-cutters and camp followers, strayed into the lines of the Horse Artillery.

In a few minutes their whole camp was in an uproar. The troop horses struggled, and screamed, and fought as though they were possessed. Every man, whether native or European, ran to join in the furious fray; for to quell it was impossible. Horse after horse broke loose, and galloped wildly away with yards of rope and picket-posts dangling at their heels. Those that could not fasten on the ponies, rushed at each other, and fought on their own score. The combatants were knocked down, trampled upon, and torn amid an accompaniment of the most fiendish yells.

Order was restored when the belligerents were tired, and a long list of casualties was sent in to the brigadier; all the mischief being set down to the unfortunate and suffering ponies, which had strayed in search of food. Three horses were very severely injured, and limped along for many a day behind the column, in the care of their *ghorawallahs*.

We met with a misfortune at Goonah, in the lameness of my strong and good-tempered horse Prince. He ran a splinter into the coronet of his off fore foot, whilst going at a foot-pace along the Trunk Road, and being unable to put the wounded foot to the ground, he was left in the kind charge of Captain Mayne. For a long time I used to miss his large black eyes whenever I went to visit his companions; and my regret was hardly dissipated, even when Bobby, the most independent and consequential of all little round-faced, terriers, condescended to leave his master, Sir John Hill, our then brigade-major, and to honour me with a visit which he was careful not to make too long.

We expected on the following day to appear before Chandaree, but the even tenor of our way was interrupted by a violent storm. The breeze, which had been blowing strongly all the morning, became by noon a sort of burning hurricane; and at four o'clock, after the thunder had given a preparatory growl, down came the rain. I scarcely remember to have seen a fiercer squall, for the time it lasted. Tents went down like ninepins; our hospital was the first to go, and the poor sick men were transferred to the table of the mess tent. The Horse Artillery and 95th mess-tents followed, smashing in their fall glass and china, precious, because not to be replaced.

Several private tents were prostrated, and we feared greatly that the one we occupied would go also; and it would have done so, if all the establishment had not held on to the ropes and flies.

Of course there was an end of marching at 3 a. m., as the camels, fearfully diminished in numbers and in strength, could hardly stagger along even with light loads and in a light soil. We were, therefore, compelled to wait until the tents were dry. At about halt-past nine we began to strike, and at eleven commenced to march. It was imperative to move on, as we were in thick jungle, surrounded by the enemy, and within nine miles of their stronghold; but the march, directly and indirectly, cost several lives. Two men of the 95th were struck down by the sun, and perished where they fell.

One poor fellow dropped backwards as if shot, just as I rode up, and in a few moments the convulsive action commenced in all his limbs; his lips and face became black almost before life was extinct. The men of the 95th on this day, and for some time after, marched in their scarlet jackets. The fatigue of walking in such heat is enormous, and when to that is added a close-fitting cloth dress, of course it must be doubled. It seems to me most wanton to sacrifice life to appearance in such a way.

The calculation is that each European soldier costs more than one hundred pounds to equip and send out to his country. Surely, then, from economical, if not for any higher motives, everything should be done to alleviate his sufferings, and to give him a chance for his life. I would myself on no account venture out in the sun with a forage cap and thin white cover on my head, such as the men wear; but when to that is added the dress made for and stilted to an English climate, the want of commonsense becomes still more apparent.[1]

The 8th Hussars march in stable jackets, cloth overalls, and forage caps with covers—even a hotter dress than that worn by the infantry; and the officers, and most of the men, have sheepskins on their saddles, the heat and discomfort of which are very great; but being mounted, they have not to make the same exertions as a foot soldier.

The dress of the 3rd troop of Horse Artillery contrasts pleasantly enough with those which I have described. Officers and men wear the helmet covered with white, thickly padded round the temples, loose white serge jackets over their shirts, and regimental overalls. They have no sheepskins, which make the saddles of the Hussars a penance to sit on.

About half-past three we halted before Chandaree, and took up our ground. Our march was of necessity slow, as the road lay through more than one mountain pass, and infantry in skirmishing order were sent out to clear the heights.

Lieutenant Pierce, with a party of the 10th Native Infantry, took some few prisoners who were lurking about. A reconnoitring party went out with the brigadier as soon as the ground was taken up, and it was quickly discovered that if no rebels were to be seen outside the walls, there were plenty of them within. They fired with tolerable precision upon the brigadier's

1. The 95th have since been supplied. with light and suitable clothing.

party, and the quartermaster-general very narrowly escaped being wounded in the foot, the strap being torn from his overall by a bullet. Working parties went out at dusk, to make the road passable for the guns to get into position.

The fortifications looked ugly enough, as the breach made by Sir Hugh Rose was strongly repaired, and we had only 6-pounder held guns and a couple of twelve pound howitzers, wherewith to make another. I was thoroughly tired. out with my long ride in the sun, and slept as though there were no rebels in the world. Colonel Blake had kindly offered to show me a place from which I could watch all the operations of the siege, and I went to sleep, fully intending to avail myself of his offer, but the next morning I did not wake until six, when I heard two guns fired slowly one after the other, I soon learnt that these were the guns of the Horse Artillery, and that they had fired upon an empty town.

At midnight the mutinous force had fled from the place, leaving us to take possession without the opportunity of a shot or a blow. So long as the secret intelligence department is inadequately paid, the rebels must draw great advantage and impunity from our ignorance. No native thinks it worth his while to afford information which may endanger his life for the sake of three or four *rupees*, whereas he might be tempted to run a risk for 200 or 300. Meantime our servants are acting as spies for our enemies.

A *ghorawallah*, belonging to one of the troops of the 8th Hussars, deserted soon after we left Deesa. He was found at Kotah; but as he gave a good account of himself, and the regiment was in want of *ghorawallahs*, he was taken back. Shortly after we left Kotah he deserted again and was found in Chandaree, where, with six others, he was shortly afterwards hanged. Two days after the flight of the rebels, a letter was received, stating that the Ranee of Teary, anxious to manifest her friendly feeling towards the English, had despatched a force of 3,000 men, under command of Captain Maclean, to join us. As this force was supposed to be marching from the direction towards which the rebels had fled., we hoped that it might fall in with them; but day by day went by, and we heard no more tidings of it.

Sir Hugh Rose appears to possess, in an eminent degree, what the French term "*un talent pour la gloire*" and his progress through Central India must have been most triumphant. But so scanty is the information which reaches us, that we know little beyond our own adventures, and that little, as in the Crimea, chiefly through the English papers.

On the afternoon of the day following the flight of the rebels (May 27th), we rode with Sir John Hill through the town and fort, which are surrounded, by natural fortifications consisting of precipitous hills, between which lie deep valleys clothed with green. In these are massive and beautiful tombs, standing singly and in clusters, close to the walls of the city.

We have seen no town in. India which can compare with Chandaree, and no ruins which equal in beauty its temples, houses, and decaying tombs. Tall gateways carved with delicate tracery, and a large temple adorned with elaborate carvings and filled with gods in, various coloured marbles, give an idea of the former splendours of the place. But now the city is silent and deserted; our horses footfalls ring unanswered through the streets, and the presence of one or two decrepit men and women creeping in and out of the houses only makes the desolation more apparent.

We mounted its steep streets and gained the rugged road that wound upwards to the fort. Passing through the latter we rode to the breach, and saw where the guns of the Horse Artillery had been placed in the morning, and also the position of the heavy guns, during Sir Hugh Roses bombardment. We returned in the light of sunset, and I felt saddened and depressed, for the spell of the silent city was upon me; its profound and beautiful desolation reminded me of the exclamation of Jeremiah when lamenting over Jerusalem: *How doth the city sit solitary that was full of people! How is she become as a widow!*

The place is surrounded by two lines of fortification, the outer one running from hill to hill about a mile and a half in front of the actual city wall. It was taken by the English somewhere about the year 1815, and the ruins of this outer wall even now bear picturesque testimony to having been effectually breached. A short distance beyond the outer wall is a ruin, over which. we have conjectured in vain. It is cruciform, and built with double aisles formed of two tiers of arches every way. Running along the top of the highest tier is a hollow passage, resembling the "nun's walk," or cleristery of our cathedrals.

The whole building is ecclesiastical in form and appearance. But how has the ecclesiastical architecture of Europe found its way into Central India? It stands alone—there are neither figures of gods nor tombs near it. The roof has given way, and a large tree grows on the top of the wall, from whence the wide span of the centre arch originally sprung. The walls, however, are massive and almost uninjured.

General orders containing a complimentary order respecting "the very brilliant feat of arms of Kotah," have been forwarded to the column. There is however, no mention whatever made of the cavalry, nor of the valuable assistance they afforded to the escaping rebels.

On the 1st June, Brigadier Smith having heard nothing further from Captain Maclean and the Teary Contingent, resolved to break up his camp before Chandaree and march on Sepree, Cloudy days, and several smart showers, gave warning that the end. of the fine weather was approaching, and. two large rivers still lay between us and the "haven where we would be." General Roberts and the rest of our division have been stationary long ago: and we were willing to hope that only eight more marches lay between us and the shelter we had so long desired.

Our native servants also took heart, and arrived at Mahoulie, where we halted the first day, more lively than they had been for some time. We pitched by the side of a river, deep and cool, lying in the shadow of overhanging trees. A hive of bees had swarmed in one of them; and some of the *doolie wallahs* (grass-cutters), or other necessary evils of the Indian camp, disturbed them. A scene of the utmost confusion ensued, the enraged insects attacking men and horses with the greatest vigour. Several persons, including three or four officers of the 8th Hussars, were severely stung about the face, neck, and hands. We were fortunately not in the direction taken by the bees, and could laugh in safety at the energy and speed with which. the victims sought to escape.

The old hands who had been some time in India, and had profited by past experience, ran their faces and shoulders into the thickest bushes they could find, and so escaped unstung. The day after, we moved on to Esaghur, a long and tiresome road, which for the first few miles lay through a very narrow track in the hills, where the camels could only pass in single file. The baggage was, in consequence, so much delayed, that it was after one o'clock before our tents made their appearance, and I was indebted for breakfast to the kindness of Sir John Hill.

Our march was on the ascent the whole way, and at Esaghur we found ourselves on a firm hard soil, with a fine breeze, and at a healthy elevation. On the following morning, soon after we had reached our camping ground at Koosnawier, a party sent in from Colonel Owen, commanding the 1st Lancers, brought intelligence from which it appeared that the mutiny, far from being nearly quelled, has assumed a worse aspect.

The Gwalior Contingent, which revolted last year, having been joined by reinforcements under Tantia Topee, has retaken Gwalior, a place of such strength and importance as to be called the "Delhi of Central India."

Many of Scindia's troops have turned against him, and he and his family have fled: and this, when we are within a few days of the rainy season! Colonel Owen also stated that a *lac* and a half of *rupees* had arrived at Kollariss for the use of the brigade, but that the rebels were hovering so thickly round that place and its small protecting force, that he lived in dread of an attempt being made to seize it by overpowering numbers; and requested the brigadier would rejoin him with all speed.

The prospect of the *rupees* was hailed with joyful exclamations by everybody; as neither officers, men, nor camp followers, had for a month past been paid more than was absolutely necessary to carry them on. Out of shoes, out of money, out of provisions, and getting more and more out of health, it is high time that the column should go into cantonments.

CHAPTER 9

A Would-be Assassin

Says Giles: "'Tis mortal hard to go,
But if so be's I must,
I means to follow arter he
As goes hisself the first."

Tom Brown

On the 5th June we reached Kollariss, and rejoined the force of lancers and native infantry which had been detached to keep open the communications along the Trunk Road. The ill news gathered strength as we approached Sepree, from which we are now distant only fourteen miles. The head man of this place is in great alarm. He urges the brigadier to hasten to Sepree, which he tells us we shall probably find sacked and burned; and, at the same time, declares most decidedly that he will not he left behind.

He says, "I am not a soldier; I am a pundit, a scholar. why should I risk my life in the hands of these people, whom I absolutely refuse to serve? I have been brought up with the English all my life, and have always been on their side, I cannot now change."

In point of fact, the position of our column resembles very much that of a ship at sea—we pass through the rebels, and they close up behind us after we have passed. A detachment of the 8th Hussars and His Majesty's 95th is to be left at Kollariss to comfort the soul of the chief, and also to keep the road open and prevent the *dâk* being stopped.

We started at midnight for Sepree, half expecting to find the place in flames when we arrived. Everything, however, was tranquil; a large fire lit the horizon on our right hand, but we saw no signs of the enemy. The Trunk Road was almost as smooth and level as an English turnpike, so much so, that once I was surprised into a canter. Large trees pointed out the site of the town; and when we reached the cantonment we were all delighted with the beauty of its situation, the handsome, although ruinous bungalows, and the abundant shade.

Our camp was pitched on a shelving ground of hard gravel, abounding with white ants. On the first morning after we arrived we found one of our carpet-bags nearly eaten through; but the delicious feeling that here we were to sit down and rest, overbalanced all discontent at minor evils. With what feelings of thankfulness to that good Providence who had brought us all the way hitherto did we lie down to sleep that night!

Although, on inspection the bungalows proved to be in. such ruinous condition that it was impossible to occupy them at once, still the situation appeared more and more advantageous, with its good wells, and plenty of them; its fine light soil, which would not be impassable with, the heaviest rain, and its gardens with flowering shrubs; so we spent three days in peace, and rest, and self-illusion; but on the fourth day a messenger arrived with three little screws of paper hidden away in different parts of his clothing; and on each of these twisted scraps was an order to proceed immediately to Gwalior.

A despatch from Sir Hugh Rose soon followed. He, with his division, was marching on Gwalior from Calpee, and we were ordered to join Colonels Orr and Hicks, who were also marching thither, before attempting the Antree Pass, which lay between us and Gwalior. After all, we feel that we ,have become as accustomed to marching as the eels to their traditionary fate, and are glad of an opportunity of joining forces under Sir Hugh Rose.

The report, which, had reached us, of his having gone to Poonah, of course turns out to be false; but the local papers assert that he has suffered very severely from the effects of the sun, having been knocked off his horse by it three times in one day.

On the 10th June, we marched to Suttawarra. My husband had sprained his ankle on the road from Kollariss to Sepree, and was plentifully leeched the evening before; so he had to follow helplessly in the *gharry*, which, by the time he reached Suttawarra, had nearly dislocated his bones. My "Pearl" has had his hoofs much broken, and I was thinking of taking his shoes off for a month; and "Prince" is still an invalid, in the care of Captain Mayne, at Goonah.

We had fortunately been able to procure from a native shopkeeper a small store of beer and sherry; and on the evening of the 8th, seven cartloads of stores came up for the mess from Mhow before we left. On the day of our arrival, when our men crowded clown to the bazaar, a *sepoy* of the 7th Gwalior Contingent levelled his musket (an English one) at a man of the 3rd Troop Horse Artillery, and fired. Fortunately the cap snapped; but I never shall forget the excitement with which. the men crowded round their prisoner, and brought him to the brigadier's tent. He was there recognised by a trumpeter of the lancers. He was a tall, strong man, with a very bad expression of countenance; and I am told he met his death with profound indifference, mounting the cart of his own accord, and springing off it, when the noose was round his neck.

Since the 10th of June, my pen has never been in my hand. For several days and nights the noise and stir of the camp have been but as a confused and troubled dream to me. I have been lying on my bed unconscious, or communing only with my own heart. It is sad to lie in pain and weakness amidst such stirring scenes; and to be so dependent, helpless, and exhausted, as to feel that the sleep of death would scarcely be sufficiently deep to afford relief.

How vain is all human strength and courage, when in a moment, and. in the very midst of our self-reliant pride, the will of God can cast us down and leave us to be helplessly carried hither and thither at the will of others. A few hours of illness suffice to take away that power of pleasing which gives life such a charm to its possessor. The face becomes pale and wan—no witticism sparkles from the parched lips—no laughter kindles in the eyes that are filled with ever ready tears.

True heroism is not to ride gallantly amid the braying of trumpets and all the pomp and circumstance of war, but to wrestle alone, in solitary fight, with darkness and the shadow of death. Many a one may be brave before his fellows, and ride at a gallop to the very cannon's mouth, who would shrink from the sharp arrows of pain, from the weary, lonely watching, and from all the humiliation of soul and body that weakness and illness entail.

From myself, my thoughts wandered to the great ones of old, *who made themselves mountains whereon to stand, and saw the storms of life not above their heads, but rolling far beneath their feet,*—and I remembered that they, too, were of the dust.

> *What was their prosperous estate,*
> *When high, exalted, and elate,*
> *With power and pride?*
> *What but a transient gleam of light,*
> *A flame, which glaring in its height,*
> *Grew dim and died.*
>
> *The noble steed, the harness bright,*
> *The gallant lord, and stalwart knight*
> *In rich array,*
> *Where shall we seek them now? Alas!*
> *Like the bright dewdrops on the grass,*
> *They fade away.*

Individual suffering counts for nothing where the movements of an army are concerned. The strong fight through—the weak lie down and die; and the brigade marches on just the same. But, happily, above all, watches the Almighty Power, without whom nothing is strong, and without whose knowledge not a sparrow falls to the ground.

Through the kindness of the brigadier, and of Lieutenant-

Colonel Blake, my *dooley* was allowed, to be carried near the head of the column. It was many days before I was able to sit in my saddle; and, on the first attempt, I fainted from sheer pain.

At Antree, we found Lieutenant-Colonel Hicks, with details of the 71st, 86th, some Hydrabad Contingent (cavalry), a couple of mortars, and some eighteen-pounder guns. We were then nine miles from the place appointed for the brigade to encamp before Gwalior, in order to co-operate with Sir Hugh Rose. Of course, we expected that the Antree Pass would be defended; but we marched through it without let or hindrance. I was half stifled with dust in my *dooley*, until we came to an open plain with slight eminences on the left, backed by a high range of hills.

On the foremost of the lower eminences, we saw a body of cavalry; while the enemy in numbers appeared and disappeared on the ridges of the more distant heights. Our force was halted, and drawn up. Brigadier Smith, with a troop of His Majesty's 8th Hussars, and Lieutenant Harris, of the Horse Artillery, went off to reconnoitre. We saw them the whole time going down at an easy gallop. Pain was forgotten at such an exciting moment, and I got out of my *dooley* and stood to watch. When they approached the hill on which the cavalry was drawn up, a battery, hitherto masked, opened upon them, and, as they turned to gallop out of range, we saw one or two men and horses fall, and a dark spot remain stationary.

Just before the guns opened, Lieutenant Harris was riding, unconsciously, of course, straight at the battery, and it was extraordinary that he was not hit. The brigadier's horse, slightly wounded in the stifle, fell and rolled over him, bruising his rider severely on the temple, and spraining his wrist. He was not one to make the most of a grievance, and it was not until his face and hand were swelled and discoloured, that we found out he had been hurt. As soon as the reconnoitring party returned, Colonel Blake's troop of Horse Artillery clattered down at a gallop; a squadron of the 8th Hussars followed, as also part of the lancers, the 95th and the 10th Native Infantry.

It proved that the enemy's cavalry was drawn up behind a

nullah, wide, deep, and full of water. To cross this the Horse Artillery had to change their course, and. to find a fordable place; but into it, without hesitation, rushed Major Chetwode, Lieutenant and Adjutant Harding, weighing over fifteen stone, and Sir John Hill, whose horse fell and rolled over him.

The rebels, after some smart firing on both sides, galloped away to the heights taking their guns with them. It was said that they fired six-pound shot out of nine-pound guns, which accounted for the very long range at which their shot fell. The 95th and 10th then commenced skirmishing up the heights, under a heavy fire from an earthwork battery.

A troop of lancers and hussars had been sent out to scour the plain, and see that none of the rebel cavalry were lurking about. These, returning at a gallop in rear of where the baggage camels and baggage guard were drawn up, caused a momentary check to the proceedings in front, as it was reported to the brigadier that columns of dust were seen in rear of the baggage, and that the enemy were about to attack it.

About this time the wounded began dropping in, and *dooleys* were seen in the distance, bearing their freight of pain and blood to where the surgeons were awaiting them. The first contained poor Berry, a bandsman of the 8th Hussars, whose leg was so fearfully shattered that immediate amputation at the hip was considered necessary; and was, I am told, most skilfully carried out by Dr. Lockwood, 8th Hussars, the poor patient being under the influence of chloroform.

When first struck, he knew his wound was mortal, and half an hour after the operation he had ceased to live. Then an artilleryman came galloping wildly in, with bare head, and with his shoulder and his horse's quarters splashed with blood. Happily, however, his wound was slight; a shot had carried on his helmet and grazed his head and ear. But more and more came in; some wounded, some dying of sunstroke; and the doctors have full employment. Another amputation this time in the artillery hospital; and still the 95th and 10th are steadily skirmishing on, and the artillery and cavalry have advanced until they are out of our sight.

The voices of the guns (how eagerly listened to by those who were detained by duty or sickness in the camp!) told us that our force must be gaining ground, as they became less and less distinct.

Lieutenant Reilly, killed by sunstroke within a few minutes after having ridden a dashing and eager charge, was brought into hospital; and later in the day he, with poor Berry and two other men, one a non-commissioned officer, was consigned to a hastily-made grave, with as much care as circumstances would allow.

About four o'clock came an order for the baggage to move up three miles, and to halt on the very heights which in the morning had bristled with the enemy. As soon as my *dooley-wallahs* had conveyed me to the first height, I met Brigadier Smith, who told me that they had ridden right through the enemy's camp under the fort; and that if the troops had not been completely exhausted (neither man nor horse had broken fast since the previous evening), and dropping out of their saddles from the extreme heat, he would have routed the whole outlying force, and held the suburbs of the city.

This brilliant day's work was achieved solely by our tried and jaded column. Had Sir Hugh Rose been able to afford them the slightest assistance—had he even sent out one European regiment—they would have destroyed the whole of the enemy's camp. When we took up our position for the night, the evening was drawing in, but not sufficiently to prevent the enemy, who occupied the opposite heights, from annoying us with their shot. I could not help laughing at the effects of the first one that came.

It hurt nobody, but pitched in the middle of a cluster of camels and their drivers, causing the most direful confusion and dismay. One nod one way, another ran another. The *dooley-wallahs* seized their loads, and ran for their lives. But when it became dark, and the shot still came, it was not quite so amusing. Everything was avoided that could attract the notice of the enemy;

no tents were pitched, no fires were lighted, and no fires entailed no dinners.

As I had taken nothing but a biscuit and a cup of tea, kindly given to me by Lieutenant Mayne, 1st Lancers, at seven a.m., and another cup of tea charitably sent me at four p.m. by an utter stranger, Dr. Brodrick, I started in the dark in search of something to eat; and meeting my husband and Lieutenant Hanbury, both on the sick report, who were on the same errand, we at last found the messman, and secured two bottles of beer, as hot as though it had been boiled, but still better than nothing.

After this I betook myself to the *gharry*, and my husband to his *dooley* alongside. We then slept until morning, when, as there was no firing on the camp, and the sun was very hot, the tents were pitched. There was not a blade of grass for horses or bullock, but there was a little grain left, and we hoped that they would, at any rate, got a day's rest.

About eleven o'clock, as soon as the enemy saw that we had made ourselves comfortable, down came a shot close to our tent. Another and another followed; then they fired from another gun at the horses of the artillery, and afterwards at some carts in a *nullah* close by. For two hours they kept harassing us in this way, until at last an 18-pound gun, with two elephants, was sent on to our advanced height. I was not sorry when I heard his glorious voice, for it was too bad to allow the enemy to knock our camp about as they pleased.

The trail of the carnage, however, broke soon after our great friend was brought into action; and when he became silent the rebels resumed their fire, killing several horses, one in the midst of our picket, and wounding the wife of an artillery *ghorawallah*. Towards evening we rode out to see what we could, and as we were returning a shell burst so directly over our heads that it was a wonder to myself as well as to others who saw it, that neither my husband nor I was hurt.

Not long after, whilst I was superintending the packing of our camels, the load of one of them was struck by a shot nearly spent. The animal spun round and round two or three times, and then fell down, but was unhurt.

About ten o'clock the next morning Sir Hugh Rose's force made its appearance, and an order was given to shift the camp round the spur of the hill, where it would be safe from shot. The thermometer all this time ranged at 114°. In less than half an hour after we had moved our tent the shot came whistling over and about it, and all hands had to be again mustered to unpitch. Finding that quiet and comfort were out of the question, we mounted our horses, my husband with great difficulty, for his foot was enormously swelled and very painful, and rode across the heights to see what the movement in Sir Hugh's camp signified, little thinking that we were to be the spectators of a battle.

All the artillery and heavy guns were moving out of camp, also the cavalry, and plenty of infantry. Our brigade was nearly all out, and we presently saw the 86th and. 95th ascending the hill in skirmishing order to take revenge upon our enemies for the mischief done by their guns. We joyfully watched them ascending, for we knew that if Europeans cannot stand against our infantry, no native Indians would, entertain the notion for a moment. The Horse Artillery and cavalry were now slowly and steadily advancing towards the large, level plain in front of the stern fort of Gwalior, which rises on a rock, abruptly, something after the manner of Stirling Castle.

Sir Hugh Rose was very unwilling at first to bring on a general action, but soon saw that unless he drove the enemy forward they would, steal round, the hills, and fall upon our rear. The infantry gained the heights, routed the rebels, took their guns, turned them on the flying foe, and under their cover, the cavalry got quickly into the plain. Here we followed. them, in time to see the 8th, Hussars, at least one squadron of them, led by Captain Heneage and Captain Poore, fully atoning for their forced inactivity at Kotah. The rebels were driven quite to the other end of the plain, amongst some trees; the artillery then rattled in, and gave them such sharp practice, in spite of the grape and shrapnel they sent in return, that they were soon glad to leave.

Presently, away they went, hundreds of horsemen, racing as

though they were after a fox, and closely followed by the 14th Light Dragoons and 8th Hussars. In the battery from which I was watching there were two 18-pounders, one of which was quickly swung round, and opened on the flying mass. Unhappily its range was too short.

Away they sped, and soon dense clouds of dust hid from our eyes the last traces of that discomfited host. It then became necessary to scour the plains, lest any should be found lurking in houses or under topes of trees. The impulse to accompany the cavalry and artillery was irresistible; and I never, never shall forget the throbbing excitement of that short gallop, when the horse beneath one, raging in his fierce strength, and mad with excitement, scarcely touched the ground. We halted beyond the enemy's cantonment, and underneath the grim walls of the fort. Of course we expected some remonstrative guns to open on us, or some notice to be taken of this very forward movement; but all was silent and still. We could not account for this inaction on the part of the gunners in the fort.

It was now growing dusk; and as nothing more could be done, my husband and I turned our horses' heads back to the camp, promising to send out a camel laden with provisions for the officers, and another for the men, as neither had broken fast since breakfast, and there was no prospect of their doing so within any definite time.

We learned afterwards that several of the mutineers, who were unable to get away with the main rush, had hidden themselves in the village, or rather cantonment, through which we passed, but they did not fire upon us, dreading, perhaps the consequences of attracting notice. It was just by these cantonments that Sergeant Lynch, paymaster clerk, 8th Hussars, was shot during the action of the 17th.

Of course, holding the appointment he did, he had no business to have gone into action; but it must be difficult for any soldier who is worthy of the name to keep himself back in the day of battle: at any rate, there they all were, orderly-room clerk, schoolmaster sergeant, and paymaster clerk; of these volunteers one was killed, and a second wounded, in endeavouring to save the life of his comrade. The bodies of several of our non-commissioned officers and men who had fallen the day before were found in the cantonments mutilated. One was lying near some burnt haystacks, half roasted away; Sergeant Lynch was beheaded; and three others were discovered in the Lushkar, also with their heads cut off, and hanging up by their heels.

Our infantry on the evening of that triumphant day penetrated into the town of Gwalior, and in several cases were met by the servants of the Maharajah, bringing thorn champagne and beer—a most grateful draught for the parched throats of those stalwart, grim, and dusty men.

On our return I found myself terribly exhausted and in great suffering, for I could not sit in my saddle, unless under circumstances of strong excitement, without tears being forced from my eyes by sheer pain. When the *reveillée* sounded at four on the following morning, we became aware of the deep and stifling dust, which seemed more than human philosophy could endure. My *charpoy*, hair, and eyes, as well as the breakfast that we managed to secure before starting, were merely a compound of dust.

The water in the bath it was impossible to use—not only was it the colour of bitter beer, but the dust floated in a scum upon the top. So I crept on to the back of my pretty little horse, sobered after his work and scanty food of the previous day, and, with my husband and Lieutenant Hanbury, both invalids like myself, moved after the force, which had been ordered to encamp by the side of the fort, and in front of the town of Gwalior.

On asking what had occurred, I was told that about two hours after we had left the division of Horse Artillery, they were ordered back to camp. The rebels had fled; but although the soldiers were gone, the guns of the fort kept on firing at irregular and distant intervals during the night. In the morning when the troops went in to garrison the place, they discovered some eleven or twelve fanatics, only two of whom knew how to fire a cannon. They were very soon despatched by the infantry, having proved that, like the six hundred Marsellaise immortalized by Carlyle, they "knew how to die."

The two men had spent the night in going round to the various guns, all of which were loaded, and appending slow matches to them, so that, of course, when the match burned down they exploded. We reached the fort in time to see the greater part of the procession, consisting of Scindia, his family, and retainers, who, escorted by a guard of honour, composed of 8th Hussars and 14th Light Dragoons, returned in state to occupy the palace, from which he had fled some weeks previously, and to resume the government.

Sir Hugh Rose, the brigadiers, and their respective staffs in full dress, accompanied the Maharajah on his entry. He dismounted, entered his palace, and ascended to the *durbar*, leaning on the arm of Sir Hugh. Various ceremonials, more tedious than interesting, were gone through. Betel-nut and rose-water were handed round, the whole assembly was crowned with garlands of flowers, proclamations were made, and Scindia was reseated on his throne in the presence of all the chief men of Gwalior.

Our first care, on shifting ground, was for the poor sick; their numbers had increased terribly during the fatigue and exposure of the last three days. In the Hussar Hospital alone, for one wing of the regiment, there were thirty-six patients, all suffering more or less from prostration of strength. For them there was no remedy, but absolute quiet and perfect rest.

The total of the 95th Regiment then in hospital was eighty-five men, and the only two medical officers, at that time attached to them, were also sick. It was afterwards found necessary to augment the medical stair for this regiment to a principal medical officer and three assistant-surgeons. None, but those who have gone through it, can tell the effects of a hot-weather campaign upon the nervous system. The constitution becomes completely shattered and broken up.

Our own sick (8th Hussars) were placed in some handsome buildings, surrounded, by a large garden, a little to the left of the camp; and Dr. Lockwood, whose soil and kindness of heart made him of great value, took up his residence in a temple, within the same green and pleasant enclosure. The centre building in this extensive garden was left unoccupied, as it had evidently been resorted to by the wounded rebels during the three previous days, the walls and floor being splashed, and, in some places, covered with blood.

After all, I do not imagine that the slaughter on the 17th and 19th June was very great. We saw a good many bodies lying about in different directions, some of them bearing marks of frightful sword-cut wounds, but none of the masses that we remember in the foughten fields of the Crimea.

The next morning, four-and-twenty hours after the evacuation of Gwalior by Tantia Topee and his followers, the Agra Brigade, under command of Brigadier General Napier, started in pursuit; they were reinforced by a squadron of the 8th Hussars, and Sir Hugh Rose followed with a part of his division.

Very heavy firing was heard by us in camp, from about nine a.m. till noon. We could tell that some severe engagement was going on, and later in the day the information was brought that the rebels had made a stand at an entrenched camp about twelve miles from Gwalior. A division of the 3rd Troop Horse Artillery, under command of Lieutenant Le Cocq, with a troop of 8th Hussars, went out later in the day to reinforce.

The bodies of several *sepoys* and horses lying about in the vicinity of our camp soon made it advisable that we should change our ground. Before doing so my husband and I had the pleasure of dining with Sir Hugh Rose, whom we had not had an opportunity of meeting since we came into this country, and it was pleasant to renew an agreeable acquaintance commenced in the Crimea. He shows that the Indian sun is no respecter of persons, for he looks worn out with this deadly climate.

The brigadier and staff, including my husband, took possession of three bungalows which had served as habitations for the native officers of the Contingent. They were situated in front of the cantonments through which the cavalry and artillery passed on the evening of the 19th, after the rebels had fled. They were built of mud, plastered, and very thickly thatched or *chuppered*, and consisted of a small dark room in the centre and a veranda open on each side.

The strong breeze, herald of the monsoon, began to blow on the morning after we had established ourselves in. these residences, and however much reason we had to rejoice in the thick roof over our heads, we soon found that the whirlwinds of dust which came sweeping and swirling through the building, without any intermission day or night, superadded to the intolerable heat a nuisance still more insufferable. This, together with a matter that was causing me considerable worry and annoyance, made our residence in the native officer's hut at Gwalior painful beyond words.

However, time and the hour wear through the longest day, and we soon changed our camp, although perhaps not much for the better. Whilst the arrangements for shifting quarters were in progress our squadron came in, bringing with it the welcome news that not only had they overtaken the fugitives as before recorded, but they had taken from them five-and-twenty guns, besides inflicting heavy loss. These, with the guns taken in Gwalior and its neighbourhood, amount to sixty in all.

The loss on our side has been totally inadequate to the work done. The 8th Hussars lost one officer (from sunstroke), Lieutenant Reilly, and seven non-commissioned officers and men. The 3rd troop of Horse Artillery had one man killed, and I believe, three wounded, and the loss of His Majesty's 96th was proportionately slight. The Bombay Lancers sustained a loss in a favourite young officer, Lieutenant Mills, shot through the body. The sun fought against us, and proved nearly as formidable as the guns of the enemy.

On the 24th. of June we shifted camp about two miles. Gwalior and Agra are considered the two hottest places in Central India, and the ground to which we removed, barren, sandy, and surrounded by hills, afforded no advantages in the way of coolness. The rains, too, it was evident from the appearance of the sky, would not keep off much longer, and Brigadier Smith. was anxious to start on his march to Sepree before they rendered his doing so next to impracticable. Delay, however, intervened, and on the 25th of June the thunder began to peal, and down came the rain.

We were new to a tropical climate, and I shall not easily forget the first day of the Indian rains; all the morning the heat had been intense, the sky glittering and bright, and the birds gasping with open beaks. Rapidly the sky became overcast; and almost without further warning, in a moment, came down such a pour of rain that I can only compare it to a waterspout. The plain, which a quarter of an hour before had made us miserable with clouds of dust, was now a pool of muddy water, which in half an hour reached the knees of those who were adventurous enough to walk about.

The horses at their pickets were standing in a pond; the deep dry *nullahs* were transformed into rushing rivers; the 95th, who had established their cooking places in one of them, had not only their dinners but their cooking vessels carried away. A piece of undulating ground in front of the Horse Artillery lines became so full of water that the men began to bathe, and a *bheestie's* bullock had to swim across. Enormous green frogs suddenly appeared, and in such numbers that their croaking kept me awake the greater part of the night. But the most severe annoyances connected, with this deluge were the winged. ants, which appeared as soon as the lamps were lighted on the first evening of the rains; the light had. no sooner been brought than it was obscured, and nearly extinguished by these insects, which came in whole hordes at once.

At first, dinner and the ants seemed incompatible; but an officer who had served for some years in India suggested the removal of the lamp to the farthest corner of the tent, where it was placed upon the floor; the ants, following the light, clustered and buzzed round it, leaving us to eat in darkness certainly—but in peace. The next day there was a. renewal of the heavy rain, utter which the sky cleared, and no more fell for a fortnight

Sir Hugh Rose's despatch, forwarded as early as possible after the evacuation of the city, appeared in some of the local papers. It was written for the telegraph, and was necessarily concise;—

"Gwalior" (so it ran) "taken, after a general action of five hours and a half."
"The Ranee of Jhansi killed."

Now as this message was worded, the whole of the fighting on the 17th was ignored. Although there can be no doubt that the easy afternoon's raid on the 19th was attributable to the lesson taught the rebels by Brigadier Smith's force on the 17th. They were also concentrated by being driven in from the heights, and so became an easier prey when attacked by Sir Hugh Rose, in conjunction with Smith's brigade, on the 19th.

Two messengers had been despatched to Sir Hugh Rose on the 17th, during the action, but no assistance was sent; and we heard afterwards that the division could not account for the heavy firing which they heard, but concluded it was the mutineers quarrelling amongst themselves!

With regard to the Ranee of Jhansi, nothing is known with certainty, except that she was killed. Various stories got afloat; amongst others, that she was run through the body by a private of the 8th Hussars, who, as she was dressed as a man in a white turban and crimson tunic and trowsers, had no idea that his sword was pointed at the breast of a woman. Another story had it that she died, not from a sword-thrust, but from two shot wounds.

Sir Hugh Rose told me, that although mortally wounded she was not actually killed on the field, but was carried off the ground, and ordered a funeral pile to be built, which she ascended and fired with. her own hand while almost in the act of dying; an instance of fierce and desperate courage that I can only listen to with wonder. At all events, on the 17th of June her restless and intriguing spirit passed away: a subject of regret perhaps to those who admired her energy and courage, but of congratulation to all who are concerned in endeavouring to settle the intricate and disturbed affairs of this unhappy country.

CHAPTER 10

The Massacre at Gwalior

The fated hour is come—the hour whose voice
Pealing into the arch of night; must strike
These palaces with ominous tottenngs,
And rock their marbles to me corner-stone.

Byron.

While we were in camp before Gwalior news reached us that the eyes of another of England's best and bravest had. closed in death. Sir William Peel, the Bayard of our modern chivalry, who risked his life so freely in the batteries before Sebastopol, and had so many hairbreadth escapes, that he used to say, "the the bullet was not cast which was to kill him;" after distinguishing himself as nobly in India, has fallen a victim to smallpox.

Although we had changed our ground, the purer air brought no alleviation of my husband's suffering; nor did it raise me from the mental and physical prostration which overwhelmed me. The kindness of the brigadier induced him to think the situation of our tent not sufficiently healthy, so he procured for us an introduction to Major Macpherson, the political agent at Gwalior, who, with that princely hospitality which is, I suppose, only to be met with in India, immediately placed a suite of rooms at our disposal in the part of the Maharajah's palace in which he resided.

The Maharajah's palace, when I first saw it, suggested two ideas: the first was an Italian *palazzo*; the second, a feudal castle.

Its graceful arches, pillars, and flat-roofed verandas, rise round three sides of a large square. Windows It has none, the interior being screened from the sun by crimson satin *purdahs* trimmed with gold. Large *tatties* of camel thorn fill some of the spaces between the pillars, and as they are kept constantly wetted by men employed solely to dash water against them, they cause the hot air which passes through them to become of a refreshing coolness.

Natives in white robes, with turbans of crimson or green, flitted through the inner archways or sat upon the flat roofs of the verandas; while in the square or yard of the palace eighty horses were picketed, and the armed retainers waited, ready at a moment's call. Separated by a small garden from the principal building is another palace, set apart for the occupation of the Political Resident, since the frightful mutiny of 1857 destroyed his house and every vestige of his property.

The history of Gwalior, from May 1857 to June 1858, has been eventful enough. In the month of April of the former year the Maharajah and his ministry had reason to fear that an outbreak was likely to occur; and, in consequence, Major Macpherson caused all the women and children to be withdrawn from the cantonments, and placed in his apartments in the palace; an arrangement which, as the officers of the contingent steadily refused to believe in the approach of danger, was received on the part of the ladies with many complaints and much, discontent.

The cloud having apparently passed over, the ladies were let out of durance. The large cantonment, which was inhabited by the English officers of the Gwalior Contingent, with their wives and families, extended over miles of ground on either side of the city. There they lived without doubt or suspicion, in the enjoyment of every luxury, and in all the listless indolence that Indian life engenders. To the last moment they would listen to no voice warning them of the disaffection of the troops.

Day by day passed on, and as the news of other regiments having mutinied reached them, they continued to assert that they would trust their men as themselves. Suddenly, even as the flood came in the days of Noah, the hurricane of insurrection burst above their heads. So unexpectedly, indeed, did it come, and so heedless were they, that even when a messenger arrived as they were sitting down to the mess dinner, to tell them that the soldiers were loading the guns, an officer, who went out to see, returned laughing, and treated the whole affair as a jest. Fatal supineness!

In less than an hour some of them had already atoned for their blindness by death. One or two officers who rushed out at the first booming of the guns never returned again. A lady, watching from a window for her husband, saw a young lad, whom she knew, fall pierced by a ball. With that impulsive courage which some few women possess, and which lifts them above heroism, she rushed to the succour of the wounded youth. Her little child, ignorant of danger, toddled after her, and soon child and mother and the friend she tried to succour, lay in a lifeless heap together:

There did not 'scape the glaive
Man that frowned, or babe that smiled.

Meantime, by the light of the blazing bungalows, the survivors, leaving nineteen of their number beyond the reach of fear and suffering, hastened away towards Agra, some on horseback, some in carts, some in carriages, some afoot. One party of ladies was taken away by some of the friendly natives, hidden in a hovel, and sent on afterwards in a country cart, concealed beneath, the goods which it contained. But how can I, who, thank God, have never seen it, hope to convey an idea of these scenes of murder—of the blazing bungalows and the utter destruction of property—of the wild flight—the terror—the despair—and the utter desolation of many a broken heart.

Well-built and handsome houses, noble palaces, and lovely gardens, were by the next morning involved in a common wreck. The town itself received, no damage. In the long white street, with its irregular houses, ornamented, with screens of fretted stone, so elaborate as to resemble perforated cardboard, but spoiled and disguised with abominable whitewash, not a stone was broken or defaced. The admirable roadway, constructed by the Maharajah, remained entire; and the bridge of minarets, and mosque of many domes, preserved their solid and beautiful proportions.

The destruction of the Residency entailed great loss of property upon our hospitable host; a misfortune which was nearly being repeated when, in 1858, Gwalior again fell under the power of the rebels, and Scindia was obliged to fly. As soon as the Maharajah had withdrawn, the work of plundering the town began systematically and in earnest. Scindia, who had spent large sums in English and French furniture during a recent visit to Calcutta, returned, on the 20th June to find it broken to atoms. Fortunately for Major Macpherson, the part of the palace appropriated to him had been occupied by Tantia Topee, and was in consequence preserved from injury, so that the large and massive mirrors, with their frames of crimson and gold, ornamented with gilt lions and horses, the sofas, massive armchairs, carpets, chandeliers, and exquisite French lamps, as well as the numerous pictures which decorated the walls, remain in their pristine glory.

Now that my energies are dormant and my body weary, I feel as if I could easily accommodate myself to the life of an eastern princess. The cool and lofty rooms, made as dark as possible, the *punkahs* and cuscuss *tatties*, and, above all, the wide paved courtyard, which affords abundant space for exercise, seem to me most delightful. I sit leaning against the high carved parapet, in which are open spaces like windows, and ensconced in one of these like a picture in a frame, I look down at my ease upon the gay and idle crowd, which presents numberless objects to attract and amuse a European; that is, so long as he can overlook it without mixing in it.

As I watched there one day, I saw the Prime Minister (of whom more anon) on his way to pay a visit of state to Sir Robert Hamilton, the Governor of Central India, who had just arrived at another of the Maharajah's palaces, about a mile out of the town, called the Phool Bagh, or Garden of Flowers. The procession was headed by seven elephants. The first of these "huge earth-shaking beasts" was of unusual size, his housings consisting of a headpiece of crimson velvet, thickly embroidered with massive gold, and edged with deep gold bullion fringe. Two small saddles of black velvet, very like regimental saddles, were on his back, and kept in their places by a crupper, ornamented with large round bosses of silver, each as large and heavy as a small shield.

A sonorous bell hung on either side to give notice of his approach; an enormous cloth of green velvet covered him from head to tail; while round his vast neck and ample throat were six or seven silver chains or necklaces, each big enough to hold a good sized boat to its moorings. His huge unshapely fetlocks were adorned with bracelets and anklets, which tinkled as he walked. In his wake followed six officers elephants, all differently caparisoned, but none of them so gorgeous as the first. After these came the led horses the priceless horses of Cattawar.

These animals, in accordance with the ideas of Indian state, are fattened upon sugar, sheeps' heads, spices, and all sorts of food, to such excess as to be incapable of any quicker pace than an ambling, shuffling walk, while their martingales of crimson silk, and the severe bit, make them arch their necks like a bended bow. After they had passed, accompanied by a horde of foot-people, some wealthy man, a diamond merchant perhaps, followed in a richly decorated *palanquin*, escorted by a train of attendants on foot.

Native cavalry soldiers, appointed to patrol the town, clattered down the street at a canter, regardless of the dogs' toes, or the horns of the sacred buffaloes which are always wandering about an Indian town, secure alike from blows or butcher; and in many cases a great nuisance, as they never trouble themselves to get out of the way of passers-by. Merchants selling their wares, beggars screaming for alms, pariah dogs, idle soldiers, and ugly women, completed the show.

On the second morning of my residence in the palace I received, a notification from the Maharanee, that she wished to have an interview with me on the following day at six a.m. I was the more pleased with the expression of this wish as the Bhae-si-bhae, widow of a former Maharajah, and a woman of very great Indian celebrity, was one of the visitors at the court.

The Maharajah ordered an interpretress to be in attendance, and escorted by Major Macpherson, I presented myself at the *durbar* at the time appointed. After passing the Maharajah's private chapel, and ascending a broad stairway, we came to an upper gallery, branching off into numerous passages, only wide enough to admit of one person passing at a time; they were so constructed for purposes of defence. These finally led us to the *durbar* hall, one end of which was screened off by a crimson satin *purdah*, into which were inserted perforated silver plates, which serve to afford the ladies a view of everything passing in the *durbar* while they themselves remain concealed. Behind this curtain was the reception room of the Maharanee.

We arrived early, and after waiting about five minutes were admitted into the presence of the Maharanee, who with three other ladies rose from their chairs on our entrance. My interpretress *salaamed* profoundly and made offerings of gold pieces, but the ladies extended, their hands to me. The Bhae-si-bhae sat in the place of honour next the *purdah*, and arrested my attention at once, both by the simplicity of her toilette and the great dignity and self-possession of her deportment. The lustre of her still glorious eyes reminded me of the light which shines through port wine when held against the light. She is over seventy years of age, but apparently as energetic as in the days of her fiery and intriguing youth, As little is known of this remarkable woman at home, I subjoin a brief sketch of her history:—

In 1779, when young Scindia had laid Holkar at his feet, and was keeping the country round Poona in alarm, arrangements were made for his marriage with the beauty of the Deccan, daughter of Shirazee Rao Ghatgay, an important Maharatta chief at the Court of the Peishwa. The Maharajah's proposals were accepted on condition that the bride's father was to be made Prime Minister. The royal couple lived happily together. A considerable family was born to them, of whom two daughters grew up to womanhood. In 1821 their favourite daughter died, and her mother was so disconsolate that she and her husband sought for some considerable time the seclusion of the country.

Throughout, the Bhae-si-bhae has been a woman of great activity and enterprise, exercising almost unbounded influence over her husband and the ministers of the Court. She was in the habit of going out on horseback with her ladies, delighting in the chase, and amusing herself with the javelin exercise. In March, 1827, Dowlat Rao Scindia died at Gwalior, and leaving no male issue, his widow was permitted to exercise the right of adoption. He had often been urged before his death to adopt an heir, but always postponed doing so, saying he wished that his widow should hold the reins of government.

Several months after the widow adopted Moodk Rao. He soon showed symptoms of turbulence and cruelty. He naturally expected to be raised to the throne on attaining the proper age, but the Bhae-si-bhae was in no hurry to resign her authority. He attempted to enlist the Governor-General, Lord W. Bentinck, and the Resident on his side, by spreading a report that the regent had attempted to take his life by means of poison.

In July, 1834, a revolt took place at Gwalior. One half of the army joined the Bhae-si-bhae, and the other remained faithful to the Maharajah, who had the great majority of popular sympathy on his side. The regent then consented to the instalment of the Maharajah, and leaving the capital took up her residence at Dholpore, accompanied by 6,000 armed men. Military tumults followed, and the Bhae-si-bhae was strongly suspected of intriguing for the recovery of the throne.

She was, therefore, forbidden the capital, and placed in

strict sequestration. Shortly after she went to Futtyghur, where she established herself in an indigo factory, her followers being hutted round her. Some months after she was assigned a residence in the Deccan, afterwards altered to Malwa, with an income of six *lakhs* of *rupees* annually (60,000*l.*) Her worthless adopted son died in 1843, when another revolution occurred, and the country was finally taken under our closer supervision. The widow of the late chief (Moodk Rao) then adopted the present representative of the house of Scindia, and with his family the Bhae-si-bhae seems to have been staying when the Calpee rebels seized the place on the 1st of June, 1858.

The Maharanee, about eighteen years old, and dressed in black and gold, with sumptuous ornaments, was chiefly interesting on account of her little child, a girl of three years old, laden with pearl ornaments. She herself was almost entirely silent, and the widow of the late Maharajah, whose adopted son now reigns, was equally so; but the old lady and myself kindled into conversation at once, as flint and steel emit fire.

"Was I the Englishwoman who had gone with the armies to make war upon the Ruski?"

"She thought I was a much older person."

"Could I ride on horseback?"

"Had I seen a European battle between the English and the Ruski?"

"Ay," she said, her dark eyes dilating as she spoke, "I, too, have ridden at a battle: I rode when Wellesley Saib drove us from the field, with nothing but the saddles on which we sat.

She made me describe all I saw of the fight on the 19th of June, and asked to see my horses. Then suddenly telling me to take off my bracelets, she, scarcely looking at them, passed them on to the other ladies, and recommenced her conversation with me. one showed herself justly proud of the beautiful palace and town wherein she had lived and reigned so long. Presently women appeared, bearing trays of costly shawls.

"These are presents," whispered Mrs. Filose, my interpretress, and in the innocence of my heart, unaccustomed to the polite fictions of Eastern Courts, I fancied that the costly shawl of crimson and gold was destined for my future wear. How gorgeous it would have looked over a white *moire* antique! My surprise was great at being told merely to take the tray in my hand and pass it on to a woman who stood in waiting behind my chair. Seven times was I thus tantalized, but as the last tray approached, the Bhae-si-bhae, taking a piece of fine white Chandarec cambric, gave into my hands, bidding me "keep it."

Numerous offerings of fruit, betel-nut, rose-water, sweetmeats, &c., followed; when my interpretress *salaamed*, the ladies shook hands with me, and we withdrew. The numbers of women in attendance made the air hot and close. We returned to the apartments of the Resident through the lines of horses picketed in the courtyard.

Soon after I had reached my room, I received a note saying that the Maharajah had signified his intention of paying me a visit and would present himself in half an hour. Punctual to his appointment he came, attended by the Prime Minister and one or two officers of State. The Maharajah cannot be more than thirty years of age: his face is swarthy and dark, with keen, but sensual eyes; and a mouth expressing intractability and self-will.

Nevertheless, he is a good-looking man, dressed in exquisite and most simple taste, and with elaborate care. He was not conversational. He has a slight impediment in his speech, and is shy of speaking before strangers. He was good enough to inquire after my husband's arm, which he carried in a sling, and to say a few grateful and gracious words about the army which had restored him to his kingdom. He expressed great astonishment that a lady should be found (he was good enough to say) of sufficient enterprise and courage to accompany an army in the field, and said he had submitted to the Governor-General and Supreme Council a design for a decoration, which he intended, to confer on our troops, and that when it was accepted, he should have much pleasure in conferring upon me a distinction so fairly won.

These words raised in me a world of busy thoughts, To have had the Crimean medal almost in my grasp, and not to have possessed it after all, had been a disappointment the keenness and bitterness of which can be suspected only by a few. It is useless now to dwell upon that mortification. If the troops are permitted to wear the Maharajah's decoration, and I should receive it, it will at least prove to me that the Indian Prince knows how to appreciate and how to reward a woman s fortitude.

I have seldom seen a man of greater intelligence and refinement of manners, or one who impressed me so favourably as did the Prime Minister of Gwalior. There was that in his serene, half sad, yet intellectual countenance, which would have made a noble study for Fra Angelica. The face was as spiritual as those of his *confrères* were sensual and earthly.

The morning after these visits, Major Macpherson changed his residence from the Palace, in the Lushkar, to the Phool Bagh, in order to be near Sir Robert Hamilton. Here we had purer air, and a fresh breeze blowing across an open plain through long, wide corridors, shaded by crimson satin *purdahs*, and cooled by camel-thorn *tatties*. This residence is more princely than the town palace; it has such wealth of space, with handsome lofty rooms, pillars, fountains, terraces, and gardens of flowers.

During the afternoon the Maharajah hearing of my love for horses, with great consideration, sent down his state horses, fully caparisoned for me to see. The one which he rides on grand occasions is a magnificent specimen of the Cattawar breed, but so overloaded with flesh as to appear almost incapable of motion. He is a deep sorrel chesnut, with two white legs; his trappings were magnificent.

On his head was a tall plume of white cock's feathers, fastened into a jewelled head-stall. The saddle-cloth was of green velvet, bound with silver lace. He had a crimson velvet *crupper*, to which were fastened long pendent draperies falling on either side, and flowing, much as a habit-skirt would do; these, with a martingale of crimson silk, tied as tightly as possible to the nose-band and saddle-girths, completed his gorgeous costume. The bit is one of the most intensely severe I ever saw, consisting of a string of spurs, or sharp spikes of iron, the slightest pressure on which draws blood.

This instrument of torture in his mouth, and the confined position of his head, made the whole action of the animal false; and compelled me to pity as much as I admired him. Presently our attention was attracted, by the sound of a horse approaching from the further end of the terrace, but hidden by trees. In a few moments appeared, in all her self-possessed and calm magnificence, a faultless thoroughbred English mare.

What a relief it was for the eye to rest and gaze upon the long lean head, the delicate, nervous neck, the deep, sloping, and powerful shoulders, the wide, muscular arms. To measure the distance from hip to hock, and to see the genuine English quarters, which beat every Arab in the world for speed. Several other beautiful horses were passed in review; amongst them, the finest and purest bred Arab I had ever seen. How short and sturdy he looked, compared with the length and grace of the English mare; and yet, if not contrasted with her, what a noble fellow he was.

I could not but look at the mare shaking the sunlight from her golden chestnut sides, and feel that she spoke to me of home, and that I loved her better than all the Eastern horses, the "Children of the Sun." That evening we drove to Morahi, to see the cantonment which had been laid waste in 1857. It was now occupied by Sir Hugh Rose's camp; but the broken walls and smoky ruins stood like spectres among the gay white tents, and told their solemn story in voices without words.

At two o'clock on the following morning, the moon was lighting us on the first of our five marches to Sepree, where we once more hoped to be allowed to remain during the rainy season, and to obtain that rest of which the whole brigade, both men and horses, stood so greatly in need. In consequence of H. M.'s 95th Regiment being pronounced out of shoes, and in too sickly a state to march, we left it behind, and it was attached to Brigadier Napier's brigade.

About this time the 8th received some small portion of their mess stores which had been despatched from Deesa on camels, under escort of the 71st Regiment. That regiment, being short of camels, had pressed some of those which it had undertaken to escort; and the loads of the animals thus taken had been consigned to the soldiers, who had emptied twenty-four bottles out of one three-dozen case of brandy, besides drinking part of the contents of several others. With a consignment of wine at Cambay, regimental stores at Nusseerabad, and others somewhere between Bombay and Mhow, we are in want of everything. We heard of our carts being pressed, and of our bullocks being looted on the road; but when the rains began, and the black cotton soil became impassable, the remains of our stores had not arrived.

CHAPTER 11

A Hot Pursuit

Down comes a deluge of sonorous hail,
And prone descending rain.

Thomson.

On the morning of Thursday, the 8th of July, Brigadier
Smith's column marched into Sepree. This was the second time
we had entered Sepree with the idea that it was to be our resting
place. The first time our stay was of very short duration, as we
were ordered off to Gwalior at a day's notice. As we now had Sir
Robert Hamilton's assurance that we should not move until after the rains had subsided sufficiently to make the roads passable
and the rivers fordable, we felt secure of repose, and shelter, and
comparative comfort, and also ventured to hope for a restoration
to health and strength.

We did not hesitate to take possession of a tolerably large
room, situated in what must have been the back yard of a ruined bungalow. The tottering walls which came crashing down
about our ears pretty frequently as the rains wore on, gave such
an air of insecurity to the whole building, that few envied us
our habitation. There was a "*godown*," or cook-house, which our
principal servants occupied, some smaller buildings like pigsties,
where the *ghorawallahs* made themselves comfortable, and a pi-
geon-house for the treasure guard.

The brigadier gave up the compound to us, so that we had a
garden and large field, an avenue, and two entrance gates; and as
the large tent was pitched near the house, we were very com-

fortably accommodated. Our horses were picketed near a deep well of clear water, and I began to luxuriate in the quiet and the rest.

The artillery occupied the lines formerly in possession of the artillery of the Gwalior Contingent, and the 10th Native Infantry went to the still habitable native lines. The 8th Hussars were partly under cover and partly in tents, and the Bombay Lancers remained under canvas; their officers and those of the Hussars occupying a large bungalow which had been left uninjured.

It was pleasant to settle down and fancy we were going to have a little peace. I was perfectly helpless, having temporarily lost the use of my right hand, and felt that unless I was allowed to sleep, I should not last much longer. I slept all night and half the day, and for three weeks never had sufficient energy to walk as far as the garden, about twenty yards from the bungalow.

Sepree is an exceedingly pretty place. The bungalows, with trees tastefully planted round them, have almost the appearance of English villas, especially in the rains, which make India as green as England. I flattered myself with the hope of remaining for some time at this delightful spot, and even went so far as to write to Mhow for mustard and cress and lettuce seeds, which, very fortunately, did not arrive. At this time I was unable to sit up for more than a few hours daily; and about the 20th of July, when I was suffering more than ordinary pain, a Portuguese servant came to me and asked some question relative to the packing of our things.

"Why do you want to know?"

"Go march tomorrow morning—Kotah!"

When my husband returned from transacting business with the brigadier, he told me it was but too true. The rebels were supposed to be in the neighbourhood of Jeypoor, whither General Roberts was gone, from Nusseerabad, in pursuit, and it was dreaded that they would establish themselves in the strong fort of Boondee, or, worse still, in the arsenal at Ajmere.

Brigadier Smith received two imperative orders, one forwarded by Brigadier-General Napier, and the other by General

Roberts, to join the division under the latter as soon as possible. Meanwhile, the heavens were flushed with lightning, and hard and steadily came down the rain. A pleasant prospect truly, that of marching and encamping in the midst of the rains of a tropical climate, risking fever, ague, and rheumatism, when we are all, with scarcely an exception, exhausted by pain and fatigue!

Upon the discovery of a *ghaut* impracticable for guns, the brigadier resolved not to attempt the shortest route by Shahabad, but to proceed down the Trunk road *via* Goonah. This arrangement possessed two advantages; in the first place it avoided the cross country trades which are at this time simply impracticable; and in the second, by marching to Goonah we ran a chance of falling in with some money, of which the brigade was so destitute that the commissariat officer reported that he could only move along the Trunk road, where we were known, as the people on the Shahabad route would refuse to supply him on credit. I was glad to find we were to go to Goonah, as my nice horse Prince was still left there in Captain Mayne's care, and I should thus have the opportunity of recovering him without trouble.

On the 30th July we still found ourselves at Sepree, and as the rains were incessant, there seemed to be no immediate prospect of leaving it. A few days before, Sir Robert Hamilton went through on his way from Gwalior to Indore; his train was three days passing through Sepree, and very soon after leaving it, in spite of his elephants, he stuck fast in the mud.

This news we heard with rather more satisfaction than the misfortunes of our friends generally afford us; for if Sir Robert Hamilton could not get on with elephants, how could we hope to get on with camels, which fall down on slippery or muddy soils and never rise again. He brought us, under an escort of Meade's Horse, a *lakh*, and a half of *rupees*, which replenished our exhausted treasury. The miserable condition of the camels which conveyed it reminded us of the gaunt specimens of that annual in the Crimea, and the poor horses too looked regularly sodden with the wet.

The brigadier having represented the inefficiency of our bri-

310

gade without European infantry, the unfortunate 95th was again detached from Gwalior, and sent down to us in carts. They were much delayed *en route* in consequence of rain, and the brigadier ordered a bungalow, with two or three large rooms, to be fitted up as a hospital for them; for he knew that by the time they reached Sepree they would require one. Two days after their arrival, as I was taking a drive in the *gharry* for the purpose of inhaling some fresh air, I met my dear Prince walking up the road, attended by his *ghorawallah*, who had brought him from Goonah without an escort.

The brigadier now received an order to consider himself as attached to the Gwalior division of the army. I am not aware if General Roberts knows that he is shorn of his fair proportions in the shape of our brigade; but for ourselves it does not much matter who commands us, as I am thankful to say the roads are pronounced impracticable.

If the loss of Sir William Peel was so sincerely regretted by us, how much deeper, because more personal, was the sorrow that we felt on hearing of the death of Lieutenant-colonel Morris, C. B., of the 17th Lancers. He was one of those rare combinations of true Christian and thorough soldier who raise and ennoble the profession to which they belong, and leave behind them a bright example to be followed by those who come after. Although, so young, he was a most distinguished officer. His gallantry at Balaklava, where he was severely wounded, brought his name prominently forward; and before that, he had already acquired fame in Indian warfare. On leaving England in October, 1857, he looked forward to India as a large held for future distinction, and yet hardly six months after he had landed in Bombay, all these visions had passed away; his sword was sheathed, his armour taken off, and his soul—

To Him who gave it rose,
God led it to its long repose,
Its glorious rest.
But though the warrior's sun has set,
His light shall linger round us yet,

Not long after this the brigade was engaged in ail unsuccessful attempt to capture Maun Sing, who had seized the fort of Powree, belonging to our ally the Gwalior Rajah. A feudal baron in the dominions of the latter, and also connected with him, by family ties, Maun Sing, after a great deal of quarrelling and squabbling, had been portioned off with a certain number of villages. But there are some people who cannot possibly live within their incomes, and avoid running into debt

Maun Sing appears to have been one of these unfortunates, and being out of pocket, he naturally became dissatisfied. He soon found himself surrounded by many malcontents, who flattered him and lied to him, until he allowed them to attach themselves to his train, and so from a troublesome relation he was transformed into a formidable foe. We knew he had been hovering about Sepree for some time, but as he distinctly avowed that his quarrel was not with the English, but was simply a family disagreement with the Maharajah, he was allowed to remain unmolested, until in an evil hour, tired of being wet through in his tent, he and his retainers ousted a garrison of the Maharajah's from the fort of Powree.

As soon as the intelligence of this aggressive movement against our friend and ally reached the ears of Brigadier Smith, he determined to start immediately in order to recover the fort. So one morning, about the 3rd of August, leaving behind him only a squadron of the 8th Hussars, another of lancers, and two field guns, under the command of Lieutenant Le Cocq, he set off to march eighteen miles along a cross country track, In the midst of the monsoon.

The force started at nine a.m., and by five p.m. had advanced about ten miles towards Powree. On reaching the fort the brigadier found it so much stronger than native information had led him to believe, that he was obliged to sit down before the place and to despatch a letter to Gwalior for siege guns and mortars, making his force, meanwhile, as comfortable as circumstances would, permit. Maun Sing came out of his fortress to an interview with the brigadier, who took him he was empowered to offer him his life if he would, lay down his arms.

He answered, "But I shall be a prisoner until my death. Of what advantage will my life then be to me?"

He stated again that his quarrel was solely a personal one with the Maharajah, and had the matter rested in the hands of the brigadier, he might perhaps have been turned into a valuable and grateful ally, having, as he represented, sufficient influence to keep all this part of the country quiet. The interview, however, terminated inauspiciously. It was the time at which the lancer picket was relieved, and his attendants, seeing horsemen riding towards them, raised a cry of treachery, and fled into the fort— whither Maun Sing followed them in haste. He sent an apology the next morning for entertaining doubts of our honour, but he ventured outside the walls no more, and there was an end to all hopes of an amicable arrangement.

Soon afterwards Brigadier Smith was reinforced by some details under Brigadier General Napier, and a siege train of two 18-pounders and two mortars. Entrenchments were dug, and guns were run into position; during which operations Lieutenant Fisher, His Majesty's 95th, was shot through the chest. Unfortunately, as usual, there was a loophole, an impracticable side to the fort, on which the jungle was so impenetrable, and the ground so broken by ravines and *nullahs*, that it was impossible to place either guns or troops there.

Moreover, the fort was large, and the attacking force was small; but, nevertheless, on the 19th of August, so sanguine were our people, that a message was despatched to Sepree for the rest of the 8th Hussars, the two guns, the 95th, and every convalescent from the hospitals; "for," said the messenger, "we have them in a trap, and only want all the hands we can get to come and kill them."

Such a message caused no little excitement amongst the few left in charge of our little cantonment. The camp was swept clean by midnight, and only the sick, and amongst them my husband and myself, remained. When morning dawned we followed the little force, so hastily sent for, in imagination, and fancied them nearly arriving at Powree to assist in the work of slaughter; but, as no news could reach us, as far as we knew, until the next day, we resolved to wait philosophically for particulars until then.

We were not a little astonished when about five pm., Lieutenant Le Cocq rode past our tent on his way to report the return of the force, sent out seventeen hours before, to Colonel Owen, 1st Lancers, left in command. The rebels had fled about the time that the little reinforcement started to cut them up; and so stealthy were their movements, and so well managed their retreat, that nobody knew either the exact time of their leaving or which way they had taken.

Consequently, the pursuing party, which was organised as quickly as possible by Sir Robert Napier, started in the opposite direction to that taken by the fugitives; and in the course of the next day word came to Sepree that Maun Sing and 1,500 of his men were at Reyghur, about six miles from us, while the other 1,500 were at Kollaris, about thirteen miles off. This news kept us on the *qui vive*, as what could be easier than to sweep our little cantonment, if they only had sufficient courage to try it? Everything was put in readiness for defence, and then we betook ourselves to sleep, undisturbed by either dreams or realities of rebels.

Meanwhile the left wing of the 8th Hussar, attached to General Roberts division at Nusseerabad, had not been idle since they left cantonments on the 27th of July, for the purpose of intercepting the rebels hovering about Jeypoor, and keeping them from taking possession of either Boondee or Ajmere. To convey an idea of the pleasures of marching in the rainy season, and also of the work they found to do, and the gallant manner in which they, in conjunction with the rest of the force, did it, I cannot do better than subjoin copies of two letters received about this time from Lieutenant-Colonel Naylor, 8th Hussars, in command of the left wing at Nusseerabad, who was in the field, although only just recovering from severe illness. The first ran as follows:—

"Two Miles from Mowgaum, July 31, 1858.

"We started from, Nusseerabad on the 27th of last month towards Jeypoor, for which place the rebels, who were reported to have increased their numbers to about 20,000, were making. They marched to within about sixteen miles of Jeypoor, and finding that we had intercepted them by going to Langaneer, about six miles from the town, they turned southwards towards Tonk. We followed them; and, on approaching Tonk, the General (Roberts) detached a flying column, consisting of about 130 lancers, 350 Belooches, part of His Majesty.'s 72nd, the 12th N.ative Infantry, B troop of Horse Artillery, and ourselves.

"We started at seven a.m. from Goonsee, where we had already arrived that morning; and, after marching all night, during which we heard a great deal of firing at Tonk, we arrived within about five miles of that place about seven o'clock on the following morning.

"The men wore becoming so exhausted from the heat, and the artillery horses so wearied, that we were obliged to halt. I never felt anything approaching to the intense sultriness of that day. We lost two of the 8th from sunstroke, which affected them whilst lying in their tents. The rebels, hearing of our approach, immediately bolted with two small guns which they had captured; and we have been following them sometimes by night, sometimes by day, without any chance of catching them. They have nothing to delay them; and can, with ease, travel twice as fast as we. They are mostly mounted; at least, what remain of them, for their numbers are greatly reduced: our continued pursuit has so disheartened them, that all their infantry have left them.

"At one place our reconnoitring party saw a body of about 500 Budmashes in the hills, who fired at them and killed a horse. They were supposed to be returning to their homes at Kotah; but the country is full of these fellows, and any camel of ours that cannot get on is immediately looted; and one of our men, when only about half a mile from camp, was fired at, the ball going through the peak of his cap, and grazing his eyebrow. We hear that there are not above three or four thousand of them left together, and their only object is to plunder towns. We have saved Jeypoor, Tonk, and Boondee, as well as several smaller places, from their depredations. We went through Boondee, and hearing that the rebels had gone through a pass further south, with the intention of endeavouring, if possible, to push on towards Adeypoor, where they have many friends, we made for Jehazpoor to cut them off. We arrived at this place (Mowgaum) on the 21st; and we have just progressed two miles in eleven days! On arriving at the river we found it was not fordable; but, after waiting three days, succeeded in crossing it.

"The following morning we attempted to march to Etonda; but, after passing through a deep *nullah*, and floundering along a road always up to our horses' knees, and many times up to their girths in black mud, the day broke, and disclosed to us the pleasing facts that we had progressed about a mile from the camp, and that the greater part of our force, and all our baggage, had been unable to cross the *nullah*, in consequence of a sudden rise in the water, already sufficiently deep; so we returned to camp; the greater' number of us, who were already over, having to wait some hours before the *nullah* was sufficiently fordable to recross once that day we have been unable to move, and have narrowly escaped starvation; we consumed our last morsel of hour on the evening of the 29th, and the horses, who were standing very nearly up to their knees in water, had not had any grain or hay for two days, so it became a most distressing matter of necessity that we should get out of that somehow.

"Unfortunately the rain, which had been pouring for some days, ceased, and enabled us to cross the *nullah* and get through about two miles of deep mud to a village where we are now encamped. We had to employ all the camels of the force to carry the baggage of the lancers and ourselves. They took over five hours doing the two miles: this was yesterday morning, and we returned the camels to bring up the rest of the force; but as they have not yet arrived, and it is late, I fancy they must have got into a fix. It is quite impossible to get the guns through the two miles we travelled yesterday. The camels suffer terribly in this muddy weather, as they slip down, with their great spongy feet, and cannot get up again. The river by which we are encamped, and which was not more than a small brook when we first arrived, became, when it rained, such a torrent, and ran with such violence, that it resembled a very heavy sea running, and one night was very nearly inundating the whole camp.

"I had to shift my tent once at midnight, as the river flooded me out, so I moved to a most attractive spot, where the water was only ankle deep instead of reaching to my knees. We have been out of beer and every other luxury for some time, and have to content ourselves with rations, and be thankful that we are not starved. We hear the rebels are at Mandulgurh, and are anxious to cross the Burnass River to Adeypoor; however, they cannot manage that yet, as the river is not fordable, and as the General (Roberts) is moving along the other bank, I suspect they will have to return to the Chumbul.

"They have, ever since we have been following them, stuck closely to the hills, never being above three miles from them, in case of being obliged to halt. We hear they are in great distress, and starving in numbers; the late weather must have told most fearfully upon them; I suppose they have been in the villages in the hills near Mandulghur. As long as they remain where they are neither cavalry nor artillery will be of much use against them."

Englishmen, however, are not easily diverted from their purpose, and a second letter received some time later, gives the result of an these troublesome marches and privations.

"Neemuch, August 21, 1858.
"We have had terribly hard work lately. On the 8th of the month we got the order to join General Roberts' force: we had been marching in the morning, but started at half-past six in the evening, and arrived at Bheelwarra about one o'clock the following day, having marched upwards of thirty miles. We then made three long marches—one of nineteen miles, one of twenty miles, and one of twenty-eight miles.

"The following day we were rewarded for our toils, by finding the enemy drawn up and waiting for us, after we had marched about seven miles. We certainly have done what no other column has, in bringing an unwilling combatant to an engagement. We had been following them up closely for seven weeks, when they became so harassed and .desperate, that they determined to fight. We found them drawn up in a magnificent position on one bank of the river, with, steep lulls down to the water.

"We, who were on the other bank, had to advance down a gentle slope, about a mile long; the Horse Artillery and Cavalry moving rapidly down to the bank of the river, where the artillery came into action, but with little effect, as the enemy s guns and troops were concealed amongst the hills; whilst we were exposed to the fire of four guns, three six–pounders and a nine-pounder, at five hundred yards range, until the infantry could get down the hill. The firing on the part of the rebels was at first very bad; but soon after, they got our range and direction perfectly.

"I moved the cavalry twice a few yards, when I found they were firing accurately; but they continued their fire on us, dropping their shot just at our horses' feet. Two shot went through the ranks without touching anybody, but we lost four horses, and my dear little gentle white horse was struck full in the chest by a round shot. I had just time to jump off him before he fell. We then crossed the river in line, and went up the hill, when the rebels ran away, leaving their guns and bullocks in our hands.

"The cavalry immediately went after them; and we had a grand gallop of about-three miles through the thick of them, as they were running along a road to a village. Their cavalry, which, with few exceptions, were well on ahead, formed on a hill. Having pretty well pumped our horses, I thought it advisable to stop until the artillery and infantry came up. By the time they arrived the cavalry had cut up all the stragglers about the plain, and the infantry had disposed of about two hundred rebels who were established on a lull round which we had passed, and from which they had fired at us as we galloped by.

"However, they made very bad shots: poor Sergeant-Major Holland was killed there, but no other person touched. I was then sent on after the enemy with cavalry and Horse Artillery, but had to leave the artillery after about eight miles, as they could not get on.

"We then went about seven miles further, and caught them on the march. As we galloped up to them they fired on us, threw away their arms, and bolted into the jungle. We skirmished through it, shooting an enormous number of rebels, who tried to conceal themselves in bushes. Very few attempted to make any resistance, as they had thrown away or concealed their arms. We took three elephants and a lot of camels, carrying the *Nawab's* kit, containing gold shawls, valued at 10,000 *rupees*.

"We then, our horses being completely exhausted, returned to the general, and arrived at eleven at night, having been in our saddles since daylight. We must have ridden a long distance. The rebels had in the morning, I should say, about nine or ten thousand men; there must have been about nine hundred killed, and they are now all scattered. We saw some of their cavalry, but beyond firing their carbines at a respectful distance, they showed no desire to fight.

"The *Nawab* and Tantia Topee are supposed to be with about seven hundred cavalry, endeavouring to cross the River Chumbul, near Rampoora. I thought that day would, perhaps, terminate our labours; but during the last week we have been so hardly worked that we are brought to a standstill, men and horses being completely exhausted. I have ceased to count marches by miles, as we generally march with infantry, and they delay us so much on the road, that I calculate by hours.

"We marched with the general on Monday and Tuesday, and then started at three a. m, on Wednesday, for Gangapoor, arriving there at eleven a.m. We started, to join Brigadier Parkes at eight p. m., and arrived at Chittore, about four p.m. On Friday morning, we started at six a.m. *via* Jawud to Neemuch, where we arrived at ten o'clock at night, doing about four ordinary marches in one. Brigadier Parkes wanted to take us out early this morning thirty-two miles; but I told him it was impossible that we could get our horses to drag their slow length over more than ten miles. Without our detachment, the brigadier had a stronger force of cavalry than we have had to pursue their entire army. I shall be glad to hear they have crossed the Chumbul. We left Stourton with General Roberts' force, sick with fever. We are all more or less shaky, but I hope rest and beer will set us right. Richards and Haynes are both quite unfit to be with us from illness. The name of the place, where we fell in with the rebels, is Kuttoria.

"But to return to ourselves, the pursuing column, which I mentioned as having been organized by Sir Robert Napier to pursue the fugitives from Powree, consisted of one squadron of His Majesty's 8th Hussars, two six-pound guns of the 3rd Troop Horse Artillery under Lieutenant Hoskins, two nine-pound guns under command of Lieutenant Strutt, some of Meade's Horse, one hundred of H. M.'s 95th, and the 10th and 25th Native Infantry; the whole under command of Lieutenant-Colonel Robertson, 25th Native Infantry.

"Before leaving Powree, Colonel Robertson expressed his intention of not returning until he had accounted for those, of whom he was sent in pursuit. The remainder of the brigade dropped into Sepree by degrees. They were detained some days for want of camels, as between three and four hundred extra ones were sent with Colonel Robertson, in order to mount the infantry; and of four hundred others sent out to Powree, two hundred went astray, and were not recovered for some days.

"At this stage of the proceedings our bandmaster, Herr König, sent in his resignation, and by way of making sure, started from Bombay in a sailing vessel bound to Liverpool, before it was accepted. His reasons, amongst others, were that "his hair was turning grey from the climate, and that the *Dhobies* had hammered his wife's linen until it was utterly destroyed." In short, he declared that it was impossible he could remain longer in "so detestable a country."

It was on the morning of the 31st August that Brigadier

Smith marched into Sepree; and the troops which accompanied him had scarcely breakfasted in their newly-pitched tents, when a telegraphic message came in from Jubra-Pattun, saying that the rebels were in possession of the town. The first idea conveyed by the news was that we were to start off without delay to Jubra-Pattun, which is six marches from Kotah. We were only kept in suspense for a day or two, and then Sir Robert Napier, who had no idea of giving us any more rest or peace, and who seems to have arrived at Sepree with a prejudice against the place, again marched us out.

CHAPTER 12

Maun Sing's Escape

Faint but pursuing.

How dull it is to pause—to make an end—
To rust unburnished—not to live in use;
As tho' to breathe were life!

Ulysses.

On the 3rd September, the force, accompanied by the siege train, marched out of Sepree about six miles, and encamped at Syssee, a village with an old-fashioned fort, half way to Kollariss. The rain did not permit us to start before half-past two in the afternoon, and our tents were not pitched on the new ground before dark. In the midst of the night the brigadier was aroused by the arrival of a despatch from Sir R. Napier, who himself remained behind at Sepree, saying that Maun Sing was again at Rajghur, and requesting that we would detach a force in pursuit. The lancers, under Lieutenant-Colonel Curtis, and the unfortunate 95th, started accordingly at daybreak, and returned next night, having seen nothing of Maun Sing, but having marched thirty-four miles.

The company of the 95th that left in the morning, piled only sixteen stand of arms on their return; the rest of the men, having fallen out by the way, came lagging and straggling into camp in the course of the night. We were detained for eleven days at Syssee, and it was only on the 7th September that news reached, us of the column under Lieutenant-Colonel Robertson, which had started from Powree in pursuit of Maun Sing. After many difficulties and disappointments, after incessant marching and terrible fatigue, they at length overtook the rebels at Beejapore. Major Chetwode, who wrote, reported nine cases of jungle fever. He also stated that Lieutenant Fawsett, 95th, was killed, and Captain Poore and Lieutenant Hanbury, of 8th Hussars, wounded.

The next rumour relative to the movements of the rebels which reached our camp, was one which ultimately affected us very considerably. It was that Tantia Topee had again assembled a numerous force at Bhopal, and was endeavouring to get southwards. At the same time we had a visit from Sir R. Napier, who alarmed us by saying that as the Gwalior and Jhansi troops were not to be disturbed, he intended to make us into a moveable column as soon as sufficient camels could be procured from Agra to enable us to move easily and to mount the infantry if required.

Soon afterwards we heard that we were to march to Goonah, then that we were to remain where we were, in order to protect Sepree and Kollaris; and, at last, hopes were raised by Sir Robert Napier that we should work our way northwards, and replace the 9th Lancers at Umballah, a hill station about sixty miles from Simla, in a most healthy and delightful climate. But the trumpeters of the brigade by sounding "orders" late in the evening of the 14th September, put to flight all our anticipations of Umballah, on the road, to which we should have again passed through beautiful Gwalior, and have seen the famous Taj at Agra, that most wonderful and beautiful tomb, in itself a commendatory epitaph.

We learned that the brigadier-general had received orders by telegraph from Sir Colin Campbell —now elevated to the peerage by the title of Lord Clyde—to send our unfortunate brigade to Goonah, without loss of time. This order upset all Sir Robert Napier's previous arrangements, and was received with dissatisfaction by us, but with pleasure by the 3rd troop Bombay Horse Artillery, who looked forward to returning to their own presidency. The siege train was taken from us at dawn, and ordered to return to Sepree. I was quite sorry when the elephants went; for being an invalid, and unable to use my foot, it was a great pleasure and entertainment to watch the odd ways and customs of these great beasts. They would dress themselves up like King Lear, in grass and straws, throwing great wisps over their heads and backs to keep away the flies.

They would then take another wisp and twist it about until it was properly shaped, when they would use it as a brush to drive away the same tormentors from their chests and legs, their great ears napping like *punkahs* all the while. It was curious to see the elephant walking to the well, carrying his own bucket and rope, and mating a staircase of his fore-leg, in order that the *mahout* might mount by it. He first raised the foot a little, bending the fetlock; when the *mahout* had raised himself upon this, the animal gradually bent his knee until the man could step easily from the foot to the fore-arm, and thence scramble up by his ears. After reading the account of Mademoiselle Djek, in Charles Reade's *Cream*, I have not been so anxious to trust myself within range of their trunks; but they appeared perfectly docile and were generally trumpeting a sign of satisfaction I believe.

On the same morning that the order arrived for us to move, the 14th September, we had sent all our sick into Sepree; and had also despatched thirty carts, and as many camels, to bring up more than one hundred sick men from. Colonel Robertson's little column. These carts, in consequence of our sudden movements, were recalled.

On the 14th and 15th of September thirteen cases of fever occurred in the squadron of the 8th Hussars only. We now heard that the rebels were not at Bhopal, but were endeavouring to reach that place; that General Mitchel had sent out his division in three columns; and that we were to march, by a route of sixteen marches, to Bhopal, joining some of General Mitchel's force by the way.

We left Syssee the day we received our orders and marched thirteen miles to Lukwassa, where we were compelled to halt, on account of the rain. It came down as soon as the column reached the ground, and before the arrival of the baggage. The ground on which our tents were to be pitched was soon flooded.

The baggage had a weary time of it, some of the carts, which started at three a.m., not arriving until five or six o'clock in the afternoon. The treasure tumbril of the 95th regiment, which had very high wheels, stuck fast in a hole opposite our tent. The pair of bullocks attached to it were utterly unable to move it, and as the blows fell a great deal faster than we liked, my husband sent a pair of powerful bullocks, used as leaders in one of the brigade treasure tumbrils, to assist. Even with this reinforcement, the wheel, which had now sunk nearly to the axle, refused to stir. Several men applied their shoulders to it, while others pushed behind, but with no better success.

Eventually, with the aid of another pair of magnificent bullocks, it was hauled out by sheer strength, the leaders pulling until they fell in the black mud. As soon as it was set in motion, the brigade treasure bullocks were detached and the tumbril started again with its own pair; they went on for about twenty yards, and then stuck fast once more. One of the mess store carts did not come in until the following morning, when five extra pairs of bullocks were required to draw it to the camp.

At this time I received the following letter from an officer of the 8th Hussars, with the squadron in pursuit, under Lieutenant-Colonel Robertson, giving the following account of the action at Beejapore, which appears to reflect the highest credit both upon, Lieutenant-Colonel Robertson for the energy and perseverance with which he followed the enemy, and upon the men who fought so well after such great fatigue.

"Goonah, September 14, 1858.
"We got over more than twenty miles the first day, and luckily hit on the track of those of whom we were in pursuit, at the village where we halted at dark. We were obliged to march almost entirely by daylight, on account of the rocky and otherwise dangerous nature of the ground, especially on account of

the guns. We followed the trade of the fugitives for five marches; and once were so close upon them, that we lighted our pipes at the fires of their encamping ground the night before. After making five marches we arrived at a village called Sangie, on the banks of a river running into the Parbuttee.

"At this place we halted one day, partly on account of having lost all trace of the rebels, and partly because our own horses, and those of the Horse Artillery urgently required rest. At Sangie it appeared that we had lost all trace of Maun Sing,[1] but that we were on the track of a number of the Gwalior Contingent and others. Our sixth march was not much more than twelve miles.

"The next day we started late, and did not get to our ground until after dark. Here Colonel Robertson got such information as induced him to think that, by pushing on with a part of his force, he might come up with the rebels. Accordingly, he started at two in the morning with fifty of our men, the irregulars, the European infantry, and part of the native. The remainder of the force he left with the guns, it being thought unsafe to leave them without protection, as Maun Sing was believed to be in our rear with 1,400 men. Those left behind followed at daylight; and, after a very long march, which took us right out of the jungle into the open country, we came up with Robertson (who had seen nothing of the rebels), and halted under the trees at the same place that we encamped in May last.

"The colonel seemed much disheartened, but resolved to make one more effort, and if that did not succeed, promised us to give up the pursuit. The horses were very much done indeed, and most of those of the artillery were without shoes. After the men had had their dinners, about five p.m., the same party started in advance as before, leaving the rest to follow at daylight.

"To the surprise of many, just at daylight the following morning the enemy were discovered. They were encamped on a rising ground, just beyond the village of Beejapore. A broad, shallow river ran past the village, and close to the ground on which the rebels were. At a short distance before arriving at the village,

---

1. He had doubled back to Rajghur and Kollariss, near Sepree.

the infantry were extended in skirmishing order along the valley of the river, and the cavalry were sent round at a trot on the far side through the village.

"The infantry first attracted the attention of the enemy, but being hidden by the houses, our fellows, and the rest of the cavalry, were upon them before they were aware of their approach, and in the thick of them before they had time to fire more than one round from their muskets which they had prepared for the infantry. They were completely taken by surprise. Down the bank and into the river they went as quick as ever they could, the mounted men being the first in, but not without leaving a good many with unmistakeable tokens of the will with which our fellows handled their swords. The infantry caught them as they crossed the river, but at a great disadvantage, as the rising sun was full in their eyes.

"After the first dash of our fellows, the work of destruction appears to have been carried on in a desultory sort of manner. The bank of the river was too perpendicular to allow of horses crossing immediately; they had to ride alongside it a little distance, and cross lower down. They then formed again, and went at the rebels, who were in a body; but from the ground being cut up by deep *nullahs* and rents, the fight was necessarily of a very scattered character. The enemy ran into the *nullahs*, and were shot down by dozens, and in some places by twenties. Many fought desperately; being driven to bay, as it were, they could not help it.

"One man in particular, although brought down to a sitting position, fought until the very last. They fired their muskets, then drew their swords, and stood, until they were either riddled by bullets or pierced by the bayonet. Our casualties, considering the desperate nature of their resistance, were very few; and some of these were caused by accidents from our own people.

"Poor Fawcett, 95th, was shot high up in the middle of the chest; he breathed for twenty minutes. He and a few men were making a rush at a lot of fellows. Poore (8th Hussars) received a cut on the wrist, severing the tendons, and he is not going on well I am sorry to say, as it will not heal. Hanbury (8th Hussars) got a slice from a sword on the fleshy part of the shoulder' and back of his arm. The enemy were all regular *sepoys*; most of them wore pouches and belts. The greater part had percussion muskets; and several had medals for Mooltan, Cabul, Pegu, &c. Their loss must have been nearly five hundred, and few could have got away without a mark of some sort.

"The 95th did the greater part of the work. The 86th were altogether too late, although they were mounted, while —— made the 95th march. The 10th Native Infantry worked right well, and kept up side by side with the 95th, and never stopped for anything. Sergeant Major Champion is going on well; he was shot in the breast.

"Tantia Topee is, as of course you know, expected to cross the road, and go to Bhopal. The country we marched through was very like parts of Herefordshire, wood and rock, with here and there an opening; and the atmosphere was that of a forcing house—so hot, steaming, and damp."

This was a brilliant day's work, of which Colonel Robertson had reason to be proud.

We marched into Goonah at about six o'clock on the morning of the 21st, and found two pieces of good fortune awaiting us, *viz.*, our letters and two *tattoos*, laden with stores from Mhow, consisting of beer, sherry, brandy, coffee, writing-paper, &c., all much needed, and most acceptable. The contents of the mail was rather amusing, as regarded the brigadier. About an hour after we had started on our march in the morning, a messenger from Sir Robert Napier had overtaken him, saying that the rebels were all gone to Shahabad, and ordering him to return and proceed to that place.

As we could only arrive at Shahabad by retracing our march along the Trunk Road to within twelve miles of Sepree, this was disheartening enough. The mail-bag, however, brought the brigadier a letter from General Roberts, desiring that, as soon as he had finished co-operating with General Michel, he should return to Rajpootana, and place himself again under General Roberts's orders. It also brought a telegraph from General Michel, desiring him to march immediately on Seronge, a fortified town, situated south-east of Goonah, where Tantia Topee has established himself.

So that in about three hours, the brigadier received as many different orders from as many different authorities, and to crown all, the telegraphic wire was discovered to be broken in two places, so that he could communicate with none of them. Sir Robert Napier would have us march due north, General Roberts wanted us almost due west, and General Michel urgently required us south-east! The hopes of the brigade were fixed enjoining General Michel, and the wish to proceed to Bhopal *via* Seronge was universal.

It was fortunate for us that we reached Goonah before the rains, which again came down in torrents, accompanied by blinding lightning and deafening thunder. These are supposed to be the finishing rains of the season; and the hard gravelly soil of Goonah enables us to trench our tent sufficiently to keep it tolerably dry.

On the morning of the 23rd, Brigadier Smith received a communication from Major Macpherson, insisting that the rebels were moving on Shahabad.

We ought to feel nattered at the anxiety evinced to retain the force in Bengal; and might do so, did we not know that we are only required to act as a police force, while the Jhansi and Gwalior troops remain undisturbed. We found Colonel Robertson very ill at Goonah; and his brigade, the command of which had devolved on Major Chetwode, 8th Hussars, absent in pursuit of some rebels supposed to be passing about forty miles to the south. The morning after we marched in, the brigadier received a despatch from Major Chetwode, saying that the information had proved entirely false, and that no rebels had ever been in the neighbourhood.

Major Chetwode then endeavoured to rejoin the brigadier at Goonah, but was much impeded by the torrents of rain. Captain Mayne had been absent with his body of Irregular Horse for some time, moving south of Ragooghur. We were detained for three days at Goonah, waiting for definite orders as to which superior was to be obeyed; and I was not sorry to be able to ride round the cantonment now that it was dressed in green. The tall, mowing grass rose to our horse's girths, and the thick tangled bushes, all agleam with recent rain, looked more English and home-like than anything I had seen in this country.

On the 25th September, at three a.m., we marched out of Goonah, leaving Captain Poore suffering from the effects of fever, in addition to his wound,, which was going on anything but well, and taking with us Sergeant-Major Champion, whose gallant bearing during the action of Beejapore deserves record. He was, as before mentioned, shot through the breast, the ball coming out beneath the shoulder-blade. He naturally believed himself mortally wounded; and although struck quite at the beginning of the fight, he continued to ride on and to fight, not knowing but that each movement of his body might cause death. On the first hasty medical inspection, it was thought that the ball had actually pierced the lungs, nor was it until after a second and very careful examination that it was found to have traversed round the ribs.

The assistant quartermaster-general attached to the brigade having reconnoitred the road to Bhadore, pronounced it totally impracticable; and we, in consequence, took a shorter route for the first three or four miles. We marched until daylight through a fen, full of holes and standing water, with long rank grass brushing the horses' sides. I had intended riding, but went the first half of the march in a *dooley*, nor was I sorry to find myself in it, as the troop horses stumbled and floundered along, sinking to their knees, and, in the effort to struggle out, falling almost on their heads.

I looked out just in time to see "The Pearl," who was saddled and led after my *dooley* by his *syce*, go headforemost down a piece of rotten ground into a sedgy hole full of water, after which I closed the *purdah*, and looked out no more. At length we gained a gravelly soil, and the latter part of the march was pleasant enough. The country was thickly wooded and hilly, with long grass and flowers; and the scenery was really picturesque and pleasing; a luxury one is rarely blest with in India.

The baggage, as might be expected, was arriving by instalments until six in the afternoon; and the next morning, the deaths of nineteen camels, which had been overloaded and had fallen during the march, were reported to the commissariat officer. The rain, which came down steadily that night and the next morning, again stopped us; and we now heard that Tantia Topee and a large force were awaiting us at Seronge. Sir Robert Hamilton reported their numbers at 10,000; and from other, but I should imagine less authentic sources, the brigadier was informed that they mustered 17,000 men.

Our brigade, reinforced by taking back most of our own men from Colonel Robertson, who gave them up unwillingly enough, numbered about 1,100. The odds are great; but no one feels any doubt about our being quite able to cope with them, especially should Brigadier Parkes and General Michel move up to help us. The 17th Lancers are at last turned out of their comfortable bungalows at Kirkee, and in squadrons and wings are marching up to Mhow. Sir William Gordon, with one squadron, arrived there some time ago; and Lieutenant Wood, weary of inactivity when real work was going forward, volunteered to serve with the 3rd Bombay Light Cavalry, and is under Captain Mayn's orders.

On the 27th September, another letter was received from Sir Robert Hamilton, urging the brigadier to hasten to Seronge. In vain did he, in his anxiety to obey the summons, ride down the road twice before twelve o'clock to see whether he could not persuade himself that it was passable. But the rain was heavy and frequent; and the baggage animals failing us so fast, with no possibility of replacement, that he was obliged to content himself with fretting and eating out his heart, until three o'clock in the afternoon of the 28th, when, as the sun shone and the tents were positively dry, he ventured to try a move of three miles to a piece of red soil. He accomplished it, but with severe loss. I rode almost the first of the whole column, wisely remembering that the more the ground was trodden the deeper it would be.

Presently, the horseman immediately preceding me sank in the deep black earth, up to the roots of his horse's tail; this was the first horse down. He was quickly followed by one of our own troopers, which was for some time unable to extricate himself, rolling several times over, and being up to his neck. The Horse Artillery had fearful work; nor would they have arrived before the next morning, had not the 95th Regiment assisted them.

One horse remained, head under for so long that, when first dragged out, he was supposed to be dying. None of the baggage-train, except a few camels, nor the treasure tumbrils, nor the mortars, came in before the next day. Twenty camels were reported "dead," and the road "a wreck of carts." The change, however, was much for the better, as far as the health of the troops was concerned; they were camped on fine, high, dry ground, and no longer laid down to sleep in odorous and slushy mud. A *jemadar*, of the 1st Lancers, who came in soon after we reached our new ground from spying at Seronge, reported that Tantia Topee had strongly entrenched himself, and that he was aware of Brigadier Smith's approach.

A letter received the following morning from General Michel, announced his intention of making an attack, on the south side of Seronge, simultaneously with ours on the north; and added, of course, that "should the enemy escape, Brigadier Smith's column would pursue." But by noon, news had come that the Nana, with a large force, had raised his standard in the north, and that Tantia Topee had abandoned Seronge, for the purpose of joining him. The letter suggested that we should retrace our steps *via* Goonah and Sepree, towards the Nana; in which case, I may bid a fond farewell to all hopes of seeing my English box, now on the road from Bombay to Mhow, and also to the idea of resting awhile in the latter cantonment.

On the following morning we started at two a.m., to march by the large and very pretty fortified village of Bujianghur into Goonah. Colonel Robertson, who is still detained here by illness, no sooner heard of the approach of Brigadier Smith, than he telegraphed to Sir Robert Napier for leave to resume the 95th and 10th Native Infantry, but I am happy to say his application did not succeed.

Our brigadier, hearing that Tantia Topee and a large body of men were at Esaughur, started for that place as fast as the reduced state of the 95th and the baggage transport would permit. Captain Mayne accompanied us with a cavalry brigade, consisting of his own Irregular Horse and a part of the 3rd Light Cavalry. He had joined us the day before, having come one-and-twenty miles that morning to do so.

On arriving in sight of the town we saw the sky obscured with smoke. Not only had Tantia Topee stormed the place, but he had plundered and utterly desolated it. The rear-guard of his force did not move out until we drew up before it, and a party of Irregular Cavalry started at once in pursuit. But, unfortunately, there were two roads from Esaughur in the same direction, of which the rebels took one, and their pursuers the other. We learnt subsequently that Tantia had actually moved on Mahoulie that day, but as the hearts of all are with the rebels, we can procure no information in time for it to be of use. About this time the most disheartening *contretemps* of our wearisome pursuit occurred.

Our brigadier became aware that Tantia, with 12,000 men, had gone to Chandaree. After anxious deliberation the following plan, the tactics of which are shown by the accompanying map, was resolved upon. Chandaree, as the map indicates, is situated in the vicinity of the Betwa River, which being at that time so swollen as to be absolutely unfordable, was for the moment an insuperable barrier to the escape of the rebels eastward. Lieutenant-Colonel Robertson was ordered to move his force from Goonah to Shahdowra, and so to keep the Western road closed: Brigadier Smith at Esaughur would have defended the Northern and North-western roads; and General Michel was requested to move up from Seronge, in order to prevent the rebels from flying towards the South. A simultaneous attack on three sides, on a given day, with an impassable river on the fourth, seemed to offer the opportunity which had been so long sought for in vain, of putting an end at one blow to the rebel forces in Central India. The only uncertainty as to their utter destruction was the falling of the Betwa, which was not, however, likely to occur in time to enable them to escape.

We waited, anxiously to hear whether General Michel would co-operate in this well-organized plan, as in his last communication he had declared himself unable to move for nine days. His Europeans, he said, were out of groceries, and could not march, until they arrived! Without inspecting the invoice we could not tell what condiments might be considered necessary to enable this luxurious force to move, but it was almost certain that before the rune days were over the Betwa would be fordable for elephants, and in places for horses; when Tantia would probably bid farewell to beautiful, solitary Chandaree, and proceed to possess himself of the rich spoils of Teary.

The guns left by Tantia at Esaughur, nine in number, were blown up by the Horse Artillery. The *Subar*, in charge of the town, who appears from the number of dead and wounded lying in the streets to have made as stout a resistance as he could, was assisted by us with money, as Tantia had taken good care to leave nothing of any value in the town. The monsoon by this time, October 7th, had entirely passed, and the days, once more bright and cloudless, were of very great heat.

Already the first fresh tinge is off the green, and the country begins to resume its brown colour. The grass in the jungle exceeds in height and thickness anything I had ever imagined, and when we first begin to march in the morning it is saturated with dew, which makes wading through it like passing through a river; the smell, too, before sunrise is extremely offensive and injurious.

A series of misfortunes befell us at this time, for besides my being a prisoner to my tent and *dooley*, with a feverish attack which left me so weak as to be incapable of exertion, my pleasant horse "Pearl" was severely kicked on the sinew of the hind leg. There was no prospect of his being able to use his leg for a month, even if lock-jaw did not end his sufferings before that. Sad indeed it was to see his pretty head bowed down by pain, and to watch him limping slowly on three legs, and growing thinner and thinner every day.

On the morning of the 8th of October the detachment of cavalry, under Captain Mayne, quitted us at Esaughur and marched to co-operate with General Michel. They left in obedience to peremptory orders, thereby obliging Brigadier Smith to call in all his outposts of Irregular Cavalry, which were watching the country between Esaughur and the river, in a northerly direction, and so frustrating all hopes of accomplishing his plan for catching Tantia in a *cul-de-sac*. I think that were I in a subordinate command, in India, I should either throw up the whole thing, and run away in the night, or I should carry out my own plans in the teeth of everybody—*coûte qui coûte*.

The water of the Betwa, on the 7th of October, was reported not more than five feet over the ford. From what we heard subsequently, it must in reality have been much deeper. The rebels have with them several elephants laden with treasure. Grain of all kinds is scarce in their wake, as being so flush of money, they have been paying high prices for grain, instead of taking it by force, as is their usual custom. We rode through Esaughur, a mean, but in places a picturesque little town. Its desolation was as complete as that of Chandaree, but it lacked the beauty, which made that place so exquisite in its mourning.

At midnight, on the 9th of October, "boots and saddles" sounded, and by one a.m. the following morning we were again on our travels; halting once more at Mahoulie, which in its dress of tangled green was hardly recognisable. The river, with its overhanging trees, was too thick and muddy to offer a chance of success to the sportsmen, who betook themselves to fishing as soon as the camp business was concluded; the ford was three feet deep, and we were encamped in tall, rank grass and jungle, which we were not sorry to move out of on the following day. Brigade orders were to rouse at two, although the greater part of the baggage carts did not arrive until between five and six the previous evening, and the mortars only came in during the night.

It was intended to march to Serai, but despatches received about an hour previous to marching caused Brigadier Smith to direct his course to Monone. We heard that General Michel had come across a portion of the fugitive rebels, and after a fight had killed about two hundred, and taken several guns. Tantia Topee, with 2,500 followers, had escaped over the Betwa—having built boats for the purpose while the treasure and women were conveyed across on elephants. The urgency of time was so strongly insisted upon by the general, that the propriety of proceeding after the men s breakfasts was discussed, but abandoned on account of the great heat of the sun. The Bheels, who have disturbed the country below Mhow, are reported to have robbed the post; it is certain that no English letters arrived by this mail, although they are known to have been in Bombay by the 28th of September.

Some opinion of the state of the country, and of the tendencies of the people in Central India at this moment may be formed from the contents of the following letter, written by one of a party of three Englishmen travelling down to Bombay on sick leave.

"Mhow, October 3rd, 1858.

"Since I started from Sepree I have had as unpleasant a time as anyone need desire. You have no doubt heard that when we arrived at Bursode, thirty-one miles from Goonah, we learned that Tantia's advanced guard was at Keelipore, only eighteen miles from our next halting-place—Beora, on which, place he was then advanced having ordered 20,000 *sirrs* of flour and wood to be in readiness for his army. As we were struggling through the mud at the rate of nine miles in twelve hours, we took the advice of the telegraphic inspector, and returned to Goonah, whither he followed us the next day; and, in doing so, very nearly fell into the hands of the party whom Colonel Robertson cut off, and who were only five miles distant from

Ragooghur, where we breakfasted.

We had to remain at Goonah 'chewing the cud of patience' as the Persians say, until the 20th, when we accompanied Major Chetwode to Ragooghur. We reached Beora, sixty-one miles from Goonah, in two days, and were highly elate at the prospect of a speedy journey to Bombay, when we were overtaken by one of the severest storms of thunder and rain I ever remember to have witnessed. It completely swamped the roads; nor was it without the utmost difficulty that we reached the next station of the bullock train, where we arrived about seven p.m.

The *peon* in charge there said it would be impossible to proceed any further that night, and advised our remaining in the bullock sheds until morning, adding, that he would light a fire for us, and make us as '*khoosh*' as possible. In the morning he proposed to take us by a jungle path, so that we might avoid the flooded *nullahs*. We agreed to this, and proceeded to make ourselves jolly over a cold fowl and some beer, in spite of the attacks of numerous hordes of insects, who resented our intrusion on their domains and vested rights.

Whilst thus making ourselves comfortable under difficulties, one of our servants called Captain —— out, and told him we must get away as soon as possible, as bad work was going on. Our cook being sick, did not, like the rest of the servants, leave the cart, but lay in the bottom of it covered over with *saleetas*, and so was concealed from the notice of the *peon*, who, leaning against the cart, thus addressed another man:——

'I have made the *Saibs khoosh*; and, as soon as they go to sleep, we can loot the carts.'

"'But in case they or their servants resist, you have not enough of men.'

"The *peon* replied: 'Oh, I have thought of that, and have sent to the next village for ten or twelve *budmashes* who are halting there, and who will do their business.'

"'*Bohut Atcha*' (very good), replied the other worthy.

"Our cook, on overhearing all this, was much alarmed, but remained quiet until one of our servants went to the cart, when he whispered to him to tell us directly all he had gathered of this precious plot. So I sent for the *peon*, and told him I had changed my mind, and should proceed at once. He was greatly annoyed, and tried to persuade us to remain; but, seeing we were quite determined, he left us, and went to order the bullocks; and, strangely enough, he and his friend held another consultation close to the same cart.

"'Those people say they will go on; I have ordered only one pair of bullocks to each cart, so they will get on slowly enough for you and the *budmashes* to overtake them.'

"'But how are we to attack?'

"'The drivers will have orders to upset the carts; you will then manage it easily enough.'

"This being also told me, I insisted upon two pairs of bullocks being furnished to each of the carts as usual, and then told the *peon* to get into my cart, as I wished for the pleasure of his company down the road. He refused at first, but the muzzle of my pistol applied to his ear, and a gentle *argumentum ad hominem* from the sergeant major, induced a speedy compliance. I then armed our *ghorawallahs* with swords, and told the *peon* that if any *budmashes* came near us I would shoot him that instant, while the *ghorawallahs* had instructions to cut down the first driver who upset a cart.

"You never saw such a face of terror as our friend the *peon* showed. He whispered a long time with the driver, which I permitted, as I fancied he was giving him instructions to be cautious. Whenever the gharry gave a greater lurch than usual, he exhibited the greatest agitation. So we journeyed to Puchore when I gave him over to two of Holkar's *sepoys*, who permitted him to escape; but Sir Robert Hamilton has sent people in pursuit of him. We were detained three days in a filthy native hovel at Puchore, in consequence of the rising of the river, which we ultimately crossed on *charpoys* (native bedsteads), carried on men's heads.

"We found that the Kola Sind River was also unfordable, by which. we were detained another day; and a third river, the name of which I forget, detained us the greater part of another; thus, altogether, we had a most unpleasant journey; we lived in dirty sheds, and were half starved; a mode of life not very conducive to the restoration of health.

We are now detained at Mhow in consequence of the Bheels being out on the road, joined by some 200 of Holkar's Horse. They have broken the telegraphic wire, looted the *dâk* with the English mail, seized the bullocks of the train, and smashed the carts, so our journey hitherto has not been as fortunate as adventurous.

On the 12th October General Michel rode over to our camp, which was only nine miles from Mongroulee, where his force was halted, and made arrangements with the brigadier for pursuing the enemy into Bundelcund. It was decided to form the united forces into three columns, placing cavalry and light field guns in the centre; the left wing being composed of Brigadier Smith's infantry, with 100 cavalry and two light guns, and the right column of General Michel's infantry, under command. of Colonel Lockhart.

The cavalry, so it was arranged., were to cross the river at a ford, near Mongroulee, with between four and five feet of water. Brigadier Smith was to cross at a *ghaut* near Chandaree, and Colonel Lockhart somewhat lower down. These three were to form a junction with General Whitelock, at Teary; but no sooner was the plan formed, and the arrangements made, than the rebels were found, not to have gone to Teary at all, but to have taken a northerly direction.

On the 14th of October the centre wing, consisting of three troops 8th Hussars, a squadron 17th Lancers, three troops 1st Bombay Lancers, a wing of 3rd Bombay Cavalry, Mayne's Horse and Horse Artillery, marched to a ford on the river Betwa, about thirteen miles from Serai; and as Brigadier Smith had received, information that the *ghaut* at Chandaree was utterly unfordable, he marched his infantry to the same place, hoping to get across. But on the evening of the day on which we arrived, General Michel decided, that the river was quite impracticable for infantry and for baggage carts, and ordered Brigadier Smith not to attempt to cross it at all; but to proceed along its left bank as far as Chandaree, from which place he could watch two fords—the one near that town and the other a few miles further down the river.

Our little force now consisted only of the brigadier and staff, H. M.'s 95th, the 10th Native Infantry, one troop of Hussars, two troops of Lancers, and two Horse Artillery guns, with five Sappers and Miners attached, together with the two mortars sent us from Sepree; and on the morning on which General Michel crossed the river, we returned to Serai, not a little pleased that our baggage had escaped being drenched and drowned, and delighted to find ourselves moving independently, as we, ourselves particularly, were thereby relieved from, a great deal of worry and annoyance.

We heard at this time of the arrival of Major Seager in Bombay, which, as he is anxious to purchase, may perhaps cause great and, on some accounts, very beneficial changes in the regiment, although, should they involve the loss of Lieutenant-Colonel Naylor, they will cause universal regret.

On the morning of the 17th of October we again, pitched our tents amongst the hills that surround Chandaree, where we halted for some days to watch the fords of the Betwa. If the country was beautiful in May, when the trees were leafless and the ground barren and bare, it acquired a double charm now that the earth was green and the trees bent down with foliage, and in many cases with flowers. A beautiful ruin of what had once been a *serai* or resting-place for travellers, lay on the right of our camp, and before us were the hills topped with the fortifications that defend, the town.

This evening the mail of the 30th August reached the camp, and a sergeant brought letters to our tent, containing intelligence of the death of my Crimean companion and friend, the chesnut horse Bob. When we left England he had been committed to the care of friends whose kindness he had enjoyed for nearly twelve months, and from them we received the following account of his death: ——

I have to tell you of what I fear will give you pain—poor
Bob's sudden death not by bullet, but in the common
course of nature. He had never had ache or ailment since
he came into our stable, and on Sunday, 29th August, he
took his morning's feed at eight o'clock, and went out to
exercise in the park as usual. Suddenly he staggered and
fell, and was dead in less than five minutes. He was only
being walked round, the groom riding him, and leading
another horse. He was buried in Park Coppice, where several other old favourites lie. We are almost as sorry for his
death as you will be; he led an easy life whilst in our care.
'The 'Squire' very seldom worked him, and he ranged
about in his large loose box, more a show horse than anything else; for everyone who came to the house was taken
to see him.

The next morning we moved down a steep and rocky road,
which cut the horses' feet very much, to the east side of Chandaree, nearer the fords and encamped on more open ground.
Receiving vague intelligence of some Bundealahs on the opposite side of the river, the brigadier sent a party of the 95th, under
command of Major the Hon. E. C. H. Massey, to reconnoitre. It
was found that they were encamped and had with them two or
three small boats, which were soon after taken by us. They fled
as soon as the white faces became visible, although they were on
the other side of water between seven and eight feet deep.

We are urgently looking for a reinforcement of camels, as
there is actually not a spare camel in the force; and of the few
that are left some die daily, while others can hardly carry their
loads, owing to the frightful sores on their backs. For these the
natives know no remedy but the actual cautery, and one is nearly
deafened at times by the roars of the unfortunate victim whose
wounds are being comforted by the application of a red-hot
iron.

The beautiful comet, which has been visible to us for many

nights, is now passing out of sight. Its first appearance was on the evening of the 29th of September, soon after sunset. Since then it has been seen nightly with more or less distinctness. At first it caused a great sensation among the camp followers, who were anxiously inquiring whether it was a star of good or evil omen. For my part I cling to the hope that it will prove the herald of peace if not of goodwill, and that as its splendour has witnessed the decline, its departure may mark the suppression of the mutiny.

On the evening of the 22nd of October, as we were still resting—four whole days of rest—beneath the shadow of the hills round Chandaree, a native arrived with intelligence that the rebels intended to cross the river at the Rhait Ghaut. As the information was given by a man who had offered himself as a spy, and as nothing was more probable than that the enemy, knowing Scindia's force in Chandaree to be short of ammunition, should endeavour to draw off the European brigade, in order to gain an opportunity of crossing the river at the ford opposite the town,

It was decided to wait until the spies of our own camp returned. In the meantime it was intimated to our informant, that if his intelligence proved correct he would be well rewarded, but if on the contrary, he was found to have spoken falsely, he would be hanged, a consummation he appeared to contemplate with the most frigid indifference.

Next morning, however, his news was so far confirmed, that the enemy were found to be hovering on the banks of the river, undecided, whether to cross or not; and in consequence of orders, which arrived shortly before noon from General Michel, Brigadier Smith marched at three p.m. for Bhorassa, in order to guard that ford, which was only knee-deep.

The brigade reached Serai about half-past nine o'clock in the evening, having marched over a terrible road, up a very steep and rocky *ghaut*. No tents were pitched, the men laid down in the open air, and by five o'clock the next morning after this sixteen-mile march, were again on the tramp, ten miles further to Mongroulee, where no carts, commissariat or private, appeared until four or five o'clock in the afternoon. The English infantry had proved themselves more enduring than the native cattle, which were unable, without rest, to accomplish the severe work over the incredibly bad roads. The men lay down until midnight, when *reveillée* sounded, and the brigade then completed the remaining twenty miles which lay between them and Bhorassa, thus performing a forced march of forty-six miles in forty-two hours.

Enough cannot be said in praise of the endurance and fortitude of the non-commissioned officers, and men of the 95th——I do not include their officers, as they were, I believe without exception, mounted, and so incurred no more fatigue than the cavalry; but when it is considered that on this occasion the regiment accomplished, beneath an Indian sun, a march far beyond anything that ever was required of them in their native country, it becomes a matter of regret that men, so heroic in endurance, should have been so severely tried.

We encamped at the village of Bhorassa on the left bank of the Betwa, opposite the fort of Koozwye, wherein resides a friendly *Begum*, who sent her younger brother, the Nawab, accompanied by trays of sweetmeats, to make his *salaam* to the brigadier.

Just before we reached the end. of the march we heard that General Michel had encountered, the rebels, under Tantia Topee, at a place called Sindwaha, on the right bank of the Betwa; and the next day more detailed accounts arrived, by *dâk*, and we learned, that on the 19th a severe battle was fought, wherein the enemy mustered, about ten to one. They attempted to charge the Horse Artillery guns, but were driven back by the Hussars. Lieutenant Harding, 8th Hussars, was very severely wounded in the right side, Captain Heneage's troop lost eight men killed, and wounded, and Captain Penton's troop also suffered loss. A *nullah*, which ran in front of our men, saved a good many of the enemy, and the broken nature of the ground made it very difficult for cavalry to work. But every account that has as yet reached us agrees in saying that had the cavalry been permitted to pursue as energetically as it was their wish to do, the loss of the enemy would have been far more considerable.

At Bhorassa-Koozwye, we remained four days, spent by the brigadier and staff in endeavouring to collect intelligence of the whereabouts of Tantia and his treasure, and by me, in riding about in the vicinity of the camp.

One evening we rode to look at the Betwa, of which so much has been said. We found a wide river, with a bed composed partly of sand and partly of rock, The water had sunk so much that the ford was easily passable on horseback. As we returned we met a wild boar, who like ourselves was taking his exercise in the cool of the day. The broken nature of the ground, and the number of large holes, made it impossible to give him chase, without more danger to our horses and ourselves than the fun of the gallop was worth.

In India the ground is in very many places perforated with deep holes, which are never filled even with the mud caused by the rains. Some of them, just large enough to admit a horse's leg, are from two to three feet deep, others are larger and deeper. In places the land is honeycombed with them, so that it is necessary to ascertain the nature of the soil before attempting even a trot.

At the same time, the dexterity with which a horse will gallop over ground covered with holes is very wonderful—that is to say, if his rider gives him his head, and lets him trust to his own eyes and feet; should the rider, however, attempt to put ins judgment in place of that of his steed, the chances are that he earns a fall, upon ground which for eight months of the year is as hard its brass.

CHAPTER 13

The Value of a Treaty

The two corps of this army, particularly that which has been in the north, are in want of rest. They have been in the field, and almost constantly marching since January last; their clothes and equipments are much worn, and a short period in cantonment would be very useful to them. The cavalry likewise are weak in numbers, and the horses low in condition. I should wish therefore to be able to canton the troops for a short time.

The Wellington Despatches

No communication was received from General Michel from the time of the arrival of the order to move from Chandaree until the 31st October, when a letter reached us at Malaghur, informing us that General Michel, who was now marching south, had, on the 25th inst, come across and dispersed a body of 3,000 rebels. He desired the brigadier to proceed by easy marches to Seronge. We hear that, three *lakhs* of *rupees* are at Saugor, awaiting "a strong escort" to be supplied by Brigadier Smith; two *lakhs* for our own column, and one for that under General Michel.

On the 30th October the 10th Regiment of Native Infantry received, a reinforcement of 250 men and four officers, and on the following day the brigade was joined by 500 irregular cavalry, under Captain Buckle.

On the 1st of November we marched to Moundalh, and the day following to Taal. Both these marches were in the direction of Seronge, to which place we were proceeding in order to cover Goonah. General Michel himself had hastened south, and we heard of his force as being near the Nerbudda River. Great diversity of opinion exists as to whether the force under Tantia Topee will cross that river. Crossing the Nerbudda is like crossing the Rhine—the opposite shores are inhabited by people of different race, prejudices, and opinions. Some say that once across the Nerbudda Tantia Topee would meet with very little sympathy or encouragement.

A letter from an officer of the 8th Hussars shows that the cavalry brigade has been well worked in the pursuit. He says:—

"After we left the old brigade we crossed the Betwa River with less difficulty than we expected, and marched for a great distance southward. We met Lockhart's brigade, and the two went on together in the direction of Teary. The enemy were known to be somewhere in our neighbourhood, but few suspected them to be so near as they afterwards proved.

"We marched about twelve miles through an open cultivated country, and had forced some little distance ahead of the infantry, when all at once, the enemy's picquets were seen galloping in, and in a few moments we came in sight of the whole army, extended in line, on some open ground near the village of Lindwaha. We went steadily on, and the enemy fell back upon some ridges, with fields of very high standing grain towards the centre.

"A squadron of 8th Hussars, the 17th Lancers, and native regular cavalry were on our right; the Horse Artillery, one troop of 8th, and Mayne's Horse, went away to the left. We rather hurried up into action; hut I rather think the general was afraid of their slipping through his fingers. The action began on the left, by the enemy opening fire upon us from four guns. We were so short of men that we could only reply with three, I could not tell what was doing on our right, on account of the high grain.

"After a short cannonade, the enemy, possibly emboldened by our apparently insignificant force, made a demonstration of attacking the guns, and our position, for a short tune, was very critical. Not only was there a large force in front, but a lot of skirmishers had very pluckily crept close to us in the grain" (grain grows sometimes to the height of ten or twelve feet), "and the bullets and shot came in very smart.

"The body, who menaced us in front, had got much less than 300 yards from us, when luckily for us the infantry and 9-pounder battery came up. Grape and round shot soon made the enemy hesitate, and before the rifles could begin to tell, they moved off. Those on the right were not idle, but owing to the broken nature of the ground the charge was not very effective. Men and horses fell in the *nullahs*, and two of our men were cut to pieces, from being dismounted. As soon as the enemy took decidedly to flight, Colonel Blake ordered, me to remain and protect the baggage, which I did; and having luckily found my camels, was able to feed my horse. The pursuit was continued, for seven miles, being finished at the banks of a deep river.

"Had the existence of the river in front only been known to the general, we could have driven the enemy pell-mell into it, and the slaughter would have been immense; as it was, I dare say 500 is about the number killed. We found four guns abandoned, near the river. Tantia Topee was present, but made off with his elephants early in the day.

"Our loss (8th Hussars) was two killed. and seven wounded; six horses wounded, and nine missing; the 17th Lancers had. two or three wounded, and the Bombay Lancers lost two men."

When within a march of Seronge we received orders again to change our course, but nevertheless we did go there, for not only were nearly all the troop and artillery horses in need of shoes, but several of the officers' horses could not be ridden, as their feet were in so bad. a state. The horses were also many of them without clothing, which proved very injurious during the intensely cold night.

The monotony of our domestic life was at this time disturbed by the discovery that our Portuguese butler, hitherto deemed a respectable man, had been carrying on a system of gross extortion. We found that we could be supplied with the only procurable luxuries, bread and meat for ourselves, and grass and grain for our horses, at about 200 *rupees* a month less than the rate at which he had been charging us. European stores such as wine, brandy, beer, coffee, tea, sugar, cheese, bacon, &c., are only to be obtained at rare intervals from the Parsee merchants at Agra, Mhow, or Bombay; and as to potatoes, we have not seen any since we left Major Macpherson's hospitable roof in the Phool-Bagh at Gwalior.

On the 4th of November, the day on which we reach Seronge, with its tall and goodly trees and its fretted buildings, we heard officially that General Michel intended to return the larger part of the cavalry and the artillery to this brigade. Captain Heneage remains with his troop of Hussars, nor can we regret that an officer who has proved himself so energetic, yet so steady and cool when in action, and so efficient and popular when in camp, should have the advantage of seeing active service in the field.

The remainder of the cavalry, under command of Acting Brigadier Colonel de Salis, were to have rejoined us on the 7th of November; but the colonel sent word that they were so tired, and their horses in such an exhausted condition, that they were unable to proceed, adding, "that a three weeks' halt at least was required;" but as his men and horses cannot be more exhausted than the rest of the brigade, I do not imagine that his reasons for a three weeks' halt will be considered satisfactory.

Captain Buckle, in command of the Irregular Horse, has given my husband some curious information respecting the habits of the Bheels, who have made themselves so troublesome lately. They are believers in witchcraft; and there are persons amongst them who obtain their livelihood by witch-finding. A misfortune occurring to one of their community, the witch-finder is sent for to discover through whose evil agency the victim suffers.

This man artfully discovers some female who is the "pet aversion" of his employer, and at once declares her to have bewitched him; upon which she is seized and hung up by her heels. If the torture drives her to confession, she is burnt without any further ceremony. If, on the contrary, she persists in her innocence, she is sure, soon after, mysteriously to disappear.

We have been much interested lately by a history of the Nana and his family, previous to the rebellion; and I venture to make a few extracts which may throw some light on the apparently unprovoked atrocities of this monster.

"Nana Sahib, Rajah of Bithoor, is the eldest son, by adoption, of Badjee Rao, ex-Peishwa of the Mahrattas. For many years previous to his death, Badjee Rao had been a dethroned pensioner of the East India Company. When in the fulness of his power, he had, as a native prince, assisted the East India Company in their war against Tippoo Saib, the tiger of Seringapatam; and as a reward for doing so, the Company, after years of strife with him—after negotiations, exactions, and treaties, and violations of these treaties on their parts—contrived in 1817 to get hold of his dominions. After numerous and fierce conflicts, Badjee Rao, at the head of 8,000 men, with an advantageous post, was prepared to do battle for the sovereignty of the Deccan; when Brigadier-General Sir John Malcolm, who commanded the British force, sent a flag of truce to him with proposals of surrender.

"The proposals on the part of Sir John Malcolm were—that Badjee Rao, the Peishwa of the Mahrattas, should renounce his sovereignty altogether; that he should come within twenty-four hours, with his family, and a limited number of adherents and attendants, into the British camp; that they should be received with honour and respect; that he should be located in the holy city of Benares, or some other sacred place of Hindoostan; that he should have a liberal pension from the East India Company for himself and his family; that his old and attached adherents should be provided for; and that the pension, which was to be settled upon himself and his family, should not be less than eight *lakhs* of *rupees*, that is, 80,000*l. per annum.*

"After long deliberations with, his prime minister and other great officers of state, the Peishwa accepted these proposals, went with his family and adherents into the British camp, and Bithoor was afterwards assigned him as a residence. The East India

Company, with their usual grasping and illiberal spirit of covetousness, were displeased with Sir John Malcolm for granting these terms. They could not recede from them; but they, and the Governor-General, Lord Hardinge, took care to limit the stipulated allowance to the smallest sum mentioned in the treaty namely, eight *lakhs* of *rupees*, or 80,000*l. per annum*. In his day, Badjee Rao, as chief of the powerful Mahratta nation, had been a great sovereign. He survived his downfall exercising civil and criminal jurisdiction on a limited scale at Bithoor—thirty-five years. On the 28th January, 1851, he died.

"No sooner was his death made officially known, than Lord Dalhousie tabled a minute at the Council Board of Calcutta, ruling that the pension, expressly guaranteed to the great Badjee Rao and his family, should be withdrawn. Nana Sahib, Badjee Rao's widows, and the other members of his family were naturally stricken with grief and terror. They saw themselves reduced to poverty. They had no other pecuniary support, than some trifling sum Badjee Rao had left behind him.

"On the 24th June, 1851, Nana Sahib forwarded a memorial to the Lieutenant-Governor of the North-Western Provinces of India, on the subject. He was told the pension could not be continued; but that a certain tract of land would be his for life. The Commissioner of Bithoor, a man of high rank and standing, and who knew the circumstances and claims of the ex-Peishwa's family, forwarded an urgent and earnest appeal on their behalf; but in a letter from the Secretary of the Governor-General, dated September 24th, 1851, he received a severe reprimand for so doing. His recommendation was stigmatized as 'uncalled for and unwarrantable.'

"After some further efforts, Nana Sahib addressed the Court of Directors at Leadenhall Street, in England. His appeal was dated 29th December, 1852. The Company appear to have considered that it added to their dignity to have the advocates of Eastern princes waiting in their ante-rooms. Somewhere about December, 1853, the Company sent back Nana Sahibs memorial to the Government of India, and the result was that nothing was done. It would appear that Nana Sahib, with smooth and gentlemanly manners, unites superior abilities and passions of the strongest and most vindictive nature. His spirit is high—his vehemence of the most determined character. At the breaking out of the mutiny, which has rendered his name so infamous, he appears to have become a monomaniac on the subject of his wrongs."

Three or four officers of the Indian army. to whom I have applied for information on this subject, tell me that the pension was not guaranteed to the family of Badjee Rao; but I gather from their answers that there might have been some flaw in the wording of the agreement which was taken advantage of by Lord Dalhousie. Of course, nothing can for a moment palliate the fiend-like atrocities of this man; but who, or what aroused, the devil in his breast?

CHAPTER 14

An Hour too Late

I cannot rest, from travel. I will drink
Life to the lees. all times I have enjoyed
Greatly; have suffered greatly; both with those
That loved me, and alone on shore, and when
Thro' scudding drifts the rainy Hyades
Vext the dim sea

Ulysses.

On the 8th November we left our camping ground at Deepna Kaira, where we had halted during two pleasant days, and came to within six miles of Mongroulee, as Maun Sing was reported to have joined a large body of *bundealahs* at Jacklown, and to be meditating the plunder of the former place.

On the 9th we were rejoined by part of the cavalry, and all the Horse Artillery which had been detached with General Michel on the banks of the Betwa. They returned none the better for long marches of thirty miles, and sometimes more, a day. The state of forty-four of the artillery horses brought vividly before me reminiscences of the famous Danubian reconnaissance. Their backs will not be able to bear a saddle for many weeks to come.

The Queen's proclamation will, it is conjectured, cause many of the Bengal *sepoys* to lay down their arms. Maun Sing might also avail himself of it, as he has committed no cruelties on the English, but, on the contrary, I am glad to say, protected and assisted several ladies, fugitives from the Gwalior rebels, and forwarded them to places of security. It was well for him that he declined to surrender on the terms offered him in his interview with our brigadier before Powree. They were, "Your life shall be spared, and you shall have the same conditions which are granted to the Rajah of ——"

"What are those conditions?"

"Oh! I believe they are not settled yet"

The Rajah of —— was made a state prisoner, and sent to Sind for life; a punishment greater in the eyes of a Hindoo than banishment to Siberia in the eyes of a Russian.

We were returning from a ride, late in the evening of Friday, 12th November, when, to our surprise, we found the brigadier had struck his tent. This betokened a move, and we hastened to ascertain the why and the whither? In consequence of some information received about four o'clock, it was decided to move instantly to a place called Dum-dum, where Maun Sing, with a large force, was said to be encamped.

We started not very hopefully, as we had been cried wolf to so often before; but as the day broke and deepened into sunrise, and then wore on towards noon, the march became more and more interesting. At half-past ten some spies, sent out by the assistant quartermaster-general, met us, with the news that Maun Sing's force had been that morning at a village a short distance ahead of us; and on our reaching the place we found it plundered and deserted, Information was now eagerly proffered, and we found that the enemy were encamped on the opposite side of the river, distant from us about a mile.

After halting for breakfast, under the grateful shade of some spreading tees, we resumed our route, and crossed the river, though not without delay and difficulty, as we had to find a fordable place as well as a pathway down its precipitous banks. Presently we saw, in the long beaten jungle grass, unmistakeable tracks of the enemy we were in search of. The trodden grass showed every turn they had taken. The scent might now be said to have been breast high; and it was followed with the eagerness of hounds. Some men running with all haste were speedily overtaken by four or five horsemen, who dashed after them at a gallop, regardless of holes, and stones, and hidden *nullahs*. They turned out to be Maun Sing's fishermen, and stated that the main body were about two *cos* (four miles) in front.

The sight of a poor old man, with his arm slashed and bleeding from a sword cut, proved that we were still on the right track. At seven o'clock the brigadier halted his men for a few hours' repose, which was absolutely necessary after being nearly seventeen hours on the line of march, during which only one man of the 95th had fallen out, and he was but lately discharged from hospital.

At the village where we rested, the monsters were said to have burnt a woman and two children about two hours before our arrival; and the inhabitants, who were eager for revenge, gave us, for once, truthful intelligence. The camp was pitched, and the troops allowed to sleep until half-past two: at half-past three a.m., without sound of trumpet or bugle, the men fell silently in, and we marched cautiously towards the spot at which Mann Sing was encamped.

When we had proceeded about two miles the quartermaster-general's spies again met us, and said that the whole camp was asleep, being perfectly unaware of our approach. I was riding with my husband amongst the advanced guard, and could therefore note how silently the men marched; the only noise was caused by a scabbard striking against a stirrup or a spur. Just at dawn the column halted, the 95th and 10th Native Infantry went to the front; the cavalry followed, in front of and alongside the guns; and a few minutes later the artillery broke into a gallop, unlimbered, and got into action at about 300 yards without a moment's loss of time.

The enemy awoke, startled and confused. They turned and fled, leaving not only the whole of their camp equipage, but, in some cases, their very children behind. Clothes, food, arms, and burning embers strewed the ground, and several *sepoy* pouches and belts were lying about. We pursued at a gallop, the guns getting into action whenever an opportunity offered, but the execution was chiefly done by the hussars and lancers.

Between 600 and 700 were computed to have been slain; and the jungles were filled with wounded men. Maun Sing, aroused by the first gun, threw himself on his fast and famous cream-coloured horse, and galloped for his life. His tents, camels, cooking vessels, and clothing, all fell into our hands.

Our casualties were chiefly among the horses. Captain Harris, Bombay Horse Artillery, was the only officer wounded. He was shot through the arm from behind a bush, in some jungle. There would, doubtless, have been many more casualties, but the matchlock-men had no time to light their matches; consequently, the only shots were those fired from *sepoy* muskets. Two Enfield rifles were picked up, marked Grenadier Company, 88th Regiment, and between fifty and sixty prisoners were taken. We heard the next day that Runjeet Sing, Maun Sing's uncle, was among the slain.

Some circumstances that came under my notice were very distressing. A man shot in the head, and who was bleeding profusely from his wound, was tended by his little daughter, apparently about twelve years old, who held up her hands imploring mercy and pity as we passed. Nor was I the only one who tried to reassure and comfort her.

One of our servants, when he joined us later in the day, brought with him a little boy, about seven years old, whom he found standing by his dead father, who had been shot and had fallen from his horse. The dead man, the child and horse were in a group, and our servant charitably took the child and placing him before him on his own horse, brought him into camp. I became possessed too of a small white dog, which; together with a baby of six or seven months old, was found lying on a bed, from whence the mother, frenzied, I suppose, by terror, had fled, and left her child behind!

The little one was sitting up and laughing, pleased at the horses and soldiers as they passed. This child was also brought on and given to the care of a woman in our camp, and the little dog was sent to me. I was told of a woman who, in the action of Beejapore, was endeavouring to escape with her child, but in the agony of fear she clasped it so closely to her side, that in her passionate efforts to save its life, she had squeezed it to death, and was still flying with it hanging over her arm, and pressed as closely as ever, but dead and cold.

We halted for one day after the fight at Koondrye, where nine of the prisoners were shot before marching on the 16th towards Mongroulee, which we reached on the 18th. It seems to me that all this Indian warfare is unsatisfactory work, and although it may be true that in this rebellion severity is mercy, yet, on the other hand, there have been cases of ruthless slaughter, of which perhaps the less said the better.

We heard on the 16th that Tantia Topee had sent from the other side of the Nerboudda to know on what terms, under the Queen's Proclamation, he could give himself up. He was then making his way to Poona, near Bombay. It seems that his race, as well as that of Maun Sing, is nearly run, and with them will probably end all the disturbances south of Oude.

A ridiculous report that Amba-Paniwallah, who is supposed to be at Serai with 4,000 men, has sent to challenge Brigadier Smith to single combat, has obtained circulation in our camp, and caused great excitement amongst the men. We remained three days at Mongroulee, as a halt was most urgently needed. Not only were there seventy horses of the troop of Horse Artillery unfit for work, but we were carrying about with us the men wounded in this action of Koondrye, and also Lieutenant Harding, dangerously wounded at Sindwaha.

Persons who are not actually in the position of the sufferer little know what a man, weakened by pain, loss of blood, und want of sleep, endures—who, besides being exposed to all the unavoidable noises of the camp, is shaken up in a *dooley* for several hours every day.

The state of Lieutenant Harding was at this time most critical, as the wound, inflicted nearly a month before, began to bleed afresh. It was impossible to leave the sick in any place of safety, and as the brigade was so short of medical officers, it was equally impossible to send them away to cantonments at Saugor under medical escort.

Letters from Colonel Lockhart give information of the rebels being at Bersea, not far from Bhilsa, but local intelligence reports them as much nearer. A body of men are said, to be between Gurrah and Seronge, but I fancy they exist only in the imagination of the Nawab of Tonk, who is anxious for the presence of European troops near Seronge in order to assist him in getting in hins revenue. A few *bundealahs* and others are still collected, at Jacklown, but Maun Sing, after his flight from our brigade, immediately retired to Pardone, where he is living quietly in his own territory.

Tantia Topee has, after all, managed to elude his vigorous pursuer, General Michel, and also the troops and columns on the other side of the Nerbudda, and is reported to have doubled back towards the north. It is also said that he has detained the Rajah of Bandah a close prisoner in his camp, to prevent his surrendering himself [1] on the faith of the promised amnesty, as Madeo Sing and Beni-Madeo, two chiefs in Oude, have already done.

On the evening of the 24th of November, Lieutenant Harding died from the effects of his wound. The internal bleeding of an artery, injured by the bullet, could not be stopped without an operation, beneath which he must have sunk. He was reverently interred, beneath some wide-spreading trees, at our encampment of Deepna Kaira, nearly every officer of the brigade being present at the funeral. When, on the day but one following, we left the place, the tree above him bore an admirably carved inscription to his memory, stating name, age, date and cause of death.

On the 26th November, we moved on to Seronge, intending to halt for a few days, as so many repairs of tents, saddlery, gun-carriages, &c., were absolutely necessary. Colonel Scudamore, with a small field force, occupies our vacated ground at Mongroulee, in order to check any predatory incursions on that

---

1. He soon after surrendered

village. We rode over to see his camp, and in this land, of wilderness and jungle, it seemed to us a, positive blessing to see the fresh English faces of the 14th Light Dragoons and the 86th Regiment.

When we arrived at Seronge, a rumour reached us, through the medium of the *dâk*, that Brigadier Smith's column had come under the merciful consideration of the authorities. That the lengthened and unprecedented period during which it has been serving in the field, and the wear and. tear of eleven months unceasing work, on men, horses, and camp equipage, has induced the commander-in-chief to order the troops composing it to be relieved from active service, until such time as they shall be rendered thoroughly efficient by rest and reinforcements, or until it becomes again their turn to take the places of the relieving regiments in the field.

On the 10th of December, whilst the brigade was halting at Beora, we heard that the Nana had crossed the Ganges, and, in company with Feroze Shah, was bearing clown upon Bundelcund. Beora is a telegraphic station on the Great Trunk Road; and. as we halted there for a week. Captain Shakespear, the political agent, who had lately accompanied the brigade, was in constant and easy communication with Sir Robert Hamilton at Indore.

We, therefore, received early intimation that the report wanted official confirmation. When it first reached us, it effectually scattered our visions of Neemuch, to which place we had a few days before received a telegraphic order from General Michel that three squadrons of the 8th Hussars should proceed, the fourth squadron going to Nusserabad. I sincerely hope it win not be our lot to be stationed at the latter place, of which an officer, writing a short time ago, says:

I trust it may never be your fate to be stationed here. It is, of all places, the most disagreeable. There is no drinkable water nearer than a mile, and no gardens or anything else to make life pleasant. We suffer torments from the mosquitoes, of which there are two sorts—one, a small lively kind, with curly legs, that flies about by day; the other, a large black fiend, which comes prowling out at night.

Still it will be something to have "a local habitation," which is not taken to pieces and set up again every day.

It is certain that a body of rebels has escaped from Oude; and, in consequence, the brigadier marched from Beora to Seronge, on the 12th December, in order to cover Bhilsa and Bhopal. We arrived at Seronge on the 16th, and soon after learnt that Sir Robert Napier had been in pursuit of a party of rebels from Gwalior, but had not succeeded in coming up with them.

We now begin to understand the object of Tantia Topee's erratic marches. He has evidently been endeavouring, by the rapidity of his transits from place to place, to draw away or separate the British forces, so that a passage might be left open for the Nana, should he be able to escape from Oude, and desire to make an attempt to raise his standard in the south amongst the Mahrattas.

The fate of Tantia appears to be sealed: his gallant course must be nearly run; and however we may abhor the crimes which he has committed, we cannot refuse our respect to his good generalship and brilliant talents. The chances are that, finding all attempts at further resistance vain, he will retire to some holy place, and, changing his name and dress, will seek safety in obscurity. In General Michel he met with an antagonist as indefatigable as himself.

No march appeared too long or too difficult for this division of our army: nor is it out of place to observe that the portion of Smith's Brigade which accompanied the major-general across the Betwa had, on its return, accomplished a distance of more than 2,600 miles within twelve months. And a squadron of the 8th Hussars, which is still away far below Mhow, under the command of Major Chetwode, has marched even a greater distance than this.

We have just heard of the death of Brigadier-General John Jacob, who expired, after a short illness, of fever, at Jacobabad, on the 6th of December. He is universally regretted as a valuable officer and an eminently practical man; and it is those who knew him best who mourn for him most deeply.

The Queens most merciful Proclamation, winch does credit to the head and heart of Lord Stanley, or whoever dictated its gracious words, although it in believed in and accepted by some, is received by others with contemptuous incredulity or with open defiance.

> *The Bombay Standard* says—"The rebels in Bundelcund appear cursed with a disbelief of virtue in human nature, and cannot conceive such a forgiving spirit as our gracious Queen breathes in her amnesty to her rebellious subjects. Des Put, the leader hereabouts (Srinuggur), on receiving the Proclamation, deliberately put it into his pipe and smoked it, by which he set fire to his own beard, as my respected friend of the secret intelligence department observed. But worse occurred at the village of Koolpahar, under the joint noses of the general, two civilians, and a deputy. Eight men-at-arms proceeded thither to read her Majesty's Proclamation; the rebels slew seven out of the eight, and the other they most fearfully wounded. Such was the bloody answer these monsters deigned to give; and these are Hindoos—gentle Hindoos—the mild Hindoo with whose morals Mr. Layard declares we have played the deuce."

As far as the last line goes, I, to a certain extent, must agree with the gentleman whose name is quoted; but the Englishmen in India are not all evil, if they are not all good; and we must hope that the new administration will encourage and strengthen all that is good, and set its face against the evil.

On the afternoon of Monday the 20th of December, some lancers came into camp and reported that a, party consisting of *sepoys* with remount horses, stores, spare camels, kit, &c, under command of Lieutenant Stack, 1st Bombay Lancers, had been attacked by a body of rebels, and that fifty camels and a considerable part of the kit had fallen into their hands. These men were reported to number 2,000 or 3,000, and to be encamped about twenty-five miles to the north-west of us.

Brigadier Smith determined on starting immediately to punish them; and as soon as the camels, which were grazing in the jungle, could be recalled, the whole brigade moved, at eight p. m., to march all night. How cold it was! Those who were mounted found it impossible to keep themselves warm, and as far as comfort was concerned, the infantry had much the best of it. About six o'clock the following morning we halted at a village, and on making inquiries as to the exact spot where we hoped to surprise the enemy's camp, we learnt to our mortification that they had left on the previous Saturday evening, and were marching west! As they had two days' start and were all mounted, it was useless to attempt a pursuit, our infantry being already exhausted and footsore with a ten hours' march.

On our return to Seronge, we learnt that Captain Rice, at the head of a very small body of men, partly European and partly native, had succeeded in coming up with these same rebels from his camp at Arone, and had recaptured our looted camels, besides taking the enemy's camp equipage. Central India seems absolutely infested with fresh insurgent forces escaped from Oude.

Whether the object is still to effect a junction with Tantia Topee, or not, we cannot at present tell; but we hear of rebels congregating on all sides of us. As General Michel is expected to move out from Mhow to Beora, we have sent out a party to Bhilsa. How much longer this desultory police warfare may be carried on, no one can at this moment conjecture. We returned to Seronge on the 23rd of December, but the brilliant weather and our unsettled movements destroyed all the peace and happiness of holy Christmas-tide.

From Bursad we continued our route, and after two long and fatiguing days we arrived at Chuppra. It was on the 1st of May, 1858, that we reached it for the first time, and on the 1st of January, 1859, about four o'clock in the evening, prostrated with fatigue, we again sought a temporary shelter beneath its walls. Our march had been an unusually distressing one, as the brigadier having received information that Feroze Shah was in the neighbourhood with a large force, was anxious to lose no time. The worn-out baggage animals refused to answer to this call upon their exhausted strength, consequently those of the 10th Native Infantry were two days behind, and for those two days the unfortunates of that regiment went without food, performing on the first day fourteen, and on the second day twenty-two miles.

Fortunately we found Chuppra well supplied and hospitable, but the news which greeted us was little calculated to allow of halting. Tantia Topee had that morning been encamped only four *cos* (eight miles) from Chuppra, and Colonel Somerset at the head of a squadron of cavalry, four guns, and 180 Europeans mounted on camels, had come across the rear guard of his army, without doing them much damage. This interruption had, however, the effect of making the enemy hasten beyond our reach; and it was agreed at a council of war that the only plan remaining for us was to hasten with all speed towards Pooree, to which place they were supposed to be doubling back.

The brigadier, in consequence of a communication from Sir R. Napier, changed his course; and in order to strike into the Trunk Road at Budderwas, near Sepree, marched the next morning on Shikarpoor, and the following day reached Futtyghur. Here the clouds which had been gathering for some days came down upon us in copious showers of rain, accompanied by continuous thunder and lightning, effectually stopping our movements. So far as I was personally concerned I was not sorry, for the axle of our bullock *gharry* had broken ten miles on the other side of Chuppra, and the contents—my pet hare, dressing-case, little white dog, and sundry other valuables—were left on the road.

Some invalid hussars following in a cart recognised the little dog and brought it on; but I was greatly afraid lest the *budmashes*, or hangers-on of the rebel army, would find the wreck, and, after having looted the cart and walked off with the bullocks, would proceed to murder the driver. We were greatly indebted to the kindness of Captain Shakespear, who put himself in communication with the *Resildar* about it; and by his orders the cart was conveyed to Chuppra, and there left to be repaired.

We sent one of our servants bade on horseback to Chuppra to bring on the contents of the *gharry* in a native cart, and he did not catch us up for three days, causing us great anxiety as to what had befallen him; but he eventually appeared at Futtyghur, bringing the little hare uninjured, and the dressing-case, with its contents untouched. The same good luck did not attend one of my husband's brother officers, whose cart, containing all his stores—beer, wine, and a good deal of kit—none of which he will ever see again—broke down on the other side of Bursad. Another told me he believed his cart had been going on the spokes of one wheel for a week, as it had lost the felloes. Some things are irresistibly funny, although bitterly vexatious.

On the evening of the 5th we were aroused from sleep at eleven o'clock, and started soon after twelve. We marched by an exceedingly rough and bad road, over three or four rocky *nullahs* full of water, to Kailwarra, and about three miles from that place came upon horses' hoof-tracks, and several dead bodies, affording unmistakeable evidence of the presence of *budmashes*. The information of the spies led the brigadier to believe that they were still actually encamped at the village below us, and he formed up his brigade in consequence, bringing infantry and cavalry to the front, leaving the guns in reserve until required.

The hope, however, proved a fallacious one; the enemy had left about an hour previously, and were rapidly in flight. I believe they gained information of our movements from the head man at Naharghur, who had proved himself a suspicious character before. As it was, we could not pursue with infantry after so long a march, and the brigadier determined on letting the men rest that day. We accordingly pitched our camp, and on the next day we tracked the enemy about sixteen miles further. At the village where we halted several horses were found, which had been left behind in the hurry of flight; they were fine animals, but all excessively sore-backed, and in very low condition.

On the 8th the brigadier learnt that Brigadier Showers was moving down from Agra to Jeypoor, which movement, if we progressed steadily in his rear, might cause Tantia to be headed back and so to fall into our hands. It would, be a proud, thng, if, after all, Tantia should be taken by this indefatigable brigade.

On the 9th and 10th we still followed the foot-prints, and on the latter day the brigade crossed the wide and deep ford of the River Chumbul. I watched a portion of the brigade crossing before me, in order to see which was the shallowest part, but as I saw several horses disappear in holes and deep water, and a gun carriage go in over the wheels, I very gratefully accepted the offer of a seat on Captain Shakespear's elephant, winch carried over a party of five with great unconcern; causing, as he ploughed through the deep water with his enormous legs, almost as much noise as is made by the rush of water under the stern of a ship.

At the village where we halted, we were told, that the enemy had on the previous day but one looted, all their camels, doubtless a valuable addition to their carriage. This part of Rajpootana is a great camel-breeding country, especially among the Boondee hills, where we now are. On the 11th of January we were only about twenty miles from Kotah, and seventy-seven from Nusserabad; thus we have come round to the same point at which we were this time last year.

I imagine the Rajah of Kotah knows better than to admit the rebel army a second time inside his walls. The rich pastures of Rajpootana contrast very pleasantly with the sterile country we have left. The numerous and wealthy villages are picturesquely situated, each on the borders of a large tank, abounding with wild-fowl. As we pass them before daylight they rise with a noise resembling the whirr of machinery, and wheel high in the air over our heads. Vast fields of wheat stretch to the wide horizon, and give a cheerful aspect to the plains.

A gang of thieves have been busy in our camp. They robbed the brigadier of his helmet, all over feathers and gold, and then tried the tent of the quartermaster-general. He had a light burning, and seeing the man's hand feeling under the wall of his tent, made a thrust at him with a sword, *à la Hamlet,* but missed him.

The thief then came to our tent; but my small dog, sharp as a needle, woke me when the man was within a foot of me, and I could have cut off his hand with my Bhooj dagger. He afterwards ripped open another part of the wall of the tent with a knife, and took out a portmanteau, containing my husband's office papers. Disgusted at finding nothing of value, he scattered them all about, and walked off with three bottles of English ink. There were fifteen servants sleeping round the tent, and a corporal and six men on guard at the time.

I must now, for the present at any rate, bid *adieu* to my readers; but I cannot conclude without expressing my gratitude to that good Providence which has brought us thus far safely, when so many have fallen round us, the victims either of accident or disease. Animated with this feeling, I close the record of our first year's Field Service in India, wherein that part of the brigade, which was accompanied by my husband and myself, passed only one European station, Deesa, and marched in spite of Indian sun and Indian rain, and in the toilsome pursuit of an ever flying foe, a distance of 2,028 miles, more than 1,800 of which I have myself accomplished on horseback.

LEONAUR

ALSO FROM LEONAUR
AVAILABLE IN SOFTCOVER OR HARDCOVER WITH DUST JACKET

A JOURNAL OF THE SECOND SIKH WAR by *Daniel A. Sandford*—The Experiences of an Ensign of the 2nd Bengal European Regiment During the Campaign in the Punjab, India, 1848-49.

LAKE'S CAMPAIGNS IN INDIA by *Hugh Pearse*—The Second Anglo Maratha War, 1803-1807. Often neglected by historians and students alike, Lake's Indian campaign was fought against a resourceful and ruthless enemy-almost always superior in numbers to his own forces.

BRITAIN IN AFGHANISTAN 1: THE FIRST AFGHAN WAR 1839-42 by *Archibald Forbes*—Following over a century of the gradual assumption of sovereignty of the Indian Sub-Continent, the British Empire, in the form of the Honourable East India Company, supported by troops of the new Queen Victoria's army, found itself inevitably at the natural boundaries that surround Afghanistan. There it set in motion a series of disastrous events-the first of which was to march into the country at all.

BRITAIN IN AFGHANISTAN 2: THE SECOND AFGHAN WAR 1878-80 by *Archibald Forbes*—This the history of the Second Afghan War-another episode of British military history typified by savagery, massacre, siege and battles.

UP AMONG THE PANDIES by *Vivian Dering Majendie*—An outstanding account of the campaign for the fall of Lucknow. This is a vital book of war as fought by the British Army of the mid-nineteenth century, but in truth it is also an essential book of war that will enthral.

BLOW THE BUGLE, DRAW THE SWORD by *W. H. G. Kingston*—The Wars, Campaigns, Regiments and Soldiers of the British & Indian Armies During the Victorian Era, 1839-1898.

INDIAN MUTINY 150th ANNIVERSARY: A LEONAUR ORIGINAL

MUTINY: 1857 by *James Humphries*—It is now 150 years since the 'Indian Mutiny' burst like an engulfing flame on the British soldiers, their families and the civilians of the Empire in North East India. The Bengal Native army arose in violent rebellion, and the once peaceful countryside became a battleground as Native sepoys and elements of the Indian population massacred their British masters and defeated them in open battle. As the tide turned, a vengeful army of British and loyal Indian troops repressed the insurgency with a savagery that knew no mercy. It was a time of fear and slaughter. James Humphries has drawn together the voices of those dreadful days for this commemorative book.

Lightning Source UK Ltd.
Milton Keynes UK
UKHW010633051022
409964UK00002B/272